D0451205

Ways of Staying

KEVIN BLOOM is an award-winning South African journalist who has written for many of the country's mainstream publications. He has been editor-at-large of *Maverick* magazine, co-editor of *Empire* magazine and founding editor of *The Media* magazine. He completed *Ways of Staying*, his first book, as a Writing Fellow at the Wits Institute of Social and Economic Research (WISER) in Johannesburg.

Ways of Staying

Kevin Bloom

Portobello
BOOKS

Published by Portobello Books Ltd 2010

Portobello Books
Twelve Addison Avenue
London
W11 4QR

First published 2009 by Picador Africa, an imprint of Pan Macmillan South Africa

Copyright © Kevin Bloom 2009

The right of Kevin Bloom to be identified as the author of this work has been asserted by him
in accordance with the Copyright, Designs and Patents Act 1988

A CIP catalogue record is available from the British Library

9 8 7 6 5 4 3 2 1

ISBN 978 1 84627 265 3

www.portobellobooks.com

Editing by Ivan Vladislavić and Andrea Nattrass
Proofreading by Jeannie van den Heever

Offset by Avon DataSet Ltd, Bidford on Avon, Warwickshire
Printed in the UK by CPI William Clowes Beccles NR34 7TL

Contents

For the Blooms

'Yes, they have a story to tell. Its setting is in the interstice between power and indifferent or supportive agency. In that interstice, the English-speaking South African has conducted the business of his life. Now he was indignant and guilty; now he was thriving. This no-man's land ensured a fundamental lack of character. With a foreign passport in the back pocket of the trousers, now they belong – now they do not. When will they tell this story?'

         – NJABULO NDEBELE, *Fine Lines from the Box*

'For the circulation of horror stories is the very mechanism that drives white paranoia about being chased off the land and ultimately into the sea.'

         – JM COETZEE, *Stranger Shores*

PROLOGUE

UMBRELLAS ARE UNFURLED, yellow and blue and bright orange. The Johannesburg sun is fierce and the men wear dark suits, the women heavy dresses. Laurie and I don't have an umbrella. We stand at the back, in the sun's full glare. The rabbi is far away, concealed in the crowd, and his voice fades and resurfaces on the wind. We catch excerpts of psalms, the eulogy, the *Kaddish*. By rights we should be nearer the grave: Laurie's grandfather and Brett's grandfather were brothers. But we must leave soon so I can stand with my own family at the next funeral. At the next funeral they are burying my cousin Richard.

I turn around again to make sure we can get away. We're still in the clear, I see. We can walk up the hill and onto the path between the conifers. I see a lone worker up there, a gravedigger perhaps, waiting in the shade with his newspaper.

The story is no doubt on the front page.

'Slain actor and fashion designer to be buried this morning in Westpark Cemetery … the bodies of Brett Goldin (twenty-eight) and Richard Bloom (twenty-seven) were discovered on Monday beside the M5 freeway in Cape Town …'

Discovered, that is, four days ago. The funerals should have happened sooner, I'm thinking, in accordance with the custom of returning the dead to the earth without delay. Of course custom – whatever its virtues – must occasionally bow to the laws of the state.

And who can complain that the state has been tardy?

Post-mortem completed, evidence filed, corpses 'reconstituted' and flown up to Johannesburg for burial. Now, while a long queue of mourners performs the *mitzvah* of shovelling soil – three spades each – into Brett's grave, Laurie and I hurry

I

back to the *ohel*, where in the middle of a bare anteroom Richard's coffin lies on an old steel gurney.

My name is called as a pallbearer. I take my place on the left, behind my father and my uncle Jonathan. My father sobs once, a deep sharp heave, and then he is quiet. We wheel the casket out of the room.

We stop in the central hall, where the rabbi speaks briefly about Torah and 'the world to come'. The next pallbearers are called; the casket is wheeled out the back door and into the sun. More than two hundred mourners follow, the only sound in the procession the rattle and clank of steel and rubber on broken tar.

I walk with Laurie, beside my parents and my sister. My uncle Tony and aunt Sandy walk just ahead. Tony's shirt is torn, a sign that today he is burying a son. Between Tony and Sandy walks Derek, Richard's twin. I can barely look at my cousin.

Later, in the car on the way home, Laurie and I don't say a word. We've been fighting all week, venting at each other, and now our anger is spent. When we get to the apartment I head for the couch. Laurie goes to the bedroom with her guitar.

She can't know it yet, but the song my girlfriend composes will be broadcast one day to a large international audience. She writes it in minor chords, a Patty Griffin-type sound, spare and precise. She names it for a line in the chorus – 'What else is there?' – and decides not to include in her lyrics a reference to the fact that Brett and Richard were murdered.

They're gone, she sings. That's all.

CHAPTER 1

City in Disguise

AT THE FAR END of downtown Johannesburg, where a six-lane high-way separates the city from the industrial suburbs to the south, stands an invisible skyscraper. The building rises twenty floors and boasts almost two thousand windows, and nobody has seen it in months. Instead of a chocolate-brown seventy-eight-metre-tall office block, what you see when you drive past Penmor Tower – 1 Rissik Street, completed 1974 – are skyscraper-sized billboards for an insurance company.

It is only when you leave the safety of your car – to peer into the building's empty lobby, to walk on its crumbling concourse – that you notice the other, smaller billboards. There are two of them: one facing north, where there is a fenced-up tavern called Bender's Arms, the other facing east, where a forbidding concrete monolith houses the deeds registry office.

The smaller billboards show a picture of a smiling and attractive woman, and extend the following invitation: 'Sexy Space to Let! Live, Work & Play in the City!'

———

A Monday morning in late summer 2007. From where I wait Penmor Tower is one block to the south. I wait in my silver Alfa Romeo, a 156 Selespeed, with a sunroof and spoilers and red and black leather seats. The car – which hides beneath its racing exterior perhaps the worst gearbox in the history of the marque – is parked on Anderson Street, just off the corner of Loveday. On the corner opposite is Johannesburg's newest street sign, a diagonal red line through a man next to a table stacked with goods: no hawking.

Themba Jacky Koketi, aged twenty-seven, is on foot. He has walked to this end of town from Saratoga Avenue, from his room in an old carpet factory more than three kilometres away. He arrived at the municipal office in Loveday Street at eight, at opening time, to ask the people there to reconnect his water supply. Now he is walking up from the office to my car. I call Themba on his cellphone and say, again, that I can come to him.

'No,' Themba says. 'Wait where you are.'

In five minutes he appears, a face at the passenger window. I grab my pen and notebook and lock the car. We head south down Loveday for three blocks and cross the street at Argent House.

'Themba,' I say, following his short frame up the entrance steps, 'you don't think I could have found this place on my own?'

He stops and turns, his face vacant. I let the question go. We enter the building.

It's a flawed assumption, I'm thinking, it endorses a myth – but I have no better way to explain to myself Themba's courtesy: he was raised by his grandmother in a mud hut in a place called eMondlo, deep in the hills of KwaZulu-Natal; he has brought his rural manners with him to the city.

There are, to recast the myth, other rural habits Themba still practises. For instance: every morning the residents of the former carpet factory go out to fetch water. These days the closest source is the railway station. The residents take it in turns to make the kilometre round-trip. The water is hauled back in as many buckets as their trolleys can carry.

'In my room we used to need three buckets a day,' says Themba. 'But that was when we were cooking.'

They are no longer cooking, I already know, because the owner of the building has cut off the electricity.

We are sitting now in a pair of plush blue chairs, in a waiting area with a thick cream carpet. On a side table is a pamphlet showing a group of children cavorting under a sprinkler. Tacked to the wall is a press clipping: 'Joburg targets water crooks'.

A squat man with a blonde moustache and pink skin strides across the room. 'Have you got a number?' he barks at Themba. Themba nods. At me he barks a bit softer. 'And you?'

We watch the man squeeze into his cubicle. I turn to Themba and tell him, once more, what I am doing here. When I am finished, he says, 'Even myself, I don't understand this thing of inner city renewal. I mean seriously, I don't understand. They say they are renewing the city, but they don't give us other places to go.'

———

Three weeks earlier, a warm afternoon. Stuart Wilson, a human rights paralegal from Manchester, steers my Alfa through a wrought-iron gate and up a slight hill to the end of a rubble-strewn alley. He turns off the ignition, leans his head against the steering wheel and exhales.

Although this is one of the city's most violent districts, a part of Johannesburg white people no longer visit, the source of Stuart's concern is my car. On the way here, at three consecutive traffic lights, he failed to engage the semi-automatic gears. He kept gearing down instead of up, jerking the Alfa to a stop, laughing madly.

'You can have the thing if it's so much fun for you,' I said.

I have asked Stuart to drive so I can take notes. Stuart's clients are the inner city poor; he is an expert on the fallout from urban renewal. One fact that he has taught me this morning already: 'If you are evicted from a building in the inner city, you join a housing queue that's fifteen years long.'

Now, at the end of the alley behind the old carpet factory, Stuart wrestles with the Alfa's alarm. I take the keys from him and press the button, which must be pushed a special way. A short black man is standing beside the boot, and Stuart walks around the car and embraces the man and says, 'Themba, this is Kevin, the journalist.'

Themba Jacky Koketi, dressed in new jeans and white takkies and a sweater with stripes down the sleeves, pronounces for me his full name. He says he has been waiting. He shakes my hand and smiles. 'Follow me,' he says.

There are four buildings at 7 Saratoga Avenue. The buildings surround a courtyard, a small concrete square that evokes the idyll of the African village. Young men lean against doorposts, buxom women in bright-coloured skirts hang up washing, barefoot boys play soccer with a plastic colddrink bottle.

Themba leads me into the old factory building first. The village idyll – the perennial pastoral myth – evaporates.

The stairs are disintegrating; I steady myself in the darkness against a damp wall. 'The toilets aren't working this side,' says Themba. 'On the other side are buckets of water.'

We are in a corridor suffused with shafts of pale light, a two-foot wide walkway that runs between walls made of chipboard and plywood. A woman with an infant strapped to her back emerges from the door at the end of the passage. She greets Themba and disappears down the stairwell.

'She is a hawker,' Themba says. 'She is going now to sell her sweets and cigarettes at the train station. We are all afraid, but what must we do?'

The residents of 7 Saratoga Avenue could be afraid, I'm thinking, for any reason. Fear in Johannesburg in early 2007 is an all-pervasive emotion.

'So why are you afraid?' I ask.

Last Monday, says Themba, there was a police raid. It was four o'clock in the morning and he was woken by shouts and banging. He went outside and found the residents kneeling on the pavement in rows. He was ordered by a large policeman to join them, and so the broken glass cut into his knees too. The policemen demanded identity books. A man with no documents was pushed into the back of a van. Two men who tried to run were shot with rubber bullets. The senior superintendent, an Afrikaner with close-cropped hair, called everyone a bastard. He stood on the pavement and shouted, 'You fucking bastards! You're all fucking bastards!'

Themba shakes his head. 'There are some illegal foreigners here,' he says, 'but not so many.' Themba thinks the police came for another reason. He thinks they are in cahoots with the building's owner, a white attorney who lives in Sandton.

'No, the owner wants to build a hotel,' says Themba. 'It is three years to go before the World Cup, and here we are very close to the stadium. The owner, I'm telling you, he wants to build a hotel.'

I write this information down. Maybe I know nothing about fear, I'm thinking. I ask Themba if he will show me his room.

We cross the courtyard and enter an outbuilding. Themba's room, number twenty-five, is the first one as you come through the door.

A single bed dominates the small but tidy space. On a desk by the door is an electric cooker, an object rendered useless when the owner cut the power to the building. There is a stool under the desk, and in the corner a pair of shoes. On the wall above the shoes is a poster, a pullout of Janet Jackson from *Drum* magazine. Next to the poster, typed in bold font on a white sheet of paper, is the line: 'And if you can control your body and your sexual urges, then you are a man, my son.'

The attribution confirms that these are the words of Judge VJ van der Merwe, uttered when delivering his not guilty verdict in the rape trial of South Africa's former deputy president, Jacob Zuma.

'Why's it there?' I ask.

'I like it,' Themba says. 'It sends a good message. Zuma, you can't understand the man.'

I nod. We talk politics for a bit. On a porch on the other side of the courtyard a fat baby is sitting in the sun amongst the pigeons. I think about the child's prospects and listen to Themba and scan the room again. I see that I had missed an important detail.

Themba's bags are packed. Next to the bed, ready for travel, are two suitcases and three plastic packets.

He watches as I make a note.

'I'm threatened, I'm not settled,' he says.

I write down these words. I stare at them on the page.

In the last ten months there have been a few moments like this. Since April 16th 2006, when Richard was abducted by a group of men from the Cape Flats and shot in the back of the head, there has been something new and uncomfortable about the way I live in my country. Sometimes it takes a sentence, a small thing somebody else says, to explain to me what's different.

———

In the late 1950s, Es'kia Mphahlele wrote in the epilogue to his memoir *Down Second Avenue*: 'I now realise what a crushing cliché the South African situation can be as literary material.'

Not much has changed in the intervening years.

Within the image of Themba's life – the sparse furniture, the man who is ready to leave at the first sign of trouble – the opposite image always lurks. It is better, maybe, to emphasise this up front: in a story motivated in part by the murder of a privileged white man at the hands of desperate and angry non-whites, the South African cliché *is* the subject.

Unlike Themba's, then, my bedroom in my apartment in Killarney is large and comfortable. It has an en suite bathroom with a shower and bath, a passage with three ample cupboards on either side, a king-size bed. There is a balcony outside my room, which is accessed through a wide sliding door. When I sit at the table on my balcony and look out over the jacarandas and pines and oaks, I can just make out tiled roofs amongst the green.

Behind my apartment, on the south side of the building, is The Wilds. This is a public park that sprawls across two koppies, a place filled with acacias and aloes and more birds than the city officials can fit on their information boards.

The nearest point of entry to the park is less than two hundred metres from my front door. In summer 2007 I visit The Wilds for the first time since childhood.

It is all still there as remembered – the clear ponds and lush grass, the stone paths leading up the hill and through the trees, the big mustard boulders. Even the feeling of the place is still there: the feeling of being on holiday in the middle of your own city.

It is my first time in The Wilds in twenty-three years. My friend, the Canadian writer, forces me to go. He isn't interested in my stories of how dangerous it's supposed to be.

In the heat of the afternoon, standing on top of the west koppie, just above the Japanese botanical gardens and a few steps from the sundial, my friend looks out to the south. 'Bro, this is one of the most beautiful city views I've ever seen,' he says.

This from a guy who, in the last year, has visited Peru, Russia, Kazakhstan,

Namibia; a guy who's never used that adjective around me before.

Below, like a river, the road carves a steep path between the koppies. In the middle ground the façade of St John's College, all brown stone and turrets and gables. In the foreground the playing fields of Roedean, mowed by some proud gardener in precise and verdant lines. Then the Upper Houghton houses, resolute mansions perched on the edge of the ridge. In the background, layered and looming, the flats of Yeoville and Berea and Hillbrow. Trees everywhere. And the flawless Highveld summer sky.

Later, on the east koppie, we watch a storm break. It's coming from the north, a grey curtain sweeping towards us over the golf course and the highway. The wind comes up and blows thick strips of bark off a row of gum trees. It smells like lemon.

The storm doesn't reach us and when the sun emerges again it's hotter than before. I see a label on a stick in the soil, next to a small succulent; it tells me I am looking at a krantz aloe. We walk on to the far side of the koppie.

On this side, too, there's a green cast-iron fence topped by razor wire blocking off access from the road. The little avenues with cobblestone gutters leading up to the old exits and entrances are cracked and sprout weeds.

Even on a Sunday afternoon in early January, the artery from the north into the inner city boils over: taxis and cars hooting and surging and growling. This is not a quiet river.

We cross the bridge back onto the west koppie, where our car is parked. Three security guards are gathered around a small radio, listening to the live broadcast of a football match between Cosmos and Amazulu. I ask the men if they've had any trouble today.

The one with the red eyes answers. 'Early this morning I heard gunshots and a man screaming. The police, they shot someone there.' He points to a place between the trees. 'I didn't go see.'

———

A restaurant on Anderson Street. It's bare inside, no attempt at decor. There is a linoleum floor, four tables at the back on a raised platform, a wooden counter on the right by the door.

We order two coffees and take a table. An enamel tray arrives bearing two cups and a silver pot. Chicory, not coffee. Frisco or Koffiehuis or something.

eMondlo, says Themba Jacky Koketi, as I blow on the scalding brown liquid, is near where the Battle of Blood River was fought. Which is to say: near where 470 Afrikaners, after holding out against thousands of Zulus on a December day in 1838, declared the day forever after a day of thanksgiving.

That afternoon I will look for eMondlo in my South Africa road atlas. I won't find it. Instead I will find a place called Vryheid (Afrikaans for 'freedom').

eMondlo was conceived by the apartheid planners as a black dormitory township. It was built away from the main transport routes, so that it would always be dependent on the white town. eMondlo is far enough removed from Vryheid so that when Themba's mother was working in town, as a domestic servant, she seldom saw her son.

Themba drops two spoons of sugar into his cup and stirs. 'People can stay in eMondlo for thirty years without a job,' he tells me. 'It's better here in Johannesburg.'

Still, *here* wasn't Themba's first choice. When he graduated from high school, with a distinction in physical science, he was offered a scholarship to the University of Zululand. He couldn't go because the grant didn't cover food and rent and blankets.

Themba has three school friends who did take up scholarships. They would call him on the phone. 'Why didn't you come?' they would ask.

'Those people are working now,' says Themba. 'The one is at Telkom. The one is teaching in Zululand. The other one is a prison warder.'

In Johannesburg, in the beginning, Themba wasn't working. He wanted to be a clerk but he didn't have computer experience. He wanted to be a police officer or a traffic cop but he didn't have a driver's licence. His brother put up the money for a learner's licence, which Themba passed first time, but when the day of the driving test came his brother couldn't afford to pay any more. And then the learner's expired.

Themba stops to reflect on that. 'I realised, no, I need skills, or I will suffer forever.'

So he waited in line at Wits University. He filled in a bunch of forms. To optimise his chances he applied for three degrees. Some weeks later he received three letters of acceptance. He took the letters to the university's financial aid department and was successful there too.

Themba chose an arts degree with a major in psychology. He did a foundation year to bridge the gap from school and improve his academic English. His results started out poor and got better in year two. Things, Themba says, were going well. But then he had to find another place to stay.

Since arriving in Johannesburg, in 2001, he had been staying with his brother in Joubert Park, on the seventh floor of a building at the corner of Smith and Edith Cavell Streets. His brother and his brother's wife and their two children occupied the main bedroom. The second bedroom was sublet to another family and Themba slept on the dining room floor.

'This brother was providing everything for us,' says Themba. 'Food and everything.' But one day his brother saw that it was better to own property than to waste money every month on rent, so with the bank's help he bought a small house in Pretoria.

Themba sought help from a man he knew from eMondlo. The man was Bonginkosi Mtetwa, and he slept in the entrance of the building in Joubert Park. Bonginkosi slept on a piece of sponge, but he had a girl-friend who slept on a bed in a room in an old carpet factory in Berea.

Themba and Bonginkosi arrived at 7 Saratoga Avenue in late 2003. Bonginkosi's girlfriend arranged it for them. They paid a deposit of R300, inclusive of the first month's rent. Themba didn't have the money so Bonginkosi took care of it.

Now, years later, Themba still talks about the urgency of his situation. 'Just one more year and I'm on my way,' he says. He thinks he can get a first-class pass this year, his honours in psychology *cum laude*. Then, while he does his masters, he can work for the Department of Social Development.

'There's a shortage of social workers,' he says. 'That's what they told me.'

But if he is evicted, his plans fall apart. He receives a living allowance from the university of R412 a month, so he can't pay rent of more than

R200. And where can you stay in the city for that? And how can you study psychology honours from the street?

———

A woman behind a desk calls Themba. He excuses himself and walks over, his hands clasped in front of his body, his neck bent slightly forward. He sits on the edge of the chair. For ten minutes he nods and listens. Once or twice he leans over to look at some figures on a printout. He thanks the woman and stands up and returns to the blue chairs in the waiting room.

'They say we need the authorisation of the owner to open a new account,' he tells me.

The owner is still refusing to talk. On this Monday in March 2007, the water bill at 7 Saratoga Avenue is R320 000. That's roughly equivalent to giving R1 to every family in Johannesburg that's on the waiting list for a house.

Themba and I leave the municipal offices and walk back to the Alfa. We pass Penmor Tower, the invisible skyscraper, whose message is suddenly obvious: the city, like the country it describes, is in drag.

While driving Themba back to Saratoga Avenue I search for more signs of disguise. Opposite the Smal Street Mall I see a matching pair, two canvas billboards flapping against the side of a building. 'Another Urban Renewal Project from City Properties,' they say.

White Settler

MY UNCLE TONY AND aunt Sandy don't know why their son was murdered. With three weeks to go before the trial, they know just a few bald facts.

They know that there are two men charged with the murder, and that their names are Clinton Davids (twenty-two) and Shavaan Marlie (twenty-five). They know that these two men belong to a racial group defined historically in South Africa as 'coloured'. They know that Clinton Davids is the younger brother of Igshaan Davids, aka Sanie the American, the alleged boss of a notorious Cape Flats gang. They know that both the accused were high on tik, a lethal form of crystallised speed, when the murder was committed. They know that Richard was not the victim of a gangland vendetta or a botched drug deal, and that his only mistake was to be on a certain street (Victoria Road, in the upmarket Cape Town suburb of Bakoven) at a certain time (late Saturday night, Easter weekend).

We see Tony and Sandy as often as we can nowadays but we never speak about what they do or don't know. At *shabbos* dinners or family birthdays or Sunday lunches it's plain in their drawn faces and sunken eyes: the last thing they want to do is go over the facts of the case again. So we discuss other things, like how Derek is adjusting to his new life in Sydney, and what their eldest son Gary is doing to help him settle in, and which of Gary's boys (Josh or Sam) talks most like an Aussie.

There's nothing in these discussions that makes *me* want to leave for Australia – no sudden awakening, no irrepressible urge to pack up and go. There are, I realise, two reasons for this: first, a tepid indifference towards my cousins' adopted home-land; and second, more important, the as-yet-unanswered question of what I now feel towards my own country. Since Richard's murder, the change in my attitude to South Africa has revealed itself gradually, incrementally, like a jigsaw puzzle materialising piece by piece at the edges. I see a picture emerging, but I can't yet say what it is.

It's in my journalism, I suspect, that this shift in perspective has been most apparent. In the stories I've recently filed for *Maverick* magazine – a feature on land disputes in Mpumalanga, a profile on the likely new leader of the political opposition, an essay on the myth of Joburg inner city renewal – I've noticed my stance becoming more tentative, my tone more sardonic and interrogative. My editor, who has noticed too, approves. As a man who fled Belgrade on pain of death in 1991, Branko Brkić places little faith in the idea that any nation (even a 'miracle nation') can free itself of its past.

Still, Slobodan Milošević is one thing, the fate of the Republic of South Africa another, and so whenever Branko and I debate the matter it's me who wears the moderate's hat.

'I've seen before,' Branko might say. 'Rule by populists and lowlifes.'

'Mate, this isn't Serbia.'

'Mate, how would *you* know?'

There's usually silence then because I can't respond.

But Branko, who knows me well, understands that I take the question seriously. He understands why I'm uncertain of my place – in my country, in my prose – and why I've decided to confront my doubts in a book.

He's happy to send me on assignments that will facilitate the project, he says. I imagine part of the reason for his generosity is that he too would like more clarity; something concrete to confirm or refute his sense of déjà vu.

———

In mid-February 2007, as my uncle and aunt return to the facts of Richard's murder in one affidavit after another, Dr Pieter Mulder, leader of the rightwing Freedom Front Plus, delivers a speech to parliament.

In his speech Dr Mulder uses the phrase 'white settler'. It is the first time in a long time that the phrase is used by someone other than a member of the ruling party, but Dr Mulder has a point to make. He is concerned, he says, about the question, 'Who is an African?'

Dr Mulder offers an anecdote. Recently, he tells the assembled parliamentarians, he visited the local branch of a government department, where he was asked to complete a form. In the first part of the form's third question, he says, he was asked to classify himself 'Asian' or 'African'; in the second part of the same question, he was asked to choose between 'white' and 'coloured'.

'It is extremely confusing,' he complains. 'You cannot compare apples with pears. Either you use continents or colours.'

But, Dr Mulder says, as long as there is a form that asks him to make such distinctions, he will continue to tick the block marked 'African'. Not to do so, he suggests, encourages the practice of name-calling.

'If your starting point is that some people are African and others not, you will end up with words such as "white settler", which ANC leaders use. This leads to words such as "maboeroe", "magoa" and "white trash", which I hear on the streets.'

Which in turn, Dr Mulder argues, leads to bloodshed. Like the murder just ten days earlier of Albie Greyling, whose friend was told by the fleeing black assailants, 'We are going to kill all you white people.'

CHAPTER 2

Ways of Beginning

FORT MISTAKE IS A DESOLATE turret on the crest of a windswept hill between the towns of Ladysmith and Newcastle in northern KwaZulu-Natal. It was built by the troops of Colonel Sir Evelyn Wood in 1881, during an armistice in imperial Britain's first war with the Boers, and it commands a strategic view of the Mkupe Pass and the Inkunzi valley beyond. The structure, despite its name, is neither fort nor mistake: it was erected as a signal station, and was once called One Tree Hill. What it is called today is believed to be the fault of a cartographer who got his bearings wrong sometime after 1910.

On the morning of March 6th 2007, as I drive a hired Toyota Corolla north along the N11 – the Alfa, my editor agrees, would never have survived this trip – I know nothing of Fort Mistake's past. All I know is that the monument on the hill to my right has an excellent name, and that it is the first sign that we are entering the territory of the battlefields.

Fugitives' Drift Lodge, where the world-famous historian David Rattray was murdered five weeks and four days ago, is now no more than an hour away.

I turn east onto the road to Dundee. With me in the car is Sally Shorkend, *Maverick*'s chief photographer, and Shizeeda Osman, her assistant. Sally is up front cleaning a camera lens and Shizeeda, faux-Gucci shades perched atop her shapely head, is in the back talking on her cellphone. Aside from driving and navigating, what I'm mainly doing is worrying about the assignment. Branko's brief to me is to explore the murder's evident symbolism, and I'm anxious, given that the story's already seen newsprint from Germany to the United Kingdom and Ireland, that I'll have nothing new to add.

Through central Dundee we pass the Talana Museum, dedicated to the Anglo-Zulu War, and we pass directions to memorials and monuments and battle sites.

We pass the Dundee Adult Centre for the Intellectually Disabled, a building in need of a coat of paint.

'I'm looking at the Isizwe funeral home,' Shizeeda says into her phone, as we reach the outskirts of the town. 'Dude, they're so Zulu here.'

Shizeeda, born in Lesotho to an Indian father and a Basotho mother, is not a fan of the Zulu. She's off the phone now, talking to Sally. She doesn't mean to generalise, she says, but she finds them arrogant, aloof. Like Xhosas, she says, they don't mix. She tells Sally about a party in Johannesburg the previous week, where a clique of Zulu girls were gathered in the garden; she asked if she could join them and they addressed her in isiZulu so, whatever, she replied in seSotho.

Shizeeda says she has Zulu ancestors on her mother's side, a result of the *Mfecane*. 'But that doesn't change anything. I still don't like them.'

At noon we arrive at our guesthouse, an old cottage on a farmstead just off the gravel road to Rorke's Drift. We drop off our bags and immediately get back on the road. We are expected at Fugitives' Drift, the luxury lodge built by David Rattray, before the guests finish lunch. The Corolla slides over loose rocks and skids in the ruts. I can't push the car any faster – the Alfa, I'm thinking, would have died out here.

We arrive as the guests are having coffee. We find Andrew Ardington, our host, on the steps between the dining room and the slate stone verandah. Andrew is a tall man with shoulder-length hair and a private school bearing; he was David's business partner and friend, and since the murder, he says, he has remained at the lodge in support of the family.

Andrew suggests an itinerary for the afternoon. We will drive the car down the hill to the village of Rorke's Drift to meet Emmanuel Mkhize, who worked for David and knew him well, and then we will attend Rob Caskie's afternoon lecture on the battle of Rorke's Drift.

Rob, says Andrew, became head lecturer after David's death. For six years he was David's understudy; he is, we are assured, as close as one can get to hearing the great man himself.

———

At 2pm, as I negotiate the road down to the village, a radio news bulletin calls to mind the other murder, the more familiar one. Yesterday Shavaan Marlie and Clinton Davids, the co-accused in the murder of my cousin and Brett, appeared in the Cape High Court, where the judge agreed to allow their lawyers extra time to prepare. The case has now been postponed to May 21st. This information, together with a list of celebrities present in the courtroom – former Miss World Anneline Kriel among them – is still being broadcast as an hourly lead.

The mention of my dead cousin's name, the enduring prominence of the story as a news item, the list of the personalities in attendance – all these things serve to remind me of the reasons I wanted the Rattray assignment in the first place. As the village comes into sight, I consider again the questions (borderline unanswerable) that have brought me out here.

In a country that averages around fifty murders a day, why have the murders of David Rattray, Brett Goldin and Richard Bloom been the most high profile of the last year? Is the focus on these murders symbolic of a national undercurrent, their front-page status a function of resurgent white fears? Or might we be affirming by our fascination that such murders are inevitable, a necessary tax of history?

———

Acacia tortilis has a distinctive spreading crown, which is why it is sometimes called the umbrella thorn. Its leaves droop downward and its top is flat, lending it the look of a portable canopy that has been wheeled onto the veld for protection from the midday sun. The tree is a popular snack on many African grasslands, its succulent pods a mainstay in the diets of insects, birds, giraffe and kudu. It is one of over a hundred African acacia species, all armed – unlike their Australian cousins – with sharp barbs that draw blood.

This land on the banks of the Buffalo River, which once marked the border between the British colony of Natal and King Cetshwayo's Zululand, is overflowing with *Acacia tortilis*.

There are specimens over fifteen metres tall and easily as wide on the grounds of the Zulu cultural village that Emmanuel Mkhize owns and operates in Rorke's Drift. I park the Corolla beneath one. Sally and Shizeeda walk towards the circle of yellow straw huts and I head for the offices at the back.

Emmanuel stands beside a wooden desk in the centre of a bare room. He has a shaved head and a neat *bokbaardjie*, and his T-shirt accentuates the cut of his triceps. He is in his late twenties, I guess, or early thirties, and his pressed jeans and leather boots complete the impression: here is a man who has risen well above his circumstance.

He has been expecting me, he says. He leads me back outside.

'Ah, David, how can I start?'

Emmanuel was thirteen when he met David Rattray, he says. David used to visit the houses around the old mission station and one day Emmanuel gathered the courage to ask for a job. For most of his teenage years, every school holiday, he worked at the Rattray lodge, fixing things and running errands and serving meals to the guests.

The story is interrupted by cries of '*uSuthu!*' I turn to see three men in Zulu warrior skins mounting a mock attack on Sally and Shizeeda and a middle-aged white couple.

Emmanuel grins and continues.

His strongest subject at school was history, he says, which David encouraged. One year, when David was due to go to London to give a series of talks on the Anglo-Zulu War, Emmanuel was invited along. He saw in London what he wanted to do with his life. On his return he went to work as a tour guide for a friend of David's. But David wanted Emmanuel to come back, to work with him, so money was raised to finance the Zulu cultural village.

Emmanuel looks up at the hills.

'I remember when he was murdered. It was a Friday. On the Monday before, he was here with his wife Nicky. They came to take pictures of this Zulu village to put in their brochures.'

Emmanuel tells me that the locals in Rorke's Drift called David *Mshweza*. It's a word that has no English equivalent, he says, but it means someone who can appear behind you at any moment. 'David cruised,' says Emmanuel. 'He was all over.'

I nod. I also look up at the hills. I ask Emmanuel how he heard the news.

'It was un-unbelievable. One of the receptionists called. She said that some men had come to the lodge demanding money. When they were told there was none, they asked to see David. They were taken to the main house, and there David was shot. "No, you can't tell me this," I said. I didn't believe it. Until I saw him lying on the ground.'

On the day of the funeral, Emmanuel says, there were three buses carrying mourners from Rorke's Drift to the service. 'More people wanted to go than the buses could carry.'

While I am aware of the rumours, Emmanuel's next words are unexpected.

'This thing, it wasn't a robbery. In my belief it's something to do with business.'

'I heard something about a land dispute,' I say.

'Zulu people will never kill David for that. David stood for his staff members, he fought for them.'

I realise I have caused offence. I begin to apologise, but Emmanuel interrupts to tell me about one of the suspects.

'The guy in the balaclava didn't work for David. He fixed the toilets for two weeks and then he was gone. If it was a robbery they should have demanded something from reception. We strongly believe we'll get the truth. David was a successful businessman. Every tour guide wished he was like David. If we find out exactly … ay!'

He pauses. Then, 'The police came to threaten us the other day. We wanted to burn those houses the other side of the Buffalo River. We said, "If you don't get them, we'll get them ourselves."'

I want to ask for more, to glean from him why he thinks there's a difference between killing a man for land and killing a man for business, to understand better why he separates himself from *those* Zulus on the other side of the river. But the time for talking is now over. Emmanuel wants to show me his village and Sally wants to take his portrait.

He gestures for me to follow. 'A village like this,' he says, spreading his right arm across the expanse of his property, 'dates back from Shaka's time, from long before Cetshwayo was king.'

Emmanuel shows me the huts on stilts on the perimeter of the village, where the lookouts would sit. He shows me the kraal in the centre of the village, for the Nguni cattle. He tells me that the floors of the huts are made from cow dung and the walls from packed straw. At the back of the largest hut, the grandmother's hut, he points out the nook for the worship of the ancestors.

'They still have these huts in deep Zululand,' Emmanuel says, 'around Ulundi and Msinga and Eshowe.'

———

At 3.30pm the whole of St Stithian's grade six is on the grass outside the Rorke's Drift museum – dozens of pre-adolescent boys laden with chocolates and bottles of Fanta and spear-and-shield souvenirs. They call to one another in clipped consonants and articulated vowels, an accent learned beneath the oaks and elms of their school grounds in Johannesburg. I stand to the side and watch. Amongst the crowd I see a black pupil tear across the lawn in pursuit of his white classmate.

'The British must die!' says the black boy, his right arm coiled, ready to hurl an imaginary assegai. A young teacher interrupts the chase. 'If you're going to kill each other,' she says, 'please do it *on* the bus.'

By 3.45pm the three coaches carrying the boys have moved off and the museum grounds are quiet. I walk up to the old church, where in a few minutes Rob Caskie will begin his lecture on the battle of Rorke's Drift. All the guests are here except one. 'Peter,' Rob says to the straggler when he arrives, 'we were speculating whether you were reading the fire evacuation procedure on the back of the museum door.'

Rob has the manner of an affable drill sergeant. He is controlling, detached, defended by a light irony. His working uniform is khaki shorts above thick red socks and leather hiking boots, a blue shirt with the lodge's logo on the pocket, and a khaki bush hat. A maroon cravat – to match the socks – is knotted at his throat. He is a big man, with a torso like a bear, and during the brief orientation session he points out the landmarks with a heavy wooden stick: the mountains where the main British army was encamped, the direction of the old Zulu capital of Ulundi, the route Cetshwayo's errant soldiers took to get here.

Orientation done, we move to two rows of foldout chairs that have been arranged behind the church. The chairs face the round dome of Shiyane, the eyebrow-shaped hill from which Rorke's Drift takes its Zulu name.

In his lecture voice now, stentorian, like a herald delivering a royal decree, Rob stands before us and announces that eleven Victoria Crosses and five Distinguished Conduct medals were awarded at the battle of Rorke's Drift. 'The most for a single action in the history of the British armed forces.'

The battle, says Rob, saw four thousand Zulu *impis* descend from the hill above us onto one hundred and thirty-nine British infantrymen, thirty-five of whom were gravely ill. The British were mostly Welshmen from coal mining towns, their average age twenty-three, and they were left here to guard the mission station and the makeshift hospital while the main army gathered at Isandlwana, five miles to the north-east.

Rob lets his words settle. He walks the length of the chairs and looks briefly at each of us. 'There is more to this that appeals to the minds of the British than just the story of a battle and a church,' he says.

Aside from myself, the twenty or so guests in the audience today are all British (Sally and Shizeeda have decided not to attend). What appeals to their minds, I'm guessing, is that their countrymen held out; that they stood and fought when a less disciplined force might have played the percentages and fled.

Rob begins to outline in detail what happened on the evening and deep into the night of January 22nd 1879.

Some time in the afternoon, he says, on a day whose signal importance for two great empires was portended by a solar eclipse of the sun, the British garrison heard shots fired in the distance. A group of officers climbed a hill to investigate, and what they saw they could not at first believe: a column of Zulu warriors appeared to be advancing towards the mission station from beyond the Buffalo River. If what the officers saw was real, if their eyes weren't deceiving them, it meant that the British camp at Isandlwana, over a thousand soldiers armed with breech-loading Martini-Henry rifles and heavy artillery, had been defeated by Zulus brandishing little more than cowhide shields and stabbing spears. The unthinkable was soon confirmed: a British lieutenant fleeing Isandlwana told the officers of the slaughter.

The Rorke's Drift garrison set about fortifying its position. The mission station was loopholed, and the church and makeshift hospital were linked and barricaded by walls of mealie bags.

Rob, I realise, is now regularly invoking the spirit of David Rattray. The further into the lecture he gets, the more he introduces facts and anecdotes with phrases like, 'David estimated ...', 'David said ...', and 'When David stood here ...'

David's voice is present as Rob moves on to the next phase in the story. 'When we go to Zulu oral history about this battle, they don't want to talk,' he says. 'Not because it was a loss, but because they disobeyed their king and brought shame and embarrassment to their nation.'

The Zulus who attacked Rorke's Drift were the youngest warriors from Isandlwana, says Rob. In the day's first battle they were ordered to guard an exit route and so they did not get to dip their spears in the blood of their enemy. Prince Dabulamanzi, Cetshwayo's brother, wanted these regiments to share in the victory – he wanted to build on the success at Isandlwana, and he knew that the young men were eager to bloody their spears so that they could marry. Dabulamanzi, by leading the men across the river into the British colony of Natal, ignored an express command of his brother: the Zulu nation was not to be seen as an aggressor.

At around 5.30pm the sun sinks below the hills. A guest in the front row wraps herself in a blanket. Rob seizes on the opportunity presented. 'Emma, you know I look at you and the image I get is of a Scarborough pensioner sitting at the station waiting for the bingo callout.'

Emma, I will find out later, is the wife of Anthony Thesiger, the great-great-grandson of Lord Chelmsford: the two are out here to see for themselves how the former commander of the British armed forces in South Africa earned his place in history.

Rob invites us all to stand, to join him behind the old hospital, where he will dedicate the remainder of his lecture to the bravery of the British soldiers who fought there.

At Rorke's Drift, says Rob, the option of deserting the sick and the injured was not entertained. He evokes for us the start of the battle: the wide eyes of the Zulus in full charge, the disciplined lines of the British, the shouting:

'Here they come, boys! Black as hell and thick as grass!'

He talks about the Martini-Henry rifle, which in capable hands could shoot six to eight rounds a minute and had the calibre to cleave a skull in half. He tells us that the battle began at 5pm and that at 7pm, with the setting of the sun, the Zulus torched the roof of the hospital.

'It gave the British in the main house two choices,' he says. 'To burn to death or die outside on a Zulu spear.'

Rob says that as many men were extracted from the hospital as possible, but a few perished in the flames. He mentions the names John Williams, Henry Hook, William Jones, Frederick Hitch and William Allen – soldiers whose dogged defence of room after room earned them all vcs.

Later, the British withdrew to the centre of the station, where a final bastion had been assembled. They picked off the Zulus by the light of the burning hospital. The attacks were resisted until midnight, when the ferocity of the assault abated. Firing continued until 4am, at which time, save for the moaning of the wounded and the dying, Rorke's Drift fell silent.

Rob ends the lecture in shouts and whispers. He recites some lines from a poem, which he dedicates to the soldiers on both sides, and to David Rattray, a man he 'grew to love as a brother, a man taken five weeks ago.' The poem is Laurence Binyon's 'For the Fallen'.

'They shall grow not old, as we that are left grow old/Age shall not weary them, nor the years condemn/At the going down of the sun and in the morning/We will remember them.'

On the way to the parking lot I speak to a man from Kent. He tells me he decided not to cancel his trip because of the murder. He got an email from Nicky Rattray, explaining that it was an isolated incident.

'It was an isolated incident, wasn't it?' he asks.

———

The next morning, I step out the back door of the guesthouse to watch the sunrise. It's a cold morning and mist has settled at the bottom of the valley. The sun is feeble and disappointing, a vague orange disc.

An alarm clock rings inside. Through the open door I hear Shizeeda. She informs Sally how she slept: woke at twelve, woke at one, woke at three.

Then I hear laughing. I join the women in the kitchen. 'What's so funny?'

Seems I went to bed too early. Last night, according to Sally, Shizeeda was uncontrollable. What happened was this: Wilma, the wife of the owner of the guesthouse, came in to warn us that there could be a problem with the hot water – an electricity problem, she said, the transponder got struck by lightning.

'I phoned Eskom,' Wilma explained to the women, 'and they said they had to fix the electricity at the black hospital first. But I told them I had paying guests. I did tell them.'

Which, says Sally, was when Shizeeda doubled over. 'I've got *paying* guests,' Shizeeda repeated, over and over.

She does it again now. '*Paying* guests.'

I laugh too. It is funny. Shizeeda's response to the embedded prejudices of white people, to the embedded prejudices of all South Africans, is endearing. It's possible, I'm thinking, that she's right: we're all hilarious.

An hour later we're back at Fugitives' Drift Lodge. Together with their paying guests – who pay pound-sterling rates and are never without hot water – we strike out in a convoy of four Land Rovers, our destination the battlefield of Isandlwana.

The sun has now burnt the mist away and the hills are rendered in intricate relief, the acacias cast long shadows. A recording plays on the car-audio as we bump over gravel tracks. On the recording is a male voice, imparting in lyrical cadences the distant history of the region. The Bantu tribes came down from Africa, says the voice, and thought they had found heaven. 'Which is what *amaZulu* means, the people of heaven.'

After generations of pastoral peace, the voice continues, Shaka forged an imperial force, which lasted for sixty-three years before being destroyed by the British. Woven into the narrative are hypnotic references to the place we are visiting today. 'The 22nd of January 1879 reads like a great Shakespearean tragedy,' we hear. And then: 'Isn't it strange that at the terrible battle at Isandlwana the sun should go dark like night?'

We hear that Natal was named for its beauty, a land so stunning it's as though it were the birthplace of Christ. We hear the story of Henry Francis Fynn, a colonial adventurer who arrived at Shaka's homestead seeking trading rights and ended up befriending the great king. We hear the following: 'What a pity it is that the relationship between Fynn and Shaka could not have been a lesson for the relationship between white and black in the world.'

The rise and fall of the voice, the sentence construction, is an effect of the landscape, I'm thinking. Something in it echoes Alan Paton, echoes the way liberal white men in this part of the country have been speaking and writing for decades. The line (famous, overwrought) from *Cry, the Beloved Country*: 'These hills are grass-covered and rolling, and they are lovely beyond any singing of it.' It could have been recited by the voice we're listening to, could have been referring to the hills we are bumping across now – Ixopo, where Paton's Absalom Kumalo grew up, is not much more than two hundred kilometres from here.

The Land Rovers gear down, cross a narrow bridge and climb an embankment on the far side. We're across the Buffalo River now, in what was once Cetshwayo's kingdom, and I'm wondering whether I trust the voice on the recording. For one thing, I'm dimly aware of an alternative historical version of Fynn – a version that says he was a violent rogue, a fabricator of self-serving stories about Shaka.

I'm also remembering what JM Coetzee said about the older Paton. 'As for the writing itself, one soon grows tired of his Churchillian mannerisms.'

Some put-down.

But Coetzee, I'm thinking, is from another place. And this morning, in this Land Rover, in this most mythologised corner of proto-mythical Zululand, it's hard to be unmoved by the voice – or to forget for long that its owner is recently dead.

At the first stop of the morning our driver presses the pause button on David Rattray's audio series *The Day of the Dead Moon* and we join the rest of the guests in a half-circle around Rob. We're standing on a rise, an open field slopes gently away below us, and our lecturer is soon in full throat. 'This was an unfortunate war!'

All was peaceful in the region until the 1870s, Rob explains, when gold and diamonds were discovered and the British decided to plant guard posts along the river.

'This war started on the strength of two adulterous Zulu women who were stoned to death on the river's banks in full view of the British border guards. They were looking for an excuse, spoiling for a fight. That was it.'

In mid-January 1879, says Rob, seventeen thousand British soldiers in five columns crossed the Buffalo River into Zululand. Amongst the British soldiers were a large number of Zulus from Natal; men whose crops had failed and who needed the pay, or men, like Cetshwayo's exiled half-brother Mthonga, who bore long-nurtured grudges. The Zulus on the British side were known collectively as the Natal Native Contingent, and their distinguishing mark was the red bandanna, which later became the mark of the Zulu traitor. In the violence of the early 1990s, says Rob, the red bandanna was worn by the men who threw their people from the trains.

We get back into the Land Rovers and climb a series of switchbacks, and in thirty minutes we are looking down onto the sphinx-like head of Isandlwana. 'At four thousand three hundred feet above sea level,' says Rob, 'we are higher than anything in Britain. Hundreds of feet higher than Ben Nevis.'

Rob now talks about the big mistake of the British on the day of the battle: Chelmsford's decision to split the forces. He points out where on the battlefield the armies stood, the movement of the regiments, why the British were left so vulnerable by Chelmsford's strategy.

He quotes Rudyard Kipling: 'At Isandlwana the Zulus taught the British no end of a lesson.' To emphasise the severity of the lesson, Rob invokes a *Punch* cartoon that appeared in London shortly after the defeat. In the cartoon, he says, Chelmsford and Queen Victoria are sitting on wooden stools in front of a chalkboard, and a black warrior in skins, H Rider Haggard's archetypal 'noble savage', is standing before them, giving instructions with a stick; written on the board are the words, 'Despise not thine enemies.'

Then, letting us know it's time for the main event, the intimate and detailed spoken history of Isandlwana for which David Rattray became world renowned, Rob says, 'Let's go down there and I'll explain how the Zulus took the British apart like a cheap Chinese clock.'

———

In the essay where Coetzee compares the older Paton to Churchill, an essay that first appeared in *The New Republic* magazine in 1990, Coetzee presents as evidence for his analogy the following line (from Paton's *Save the Beloved Country*): 'There are those who ask, what good has [protest] done? It has done a lot of good. It enables us to say, South Africa is a land of fear, but it is a land of courage also.'

I find the line and reread the essay when I return to Johannesburg. My flat in Killarney is not set in landscape that is *grass-covered and rolling* – The Wilds, despite its charms, is no Zululand – and I am soon won over by the force of Coetzee's argument, sceptical of the romance of Paton country. Under Coetzee's cold eye, Paton becomes one-dimensional, a caricature.

We shall fight them on the koppies.

Some months later I find another Coetzee essay on Paton. Published originally in 1980, and updated for a collection released in 1988 called *White Writing*, this one takes issue with the Zulu-language verbal exchanges (rendered in English) of *Cry, the Beloved Country*.

Dialogue like:

'You are in fear of me, but I do not know what it is. You need not be in fear of me.'

'It is true, *umnumzana*. You do not know what it is.'

'I do not know but I desire to know.'

'I doubt if I could tell it, *umnumzana*.'

And so on.

Language like this, says Coetzee, 'implies an archaic quality to the Zulu behind it, as if the Zulu language, Zulu culture, the Zulu frame of mind, belonged to a bygone and heroic age'.

Coetzee rejects what he calls 'Paton's Zulu'. He mistrusts the idea of the heroic age. The Zulu so admired by Victorian England, the man ennobled by loyalty and self-sacrifice, the figure without flaws or complexities, is for Coetzee a 'phantom'.

Still, *Cry, the Beloved Country* sold fifteen million copies before Paton's death, remains part of the curriculum in schools across the world, and is widely regarded as an African classic. Which suggests, whatever the problems with Paton's Zulu, that it takes a certain kind of person not to be enchanted.

———

The Land Rovers are parked under the canopy of the largest umbrella thorn on the veld. The beach chairs have been arranged again in rows, and glasses of water are passed around. Once more Rob begins with a quick orientation. We are sitting, he tells us, just beyond the perimeter of the main British encampment. Out in the direction we are facing is Ulundi; behind us, on the steepest slopes of the mountain, is where the fiercest fighting happened.

Rob reminds us of the battle's impact on history. Benjamin Disraeli, he says, a staunch imperialist and favourite of Queen Victoria, was so weakened by the defeat that in 1880 he was replaced as prime minister by the anti-colonialist William Gladstone.

'And Isandlwana was a pyrrhic victory for the Zulus,' says Rob. 'They lost three thousand of their strongest warriors.'

At the Battle of Ulundi in July 1879, when the Zulu army was finally overwhelmed by the British reinforcements sent to avenge Isandlwana, the absence of those warriors was keenly felt. After Ulundi, Cetshwayo was forced into exile and his kingdom broken up into thirteen chiefdoms. 'Which marked the beginning of Zulu labour for the white man.'

The stakes thus established, the end of the story told at the beginning, Rob steers his narrative in the direction of the specific: the details of life in the British camp.

He points his stick at the open field behind us. 'Most of the men began their days swilling their boots out with urine,' he says, 'to change the pH balance.' The soldiers of the Natal Native Contingent had stopped defecating, he adds, because they feared Cetshwayo's witchdoctors – 'human faeces being a well-known method of cursing an enemy.'

We inhabit, through Rob, a world of superstition, flies, fever; brutal summer heat endured in heavy canvas helmets and thick serge tunics.

We are drawn in by Rob's silences. 'The man who was left in charge of the camp here had not seen battle in twenty-three years of service.' Pause. 'Out of almost fifteen hundred of Britain's finest foot-soldiers, fifty-five got out of Isandlwana alive.' Pause.

Rob dwells on, stretches out, the tension of the moment of discovery: the instant a British patrol stumbles upon twenty thousand Zulu *impis* hiding in a ravine; the scene as the patrol fires in panic into the sea of black faces staring up at them.

'It was madness,' he whispers. 'The Zulus began to stream up the sides of the ravine.'

Rob describes how the Zulu regiments appeared at a run on the crest of the hill to the north of us, and we all turn to look, the benign ridgeline suddenly populated by the vision of a vast and swarming army. We hear the taunt of the war cries; we see the regiments forming and reforming in mass choreographed movements; we sense the fear in the British camp as the commanders realise they are being encircled on their flanks.

And then there, while we are looking up at the ridge, beyond the shadow of the acacia and in the full glare of the midday sun, we see Shizeeda. She is sitting on a rock, pulling up sheaves of grass, disinterested and disengaged, consummately bored.

———

Refreshments for the tea break have been taken out of the Land Rovers and placed on a foldout table. The guests eat and drink and discuss the lecture. Some distance away from the main group, standing with his wife Emma, is Anthony Thesiger, direct descendant of Lord Chelmsford. I approach, introduce myself and explain why I'm here. In response Thesiger says he has had the honour, five or six times, of hearing David Rattray speak at the RGS – 'the Royal Geographic Society,' he says, in clarification.

Thesiger tells me that his cousin, not he, is the current Lord Chelmsford.

He is astounded by the oratorical powers of Rob Caskie, he says. No, he is not concerned by the violence in South Africa. 'Anything can happen at any time in London.' Emma, to further disabuse me of the notion that South Africa is unique, tells me that she travelled in Africa when she was nineteen. 'Zaire and that sort of thing.'

I don't ask Thesiger how he feels about his ancestor.

When we are fed and revived and back in our chairs, Rob takes us to the final hours of the battle: an intensely primal scene, almost unreal in its power.

The sun obscured by the moon and the day going dark at the battle's height.

The looming silhouette of the *iklwa*, named for the sound it made as it was pushed in, twisted, and pulled out of the body.

The ritual disembowelment of the dead, performed to release the spirit.

The last stand of Colonel Durnford, a commander who could have escaped but who chose to fight and die, his one good arm brandishing his sword high above the encircling warriors.

The frenzy of bloodlust, the killing of even the horses, the amputation of body parts for use by the *iziNyanga* as *muti*.

Rob ends with his longest silence yet. He breathes deeply, sweats, walks up and down the first row of chairs. 'It's easy for us with our anglophile view to be shocked at the images of British officers dying,' he says. Once more, he invokes the spirit of his dead friend. 'David was alarmed how the history books tended to be the propaganda of the victor. He could not abide the default position of the Zulu as the enemy, and so he searched the area for old Zulus with a story to tell.'

Due to the practice of polygamy, says Rob, which meant men might bear children well into late middle age, David found some men in the 1980s whose fathers and uncles had fought in these wars. 'He learned from one old man that the British line almost repelled the Zulus at Isandlwana. Most Zulu regiments had taken *huge* losses.'

Rob raises his voice, stresses the point with his stick. 'This picture has been painted for too long as a terrible British defeat. We prefer to paint it as a great Zulu victory. We think the history taught at Sandhurst, that the

British line collapsed when the Native regiment fled, is absolute nonsense. There is much more to understanding this battle.'

A final remark about Cetshwayo – yet another dismissed plea for peace – and the lecture is done.

Before we return to the lodge for lunch, we are given time to explore the battlefield. With the other guests I walk up to the saddle below the crest of Isandlwana. In full daylight, amongst the cairns and the gravestones and the monuments, the sense here is of consecrated ground, of a place not to be violated. In the shade of a solar eclipse, I'm thinking, waiting to die, it must have been wholly mystical; a religious experience for even the non-believers.

I climb the path that leads up the face of Isandlwana. In twenty minutes I am at the mouth of the small cave where it is believed the last of the British soldiers died, a skeleton found months later with a fraying rope around its neck.

———

At the funeral of David Rattray, Chief Mangosuthu Buthelezi, a member of parliament and the traditional prime minister of the Zulu nation, expressed, on behalf of himself and the current Zulu king, the profound gratitude of his people to the deceased. He thanked David for his 'meticulous contribution to the recording of Anglo-Zulu history' and, more importantly, for his 'contribution to reconciliation between the descendants of those who fought on both sides of the Anglo-Zulu War'.

Throughout the tribute, Buthelezi, who had already briefed the audience on his bloodline – maternal great-grandson of Cetshwayo, 'whose kingdom was destroyed in that unjust war', paternal great-grandson of Mnyamana Buthelezi, who was the commander-in-chief of all Cetshwayo's regiments, and grandson of Mkhandumba Buthelezi, who fought at Isandlwana – emphasised his own sense of personal loss.

Near the end of his tribute Buthelezi spoke about the breakdown of the criminal justice system in South Africa. He said that David would not have died in vain if citizens were collectively to demand that the country's leaders now acknowledge the severity of the crime problem.

Buthelezi's last sentiment echoed the call of theatre personalities, fashion professionals and opposition politicians, made the previous year in the wake of the murders of actor Brett Goldin and fashion designer Richard Bloom.

While the Goldin and Bloom murders would result, for a period, in a series of anti-crime vigils (or peace marches), the response to the murder of David Rattray would find far more potent expression: in an announcement by a large bank that it had allocated twenty million rand to a national advertising campaign urging President Thabo Mbeki to make crime prevention his top priority.

But the advertising campaign was cancelled just before it was due to run. Local media reported that the government had accused the bank of 'incitement', and that the bank, fearing the consequences, had backed down.

———

Climbing Isandlwana has given me an appetite. I'm in the lodge's dining room, on my second helping of tender beef and steamed vegetables, when my phone rings. It's my father, to ask whether I know that the trial's been postponed. I tell him I've heard the news bulletins.

'What do you think?'

'I think it's dragging on too long. How's Tony?'

'As well as can be expected.'

My father has been helping his older brother prepare for the case. As a lawyer, albeit a commercial one, my father has a good working knowledge of South Africa's criminal courts; he understands the psyche of the prosecutors, what's needed if they are to be successful.

'We're doing what we can,' he says.

Then, 'Where are you? Sounds like you're miles away.'

'KwaZulu-Natal. I've been researching a piece on the Rattray murder.'

I'm tempted to spell it out, to tell him why I took the assignment, to see what he makes of my motivations. But I know what he would say. A rhetorical question: How much do you think you can learn about one murder from studying another? Part of me already sees the truth in this.

I say goodbye without bringing it up. Surrounded by these battlefields it's the other part of me, the part that sees truth in the cycles of history – in the moment (long deferred) of a reckoning – that maintains the upper hand.

———

The walls of the guest bathroom at Fugitives' Drift Lodge bear proof of the relationship between David and Nicky Rattray and the British royal family. Amongst sepia photographs of Zulu chieftains and illustrations of the battle of Isandlwana is an invitation from the British high commissioner to the hundredth birthday of the queen mother, an invitation (also from the British high commissioner) to the birthday on June 15th 2000 of Queen Elizabeth II, and an invitation from the commander of the Royal Regiment of Wales, Brigadier KJ Davey, to a regimental parade in the presence of Prince Charles.

Just outside the door to this bathroom, on the right as you come down some steps, is the window to the office where six armed men appeared at around 5pm on January 26th 2007 to demand money.

As major newspapers in South Africa, Great Britain and mainland Europe have explained, the men were told there wasn't any money. So they waved their guns and asked to see David Rattray. The men were led to the main house, and when the first man entered he saw Nicky Rattray standing in the doorway of a bathroom. The man hesitated for an instant as David pushed Nicky to the side and rushed at him. Then the man shot David.

On the afternoon of the day I visited Isandlwana, at a table not far from where David was killed, I interview Andrew Ardington, his business partner.

The table is set on the lodge's lawns with a view of the Buffalo River gorge. Bateleur eagles are riding the thermals; in the far distance is the crest of Isandlwana. I am by now fully in thrall to Paton country; I expect another tale of stoicism and intrigue.

Andrew is the first to disappoint.

My opening question to him is whether he sees a parallel between David Rattray and Neil Alcock, a white man murdered in the 1980s by members of the Zulu community he had chosen to live amongst, a story made famous by Rian Malan in his memoir *My Traitor's Heart*.

Andrew shakes his head. 'The big difference is Neil Alcock was actually involved in a dispute and got caught in the crossfire.'

Andrew likewise dismisses the theories, currently circulating in and around Rorke's Drift, that David was killed by a disgruntled former employee, that it was a hit ordered by a rival in the tourism industry, that it had something to do with a land claim.

'Never once was he outspoken on the issue of land redistribution.'

Andrew is convinced the murder was a bungled robbery, and although he admits that it might suit him as an owner to subscribe to this (the official) version of events, he refuses to acknowledge the irony.

'All my friends have said to me, back in Cape Town, "There's David, and he does so much for them, and then they shoot him." But what they don't get is, he wasn't doing all those things so that they *wouldn't* shoot him.'

———

At 10am the next morning, with Sally and Shizeeda in the car, I drive down the main gravel road that runs through Rorke's Drift and turn left onto a short track. I park the car beneath a grove of umbrella thorn. Around me, as I step out, teenagers in school uniform talk and joke.

By law Shiyane High School caters for the children of every family in the region, but despite the presence of many white farmers, all of its 520 pupils are black.

The school is a series of single-storey face-brick buildings arranged around a courtyard of dead grass. There is no name to identify the place. A sign on the side of the building nearest the wire-mesh gate says 'No Guns'.

I shut the gate behind me and find the school principal, Mr Lindani Zulu, in an office spilling over with bookshelves, work-desks and filing cabinets.

Mr Zulu is tall and lean with a beard of grey stubble. He wears a tie in a Windsor knot and an old leather jacket. He has a badge on his lapel that shows he is a man of the church, and he speaks softly, framing his sentences with bony hands.

Mr Zulu tells me, as we sit down, how he came to know David Rattray.

It was 1987, he says, when David's business was still new and had only a small clientele. David would take tourists in groups of two or three to the Rorke's Drift museum, which was next to the old school where Mr Zulu taught. Every afternoon Mr Zulu would walk home through the museum grounds, and one afternoon David invited him to tea.

'He received me very well. He offered me a topographical map of Rorke's Drift. I was a geography teacher, but I was not aware there could be a map like that of this area.'

Mr Zulu says he was wary of David at first – he didn't know what the white man wanted – but that as he walked past the museum on his way home every day, he began to think of David as a man with pure intentions.

'I would avoid David in most cases when he was lecturing. Those people are paying, I would say to myself. But he would see me passing, and he would shout "*sawubona nomzani*", and he would say to the people, "No, he is a good man." I sometimes thought I didn't deserve it.'

He pauses to think and then goes on. 'It would make me preach that gospel of his. You know, some of the tourists, especially from the UK, regard this as a sacred place. It bothers them to see the black people shouting. So David would inform me about the history. He would ask me to explain it to the people here.'

I tell Mr Zulu I don't fully get his meaning.

'I arrived in 1987,' he says, 'but I only peeped in the museum in 1993. In the beginning I hated the whole idea of seeing the tourists. I thought they were here to celebrate their victory over us.'

Mr Zulu tells me that in his heart he wanted revenge. It was David Rattray, he says, who soothed these feelings in him.

'In his life and in his efforts, he did a lot for me emotionally and spiritually. I was not aware that he was a rich man. He was always humble. He would do this' – he clasps his hands together and bows his head – 'and show, no, I am nothing before you. In most cases he would show as if I am the one who is above.'

'Okay,' I say. 'I see now.'

Mr Zulu then explains how David was instrumental in raising the funds to pay for the new high school, how he organised sponsorship for an additional building, how when the computers were stolen he gave a speech about crime in the community hall and how, when that didn't work, he arranged for the equipment to be replaced by the minister of education.

Mr Zulu sits up straight in his chair. 'He supported us in many respects. Renovations, bus trips, outings. We would find it awkward sometimes to go to him. Especially myself, I would find that he would never let me down.'

I have forgotten to turn my phone off. A shrill double-beep announces that I have received an SMS message. I apologise and reach into my pocket and press the off button.

'How did you react to the news of the murder?' I ask.

'It was a tragedy,' he says tersely, raising his voice for the first time. 'It was embarrassing. For us as the Zulus to kill him, it made me very … it made me very uncomfortable. We owe the Rattrays. All of us as the Zulus, we owe …'

He lays his hands on the table and stares at them. He talks about what has been lost.

'There were still things to learn from him. We were getting to know him … we were getting to know him better and better. Some would say he's a Boer, but I would say, no, he's different from other people, local rich whites, in the sense that what he's got he's willing to share.'

He looks up at me for a moment, and then down again at his hands.

'He was loved and respected. We really adored him. I don't think the other white people will be able to imitate David. It might be impossible. Maybe they should think about what will happen after their death. Will the whole world move like this?'

———

Sally and Shizeeda set up the tripod in the centre of the school courtyard. They position Mr Zulu in a seated pose on a work-desk that has been brought out for the purpose. A group of schoolgirls are recruited to walk across the frame of the shot. Shizeeda signals for the girls to go, to stop, to come back, to go again; she laughs each time at the catwalk strut of the joker in the group.

Back in the Corolla, on the road to Dundee, I remember I have a message. I take my phone out my pocket and switch it on.

The message – the one that came through while I was talking to Mr Zulu – reads: 'Don't know if you've heard but David Bullard was shot at his house last night. He's stable. Tom.'

Some Enchanted Evening

MY FATHER'S SIDE OF the family has never been big on the Jewishness of festivals. We celebrate them because it's an excuse to see one another. On the first night of *pesach*, a Monday night in April 2007, we go as we always do to my uncle's place, a cluster home in the oak-shaded Johannesburg suburb of Melrose. Tonight is also my mother's birthday, and my girlfriend and I have brought her a present. On the TV in the lounge as we kiss her on the cheek is Dean Martin doing 'Some Enchanted Evening'. My uncle, it appears, has a new favourite DVD.

I pour myself a scotch and open the sliding doors and step outside. The air is warm and heavy. It smells like rain. I take a long sip of my drink. The first few bars of 'Far Away Places' waft through from the lounge.

Outside still feels like a before-dinner ritual at my uncle's house. This patio, be-fore, was always filled with my cousins and their friends, and I'd always step onto it to a 'Nice one, Kev,' or a 'Whatsup, bud?' or a 'Dude, what's with the hair?' Whenever we would come for *pesach* or Friday night or whatever family thing before, Richard would be sitting there, on that chair, laughing with his partner Brian, or my sister Lara, or his twin brother Derek. He would be talking a mile a minute, smoking, ash-ing reflexively every few seconds into that silver ashtray. That same silver ashtray over there, the one with the little spring that you push if you want to hide the butts …

My mother appears in the doorway and asks if I'd like some company. Sure, I say, and as she comes out she does a little twirl to show off the gift we've bought for her (a Jo Borkett blouse, from the boutique in the Rosebank Mall). It's a perfect fit, she says, exactly her style. I kiss her on the cheek again.

We stand silently together and stare up at the oaks. I know my mother feels out here what I feel; it's impossible for her not to – the patio is haunted by absences, defined by what's no longer there. We stay like this for a while, listening to the crickets. And then for some reason I tell her about a phone call I got from David Bullard.

'I think he called as many of his friends as he could,' I say. 'A student from KwaZulu-Natal emailed him a death threat last week, promising to finish the job.'

As my mother and much of the country know, Bullard, a widely read newspaper columnist, got shot in the stomach in March. Two men broke into his house and all he could think about was his wife in the next room, so he went for the man with the gun.

'It's horrific,' my mother says, in a tone that confirms we're talking about more than just Bullard.

We go into the dining room and listen to Tony recite the *Kiddush*. The mood at the table is subdued. It's almost a year since Richard's death, and while dishing up the starters Sandy wonders aloud whether she should do anything to mark the day. Not quite knowing whether there's a right answer, the opinions we offer are hesitant and vague.

After the meal, as we're saying our goodbyes, I tell Tony and Sandy that I'd like to come past one evening for a talk. For weeks I've been waiting to tell my uncle and aunt that I intend covering the trial for *Maverick,* but the time has never seemed right. Now I can't wait any more.

The following Thursday, in Tony's upstairs study, I state my case.

'Dozens of journalists are going to be there,' says Sandy, dignified and direct despite her tears. 'I don't see why you shouldn't be one of them.'

Tony agrees, on one condition. 'You'll sit next to us in the courtroom. We'd like that a lot.'

CHAPTER 3

To Protect the Baby

AS SHE DOES MOST days, on the last Saturday of January 2006 Lisa Solomon gets out of bed at 5.30am. She walks down the passage and over to the cot where Tomer – the youngest of her four boys and already eight months old – is belting out a high-pitched wail. She picks him up and feeds him and changes his nappy. She rocks him and coos to him. She plants kisses on his forehead. When Tomer has settled, she places him back in his cot and returns to her bedroom.

Daniel Solomon is just getting up. He stretches and yawns and swings his legs to the floor. He scratches his beard. He says good morning to his wife.

Lisa sits down on the edge of the bed. 'Did the alarm turn off?'

The Solomons have a timer that automatically arms and disarms their alarm: it saves them from having to flip an electric switch, which would be a desecration of the *shabbos*. But this *shabbos* morning, Daniel has not heard the device turn off. 'I must have been asleep,' he says.

Lisa shrugs. It's probably nothing, she thinks. Maybe she was in the bathroom when the signal sounded, or the baby was crying.

She stands and walks from the bedroom. She glances in again at her two younger boys – the older boys spent the night at her sister's place – and she unlocks the internal security gate that divides the sleeping section from the rest of the Glenhazel house. As she steps into the home's eating and living section, the sharp smell of smoke assaults her nostrils. Her first thought is that she has left the heat on too high and burnt out the crock-pot (a twenty-four-hour cooker, another device for *shabbos*). But in the kitchen she sees that the pot is fine. Then she thinks that maybe the *shabbos* candles have fallen over and set the carpet alight.

It's ten short steps to the living room, a journey she makes countless times every day. Today, though, something isn't right. It's a strange sensation, as if the place is not as she left it – as if the kitchen floor is dirty, or the cutlery holder is not next to the bread bin. She ignores the feeling.

She reaches the doorway of the living room and she stops. She sees a man she doesn't know. She sees that the man is holding a knife. It's a knife from the dining room table. He's got one of my *shabbos* knives, Lisa thinks.

She's wearing her short summer nightie. To appear this way before a strange man is immodest. She sits down on the kitchen floor. And she starts to scream.

———

There are four of them. I park the Alfa on Long Avenue, forty metres off the intersection with Ridge Road. From this distance I can tell that the information I've been given is wrong: they are armed with shotguns, not semi-automatics. The barrel of each weapon is as thick as a hosepipe; there is a pump-action handle, a ribbed plastic grip, where the multiple-cartridge magazine should be.

The air, as I step out, throbs and burns. Insects drone in walled gardens; it smells of pine needles and begonia. The heat comes close to defusing my anxiety. Still, one last time, I remind myself why it will be fine.

This is Glenhazel. Those four armed black men are paid to protect people like me – they will hear my accent, assume I belong, gladly answer my questions.

They are gathered in the shade of an acacia tree, dressed in identical black fatigues. Black Kevlar vests shield their torsos and black sunglasses cover their eyes.

It is midday on *shabbos* and nobody else is on the street; they swivel on their big black boots to watch me.

I smile. From five paces away, I extend my hand to the least intimidating – the shortest, the one with the paunch – and introduce myself.

'Pietersen,' he says.

I deliver my next sentence like the opening line of a joke. 'How come you men get to carry those guns when the guys from the normal security companies are lucky to get batons?'

Pietersen is deadpan. 'We got a competency licence from Sandton.'

Maybe the informal approach isn't going to work. Maybe they don't get my accent. I hesitate – I had planned on waiting until we were further along – and then I tell them I am a journalist.

Their shoulders flare, their backs tighten – suddenly they are on parade. In minutes I know they all have special military training. One mentions 44 Parabats, one Section 20. They all fought in the Angolan civil war, as part of an elite underground unit that I'm asked not to name. Two of the men – the darker skinned, with the Portuguese accents – are in fact from Angola.

'Selezi,' the bigger Angolan says, shaking my hand. He's a giant, a head taller than me, with a neck like a buffalo. 'Military people,' he adds, 'they always give surnames.'

I ask Selezi about the three letters that appear in large white print on his vest, the 'G' and 'A' and 'P' that declare the purpose and status of his mission. He looks down. His buffalo neck folds into his chin and he underlines the letters with a fat index finger. 'Short for Glenhazel Active Patrol.'

GAP. The full version is as tame as the acronym. But what I'm thinking is that these former soldiers, these elite fighting men, are the fierce response of a fed-up community. Pietersen confirms it. 'Most people here, they're gatvol of the police services.'

In Glenhazel, 'most people' could be anyone in my family. Just past 1pm, a middle-aged white woman with shiny black hair and big sunglasses eases up to the corner in a BMW x5. She smiles, hoots and waves. The men all smile and wave back. They watch the BMW until it disappears around a bend.

'We know her,' says Pietersen. 'She is a Jew.'

Here's where I could tell the men that I am a Jew. But, whatever the advantage to be gained, I don't. Instead, I introduce myself to the two soldiers who haven't yet spoken.

The other Angolan is Maria. He patrols in a team with Selezi. 'It's like buddy buddy, attack attack,' he says, referencing a military technique that's clearly second nature.

Maria tells me a story. 'We stopped a bakkie in November, in Lyndhurst Street. There was a robbery, they stole a computer. We gave the registration number to the police.'

I don't say anything. Maybe Maria thinks that I think it's a lame story, because he tells me another one. 'Some days back they locked an old man in his house. He had nothing to eat. They stole money and jewellery. He was in there for three days. We banged down the doors and rescued him.'

The worst of the stories I've personally heard about this suburb is the story of the Solomon family, which, I know, is part of the reason the new security company was formed – but if these guys know the story too, they choose not to tell it.

The last of the four to speak is Godfrey (he has a surname with four difficult syllables, so he uses his Christian name). Thinner than the others, handsome, with a shaved head, Godfrey points to a shop up the road. 'This bakery, nearly every Tuesday or Thursday, there's been a robbery. But since we've taken over, there's been nothing. When they come, they terrorise the people with AK47s.'

I squint into the sun and look at the bakery and picture what Long Avenue would be like during a gunfight. Then I turn back and ask the men about GAP's resources.

There are twenty-eight members, says Selezi. They have four double-cab XLT Rangers, four regular undercover cars, and one unmarked Ninja. The headquarters are close by, at number 2 Elray Street, where they have a large control room equipped with state-of-the-art technology.

Godfrey extends his arm and shows me the surveillance cameras on the roof of a building across the road. They can record a registration plate from twenty metres, he says.

I ask about the shotguns. 'If you have them,' I suggest, 'surely you must use them?'

Godfrey says they shoot to stop crime. He repeats it. 'We shoot to stop crime.'

Pietersen is more direct. 'If we kill, we kill.'

No, Selezi says, they haven't killed yet. Godfrey takes a shell from his pocket and shows it to me. 'This one's got pinballs inside, but we can use real shot as well.' Pietersen explains why killing may sometimes be necessary. 'We are judged on our failures.'

At 1.15pm a red Ford Bantam bakkie, bonnet and doors emblazoned with the logo of a rival security company, tears past at high speed. The driver is speaking into the mouthpiece of a two-way radio, his forehead knotted in a frown, his left hand straining at the wheel.

'Would GAP ever hire someone like him?' I ask, as the Ford's tyres squeal around a corner.

'For them to come and join us they need to be retrained,' says Selezi. 'We prefer former military.'

Godfrey nods and indicates a shady spot down the hill. 'Like what we found the other day. A guard from that company was sleeping down there, and somebody came and stole a vehicle.'

Later, a pattern emerges. Every twenty minutes, a white man, as big as Selezi, with a crew cut and large 1980s-style Ray-Bans, drives past the patrol post in a double-cab XLT Ranger. He slows down and glares at the men and then guns the big engine up Ridge Road.

'Who's he?' I ask.

'We call him the Boertjie,' says Pietersen. 'He gets three times our salary. They've got the old apartheid system here.'

The Boertjie, I learn, is also ex-special forces – his primary job is to check on the men; check that they're doing what they're supposed to do.

At 1.30pm synagogue is out. Men in black hats and women in *sheitls* fill the street, heading home for a cold lunch or a nap. I focus on a young family walking east on Ridge Road. The bearded father is pushing a pram, the mother is one step behind in billowing skirts. Two small boys with *peiyot* scamper up ahead.

'The way you see them walk now,' says Godfrey, 'they are free.'

Pietersen elaborates. 'Like the other day when that Jew lady comes, and takes a photo of us. They just come to talk to us, to see if this thing is really happening. Because they can't believe it.'

And now, I am told, the GAP model will be copied in the crime-ridden

Jewish suburbs of Savoy and Waverley. Using the same inoffensive naming rule, the new force will be called SWAP.

Says Pietersen, 'These Jew okes want blood by blood. You can call it blood sport.'

'An eye for an eye,' I say. 'From the Bible.'

He turns away and laughs. 'Ay, you must not talk about an eye for an eye to the government.'

An old Toyota Corolla filled with five black men idles past, windows down and radio blaring. The conversation stops. Pietersen, Selezi, Maria and Godfrey look up. They squeeze their handgrips. Godfrey steps toward the car and peers at the driver, his head inches from the window.

He watches the banged-up Toyota rumble slowly down Long Avenue. 'Ya, there's trouble there.'

———

The man Lisa Solomon has seen in her living room, the man who is the reason she is sitting on her cold kitchen floor – the reason she is still screaming – is now standing over her and telling her to shut up. The man is demanding that she hand over her jewellery. He is shouting and swearing.

Lisa stops screaming. She breathes in deeply and regains her composure. She removes her engagement and wedding rings and hands them to the man. Now he demands money.

'I don't have any money,' Lisa says.

From somewhere a second man arrives. He is more aggressive than the first. He has a more abrupt manner, he shouts louder. *He* now asks for money. The second man touches Lisa's thigh. 'Show me where the money is.'

The two men lift Lisa to her feet and point her in the direction of the bedroom. They walk her up the passage. Tomer, the baby, is crawling down the passage towards them. He is looking up at Lisa and howling.

The following few minutes are erased from Lisa's memory. In the weeks to come her mind will tell her that, logically, she must have heard a gun shot go off. But she does not remember the sound, nor how two of her children came to be in the bedroom with her.

Lisa is now sitting on her bed. She has her baby, Tomer, and her four-year-old, Akiva, on her lap. She is comforting them. She rocks Tomer and pats Akiva on the back.

Strange, Lisa thinks to herself, Akiva's back is wet. She looks down and sees blood. She lifts Akiva's pyjama shirt to trace where the blood is coming from. There is a large hole in her son's back. She doesn't know how it happened.

She scans the bedroom and sees a third man, who has bound Daniel's hands and feet. This third man has a gun.

One of the men – neither the man with the gun nor the aggressive man – walks over and sits on the bed next to Lisa. He begins to bind her own hands and feet.

'I need to hold the children,' Lisa protests.

The man hesitates, then tightens the ropes anyway. He is not rough and he shushes and calms the baby. Lisa points with her head at Akiva.

'Look at him,' she says. 'What have you done?'

The man sees that Akiva is hurt. It seems to Lisa that he is upset and that he wants to help the boy. He calls to his colleagues in a language that Lisa does not understand.

His colleagues are not interested. They are searching the cupboards and the drawers for money.

Lisa is desperate. She tries to convince the man on the bed that she has pushed the silent panic button and that security is on its way. 'You need to leave right now,' she says, 'before the security company gets here.'

Four or five times, the man next to her looks out of the window to the driveway. But he can't leave because his colleagues want to continue searching the room for money.

Lisa screams, 'My child is hurt, I need a doctor!'

The men take a pair of ties from the rack in the cupboard, which they use to gag Lisa and her husband. Some minutes later, the man with the gun loosens Lisa's gag and asks her where she keeps the key for the bedroom.

'I don't have a key for the bedroom,' Lisa says. 'The key for the gate is in the gate.'

The man with the gun says, 'Stay in here. Be quiet. We're going for breakfast.'

———

Athol Square, a small office and shopping complex on the corner of Katherine Street and Wierda Road East in Sandton, is all chrome and glass and white tile. The clientele in its ground floor restaurants and atrium cafés have clean pores and deep, even tans. They wear sunglasses that cast their faces in exotic shadow; woodgrain red and dark tortoiseshell frames that stretch from below their cheekbones to halfway up their foreheads.

At the gift shop in Athol Square, a neon-green vacuum jug made by Alessi sells for R950. On the shelf below the jug, a black plastic Ritzenhoff tray is going for R925. Four doors up from the gift shop is 'Matispa Paris' – an embossed sign on the window announces its standing as 'Best Beauty Salon in SA'.

In the parking lot outside are two double-cab XLT Rangers. They are just like the ones in Glenhazel, except they are white and say 'Status Security', and the men inside are armed with assault rifles instead of shotguns.

On a Friday in summer 2007, a few weeks after my time in the field with GAP's Pietersen, Selezi, Maria and Godfrey, I pass the Status trucks on my way to a meeting. It's the first time I have seen such a formidable security presence in a Sandton shopping centre, but then it's possible I haven't been looking properly. I expect I will get more detail from the person I have come to visit: a former classmate, a prominent businessman, who will talk to me as long as I don't use his name.

Let's call him Bradley Miller.

Miller is an associate, a 'lieutenant', in the direct but not entirely formal employ of an influential and reclusive Jewish billionaire. Miller has an office on Athol Square's first floor, but he takes his meetings in a booth in the burger restaurant downstairs. His routine involves canvassing young entrepreneurs who need finance for their projects, sorting out the hopefuls from the hopeless, and presenting the former to his boss.

Two such young men, whose faces I vaguely recognise – they may have been a few years below me at school – are about to leave as I arrive.

Miller introduces us. They have expensive shirts and unnecessarily strong handshakes and shoes with two-inch soles. They look at me with their heads tilted back, with a nod that comes from the jaw, and they say, '*Huzzit, boet.*'

'Hello,' I say.

They leave. If Miller can tell what I think of his mendicants, he doesn't let on.

He hasn't changed much in the last fifteen years. The calm blue eyes and stocky physique are the same; he has kept most of his hair. The gentle manner is also there – although behind it now is the unmistakable weight of power.

He places his hand on my shoulder and steers me to his booth.

We study the menus and order, and catch up on mutual friends. Then I remind Miller why I am here.

'Like I said on the phone, bud, I want to talk about your business interests in GAP. But I also want to know where you think the Jews stand in this country, specially since we're now funding a private army in suburbia.'

———

The men leave the bedroom. Lisa hears the key turn in the gate. She looks down at Akiva – he is getting pale and losing blood. She tries to staunch the bleeding, but with her bound hands she can't apply enough pressure.

She twists herself into a position near the headboard and reaches for the panic button. The alarm wails sharply through the house. The sound surprises and frightens her – she had been told it was a silent device.

'Lisa, what have you done?' Daniel says, through the flimsy gag in his mouth. 'They'll come back!'

Lisa and Daniel, panicked and wide-eyed, shuffle as fast as they can to the bedroom door and push against it with their backs. They wait, breathing heavily. A few minutes elapse. 'We've got to get Akiva to a doctor,' Lisa says.

'What?'

Daniel looks over to the bed and sees that his son is covered in blood. He knew Akiva had been hurt, but he had assumed it wasn't serious – the boy was talking, he was not comatose.

Lisa pulls herself up and hops over to the stationery drawer. Shaking and sweating, she slides it open and takes out a pair of scissors. She cuts the ropes on her hands and feet and frees her husband. Then she picks up the phone to dial the emergency services.

The phone is dead. The men have severed the line.

The couple decide not to leave through the front door – the men may still be inside. Daniel unbolts a small hinge in the burglar bars and shimmies through the bedroom window. He walks carefully around the house, keeping close to the walls. In less than five minutes he calls, 'They've gone.'

In the bedroom is a spare key for the internal gate. Daniel comes down the passage and they both throw on some clothes. Daniel picks up Akiva and Lisa grabs the baby. She begins to shove nappies, wipes and formula into a bag.

'We need to go!' Daniel screams. 'We need to go! We can't take Tomer with us!'

Lisa picks up the bag and runs to the car, where Daniel is waiting with the engine running. As they leave they see a security patrol vehicle, a small Toyota. They explain to the driver what has happened. Then they speed to Lisa's sister's house, where the two older boys are. The house is also in Glenhazel, on the way to the Linksfield Clinic, and is the obvious place to leave Tomer.

But it's *shabbos* and it's complicated. Lisa's sister is *shomrei*. Her cellphone is off and she won't answer her buzzer. So Lisa decides to give the baby apparel – and the baby – to Daniel, the security guard in the street.

She knows Daniel and trusts him. As she hands Tomer over she sees he is covered in his brother's blood – she had been holding the boys together on her lap. 'Tell my sister that Tomer is not hurt, but Akiva.'

Lisa gets back in the car and Daniel drives as fast as he can to the Linksfield Clinic emergency ward. He parks outside and Lisa runs in holding Akiva and says to the doctor, 'He's bleeding. I don't know if he's been stabbed or shot.'

She asks, 'Can you just stitch him up, or do you need to admit him?'

———

Miller holds my gaze. He spreads his hands, palms upwards, in a (near Italian) gesture of goodwill. In a reasonable and measured voice he begins.

'I don't know how this looks to you, but I think the Jews are in a precarious position in South Africa. Our government has a problem. There are forty million poor people in this country, and they're black. If the government is going to preserve its power and save the economy, it must act fast. It must deliver on its promise of transferring twenty-five per cent of the wealth into the hands of the disenfranchised.'

He breaks off. 'Okay, park that.' A waitress has arrived with our burgers. She slides the steaming plates onto our placemats. She opens the flip-tops on two cans of Coke and empties the contents into a pair of ice-filled glasses. Miller waits for her to leave before continuing.

'There are sixty thousand Jews in the country, give or take,' he says, turning his plate around, so the vegetables are on the far side. 'One of them is Donald Gordon. When I was finishing up my articles I did an exercise. I unbundled the assets Gordon indirectly controlled through the Liberty group. You know, the holdings in the OK, the breweries, the hotels, Standard Bank. What I worked out is this. In 1999, based only on the figures that were publicly available, Liberty had a controlling share in more than fifteen per cent of the total market cap of the Johannesburg Stock Exchange.'

Miller leans into his burger and takes a bite. He picks up a serviette and wipes his mouth.

When he has swallowed, he continues. 'I got thinking. If Gordon is this powerful, what do the Jews control? Today, conservatively, I'd say it's twenty per cent of the economy.'

Miller takes two chips in his left hand and dips them in a bowl of mushroom sauce. He bites the tops off and repeats the process. I watch him closely.

A *fifth* of the country's wealth. There's no point making up a statistic like that, I'm thinking. Besides, while the number may be awkward, discomforting even, the prominence of Jewish industrialists in sectors like retail, motoring, property and steel – not to mention banking, insurance and finance – is an incontestable fact. In early 2007, difficult as it is to prove, twenty per cent can't be far off.

Miller comes now to his hypothesis. 'So the government has this problem. It can solve it by dealing with the Jews. Everywhere else in the world, where money and politics clash, money always wins. Here, politics always wins. I'm absolutely certain that if politics and money clash again in South Africa, politics will win again.'

I ask Miller, 'What does *dealing with* mean?'

'Who knows?'

He tells me a story. A few months back he travelled with his boss to a game lodge north of the border, for a private meeting between senior cabinet members and leading businessmen. He was privy to a debate about the wealth imbalance and the position of South African Jewry. It was clear some cabinet members were losing patience, he says.

I nod. Miller had his career mapped out at school, I'm thinking. He was quiet then, serious. He sat at the front of the class, his head deep in his books. His subjects were mathematics and the sciences. While I was cutting class, smoking, drinking, Miller was planning a life in high finance.

The waitress returns to remove our empty plates. I order a double espresso and a glass of water. Miller orders a cappuccino. We lean back and make use of the toothpicks.

We talk about all the Jews we know who have left. We agree that four generations in South Africa, measured against what came before – seven centuries in Eastern Europe, a millennium in Western Europe, countless years in Babylon, Egypt, Persia – doesn't count for much. We talk about the myth of belonging. Then, when the coffee arrives, we talk about GAP.

I ask Miller, 'What does it say about a country when some people think the best way to protect themselves is to hire professional soldiers?'

He replies, 'If the state is not providing you with education or medicine, you provide it yourself. Why can't we do that with security?'

'It's not the same thing.'

But Miller thinks it is. 'Most families in Glenhazel spend three thousand rand a month on private schools. Have a look at what they spend on medical aid. This is the next logical step.'

I quote Miller a line from the notebooks of Robert Frost, something I'd read a few weeks before: 'All the state is for is to protect the baby.' What that means to me, I say, is that protection from physical harm is the first and last job of government. When it goes, everything goes.

Miller shrugs. 'The state *should* have a monopoly on physical violence. In South Africa, it doesn't.'

I'm silent for a moment. Then I play out a scenario: the rich throw more and more money at private security; the middle class are forced to keep up as best they can; the criminals are driven back to the dirt-poor slums where most of them were born. South Africa becomes a post-apocalyptic tapestry of sparkling blue swimming pools and ungovernable feral zones.

'The ethical questions are difficult,' says Miller.

I knock back my espresso, which has gone cold. 'Dude. C'mon.'

Miller says his boss is *not* the money behind GAP. He says, 'GAP is a non-profit entity funded by the community to achieve the solution to violent crime in the area.'

'Dude.'

'We are service providers. GAP is a client.'

I don't say anything. He goes on.

'We provide GAP with armed response services. The difference between our armed response and an average armed response is that we drive better cars. And we believe, we *hope*, we've got better qualified people.'

I listen, wanting to understand.

'Most of the time, we can't afford the most highly trained staff because we can't compete with the mercenary services in Iraq. All the security companies do this, but GAP has been the best marketed. There is a firm starting the exact same thing in Sandhurst. It's not just the Jews, bud.'

I ask Miller what he knows about the XLT Rangers I saw in the parking lot on my way in, the Status Security trucks.

'That's my point, those guys are the same as GAP. The only difference is they use Ruger Mini 14s.'

One more time, I return to the consequences. 'Maybe these private armies are just the next symbol of why we are where we are. Maybe all they do is shift the problem someplace else. It may sound naive, but what if the bottom line really is that people like us have too much when there are so many with nothing?'

Says Miller, 'Breaking into a house and torturing somebody for four hours is a social problem, not an economic problem. To solve the social problem will take fifty years.'

There are over twenty synagogues in Glenhazel, from the large halls at Yeshiva College and Ohr Someach that accommodate hundreds, to the small front rooms in the houses of rabbis that take no more than thirty. By 10.15 on the morning of January 28th 2006 – even though it is a *shabbos* morning, and it is forbidden to use cellphones – the congregations in the majority of Glenhazel synagogues know about the shooting of Akiva Solomon. The community is united in prayer.

The prayers recited are *tehillim*, because it is said by the sages that in moments of crisis the psalms of King David are pleasing to God.

———

The doctor on duty at the Linksfield Clinic prods Akiva's abdomen. He suspects the tautness he feels is a sign of internal bleeding. He orders x-rays, and finds one bullet lodged in the boy's stomach and a second bullet in his leg. The doctor tells Lisa that his facility is not equipped to handle the emergency, and he instructs an aide to call for an ambulance to take Akiva to Milpark, a private hospital near the city centre. In the interim he administers fluids, blood and oxygen.

The ambulance arrives. Two paramedics jump out and attach Akiva to a life-support machine in the rear of the vehicle. One of the men warns Lisa to hold tight. 'We need to go fairly quickly, we need to put on the sirens.'

In what appears to Lisa like seconds, the ambulance banks hard into the casualty entrance at the Milpark Clinic. Two doctors are waiting: an older man with greying hair and a neat appearance, and a younger man in shorts and a collared sports shirt, as if he had been on the golf course when the call came through.

'Just tell me it's going to be okay,' Lisa says to the older man.

'I can't give you any assurances.'

Her thoughts turn to God. She remembers again that it's *shabbos*, and that she's not supposed to write. She asks a person standing beside her in reception to sign the admission documents on her behalf.

Akiva is rushed into surgery and Lisa and Daniel are ushered through to a private room. A man brings *siddurim*, so that they may *daven*. Daniel recites *tehillim*. Lisa doesn't do anything formal, she prays in an instinctive way.

Three hours pass. The door opens. A man wearing a *kippah*, a *frum* Jewish doctor, walks into the room. '*Baruch Hashem*,' he says. 'Akiva is going to be okay.'

The *frum* doctor explains what has happened. The first bullet fractured Akiva's ribs, travelled through the lung, through the diaphragm, through the spleen, and lodged in the colon. He says that Akiva is very lucky; the grey-haired doctor is one of the best paediatric surgeons in the country. 'It's a miracle, given everything that could have been.'

The surgeons, the *frum* doctor continues, have decided to leave the second bullet in Akiva's leg. They don't see it as a priority. They will deal with it later, when the boy's condition is stable.

Akiva is transferred to a ward. Lisa and Daniel go through to see him. The grey-haired surgeon is standing by the boy's bed, holding a clipboard and ticking off items with his pen.

'Will he be okay?' Lisa asks.

'He will be fine,' says the surgeon.

Lisa falls into a chair and sobs violently.

———

Frangelica's on Long Avenue, Glenhazel, is a place of bold aromas: *latkes*, cheesecake, chocolate brownies, *cholent*. Black tablecloths with pink fringes cover seven pinewood tables, and behind the counter, in a rudimentary frame, hangs a portrait of Rebbe Menachem Mendel Schneerson (of blessed memory), the last great leader of the Lubavitchers. In the corner of the establishment, against the large window fronting the street, is a makeshift shop selling stationery and *tchatchkes* – plastic beads, bottles of glue, sarongs, scissors, big sheets of coloured mounting board.

I take a seat at the table furthest from the door. There's a fridge beside me, a small white Defy, and soon a woman emerges from the kitchen to peer inside; she apologises and asks me to move my leg so she can reach for something at the back.

I swivel to the left and look out the window. A black XLT Ranger passes down Long Avenue. The woman closes the fridge door and walks back to the kitchen holding a bottle of milk. When I look towards the front again, Lisa Solomon is waving at me, approaching the table.

She places her bag on the floor and takes the seat opposite, a woman in her mid-thirties with a *sheitl* and an attractive, open face. We have already spoken twice on the phone, so she knows about my relationship to Richard Bloom – which is why, like Miller, she is adamant I use pseudonyms.

'People in Glenhazel will guess that it's us,' she says. 'But I need to insist. Mostly because I think our story is exceptional, and because I think it's miraculous. I don't want to undermine what's happened to someone else. I don't want to meet your family and have them think that this is not typically how an assault in South Africa ends. Because it's not.'

We settle on the surname Solomon, which, we agree, is appropriately generic.

It's also because Lisa knows the story of my family, though, that she's willing to share in unabridged detail the story of her own. I listen to her relive the incident, in a voice incongruously calm and detached, and at some point it strikes me how strange it all is; how I am moved but unsurprised, how odd my questions might sound to an outsider, how the sheer abundance of such stories has almost robbed the individual case of its (necessary, rightful) power to astonish.

Later, as a metallic winter dusk descends on the city, I come to my final question: Why has the family not emigrated? Daniel was born in the United States, he has a mother in North Carolina and a brother in Wisconsin. From 1995 to 1999 the Solomons lived in the States; from 1999 to 2003 they lived in Israel. Why, fifteen months after the shooting and 'miraculous' recovery of their four-year-old son, are they still in South Africa?

Lisa offers two answers.

First, she says, 'Tomer's *bris* was in Frangelica's. Every day that Akiva was in the hospital, the owners sent us a big box of food. Someone else from Glenhazel wanted to cover our medical bills. He said to Daniel that he'd had a great year financially, and that he wanted to help.'

By the time they moved back into their house, six weeks after the attack, burglar bars had been installed on all the windows. A gardening service had cut down the shrubbery; lighting and electric fencing had been set up around the perimeter; the old carpets, with Akiva's bloodstains, had been removed and replaced; palisade fencing had been erected between their property and the neighbour's.

'There wasn't a single detail we needed to take care of,' Lisa says. 'I have never lived in, or visited, a community in the world quite as selfless.'

Then there's Lisa's second answer. Soon after the incident, she says, the chief rabbi paid the family a visit. He agreed that the situation in Glenhazel had become urgent; that Akiva's escape was a waste if something was not done. The very next week the meetings began, bringing together businessmen and rabbis and community leaders. At one of the first meetings, a security force staffed by elite former soldiers was mooted (and accepted) as a solution.

'I'm not sure, if GAP wasn't around, that we would have stayed.'

Before I leave, I ask the thirty-six-year-old mother of four if she has any thoughts on GAP's downside. I test out again the scenario of the ungovernable feral zones.

'Saying "please" doesn't work any more,' she says. 'I don't see a negative to GAP. Not one. I don't see what they do, I just see that they are successful.'

A Monday afternoon in June 2007. I park the Alfa outside Rael Lissoos's 'church' in Nellie Road, Norwood. A car guard, a man with a boxer's hooded eyes and an Orlando Pirates jersey, taps on the window. 'Here, they will bash you, *foh shoh*,' he cautions. I move the Alfa to a bay a bit further off the corner.

I am early. The radio is tuned to a talk station and I listen to a middle-aged white woman tell the presenter that she really hates the malls of Johannesburg. The boulevards of Europe are more her thing, she says. 'I have family there, you know; I really love window shopping in Paris.'

This woman has called in to the show before, I'm thinking. I turn off the radio, cross the street and enter the former church.

Rael is hunched over his desk, surrounded by circuit boards and disembowelled electronic gadgets. He has some obscure software running on his Mac, and without turning away from the screen he lifts his right hand and shows me his palm. He needs five minutes.

I look around. Light grey monitors and open PC towers lie across the space where the pews used to be, an old public telephone with exposed innards stands in place of the pulpit.

Rael has been running a handful of tech companies from this repurposed church for some years now; recently he has added a new business to his repertoire – he installs the wireless networks that connect the surveillance cameras to monitors in GAP's headquarters.

He rises abruptly and pats his pockets. 'Right, let's do it.' I follow him outside to a dirty-green Jeep Cherokee and climb in the passenger seat.

'There's a difference between filter points and plain cameras,' Rael says, as we make our way east through the late afternoon traffic. 'The filter point is for when you're coming home, and you think maybe someone's following you. What you do is you drive slowly through, and you signal the guards. Cameras are more for after the fact, they record registration plates.'

On Ninth Street, just past the BP garage, as the Italian and Portuguese suburbs of Orange Grove and Highlands North become the Jewish suburbs of Sydenham and Glenhazel, Rael shows me the roofs where his aerials and transponders suck greedily at the irradiated air. He talks about the merits of line-of-sight. 'You learn quickly in this game how hilly Joburg is,' he says.

We drive down a quiet avenue. He points to a camera at the corner of Third and Sandler. 'In this place, I'm telling you, they've basically got rid of crime.'

And then we come to number 2 Elray Street. We stop at a thick metal gate topped by razor wire. Behind the gate is a three-storey concrete structure, its small barred windows framed in blue paint. A sentry approaches the Jeep. When he recognises Rael, his closed face bursts into a smile.

'For the cameras,' Rael says.

'Ya, ya, the cameras.'

Inside, 2 Elray is as neat and regimented as an army base. Three black XLT Rangers are parked in a row on a new patch of tar and a series of heavy cement barriers lie at right angles by the exit. There are no cigarette butts or sweet wrappers on the ground.

Rael parks the Jeep. I follow him up a ramp to the main building's entrance. There is a sheet of white paper pasted to a heavy glass door, offering information about combat classes in the dojo. We walk across a threadbare carpet, past open-plan offices filled with young white men in tight shirts that display their biceps and pectorals.

In the control room, GAP's nerve centre, a young man rises from his post and greets Rael. The two immediately begin a technical discussion about the cameras. I focus on the monitors. There are more than a dozen screens, some showing the position of the security vehicles on GPS tracking grids and others showing cars driving through suburban intersections. It's a mesmerising spectacle, wholly addictive, and too soon I must turn away to take in the rest of the room.

On the back wall I see a large whiteboard marked up in a thick blue pen. 'June' is written in wide capitals at the top. Just below are three sub-headers, each above its own vertical column. Arrests. Incidents. Suspicious Activity. I start at the first column, reading through the terse account of the month's activities. 'Arrested, one illegal'; 'Arrested, two illegals'; 'Possession of a stolen cellphone'; 'Possession of marijuana'.

A tall blonde man in his early twenties is watching me. I don't acknowledge his presence and continue taking down what I see on the board. Next to the date June 16, still under the arrest column, it says, 'A drunk couple fighting over their child'. As I write, I consider asking the blonde man how this couple – no doubt a black couple – threatened the safety of the residents of Glenhazel. I consider asking him what he makes of the fact that June 16th is Youth Day in South Africa, a day that recalls the police excesses of 1976.

But it isn't 1976, and the culpable are no longer so easy to identify. And so I don't ask.

––––

It is just after 11pm and we are returning home from dinner at Laurie's parents' place in Houghton. At the corner of the M1 on-ramp and Houghton

Drive, as a standard precaution against a smash-and-grab attack, I stop a few metres before the traffic light. I inch forward, leaving space for a quick pull-off, and I look around to make sure that nobody is stalking us.

Tonight, one of the coldest nights of the winter, a man has us marked.

He is crouched, bent low. He is wearing a black woollen beanie and a blue tracksuit top. He is three paces from the Alfa's back left door and he is carrying a brick. I swallow hard. I point at him with my left hand. He sees me. Maybe it looks to him as if I am pointing a gun. He stands up straight, presses his gloved hands together, and bows. We stare at each other. Then he reassumes his crouch and steps back into his hiding place in the foliage.

An End to this Thing

FOUR DAYS BEFORE THE trial is due to begin, my uncle calls to say he and my aunt have decided to accept a plea bargain.

'They've offered us a deal and we're taking it. They're going to plead guilty and they'll each get twenty-eight years. Sandy and I want an end to this thing.'

My uncle asks me not to say anything to anyone. 'Especially not anyone in the press.'

Later my father calls and repeats the instruction.

I cancel my ticket to Cape Town and tell Branko that the story's off. I make new appointments for the following week.

The next Monday, on my way to an interview in Glenhazel, I stop to pick up a newspaper. The article is on all the front pages. As part of the plea bargain, Davids and Marlie submitted lengthy statements. The full details have now emerged.

Richard Bloom and Brett Goldin were held up at gunpoint on Victoria Road after a dinner party in Bakoven. They were ordered by their assailants to point out Richard's car. Richard and Brett and the car were taken to the Table Mountain cable station. In the gravel parking area they were ordered to strip naked. They were left in only their socks while their clothes were thrown down the mountainside. One of the companions of Davids and Marlie fired off a shot by accident. Fearing that the sound might alert the police, they decided that Richard and Brett should be dumped elsewhere.

Richard and Brett were ordered to climb into the boot of Richard's car. With Davids driving and Marlie in the front passenger seat, they headed back towards the Cape Flats. The car was driven onto an open field next to the M5 freeway, where it got stuck in a patch of soft sand. The boot was opened and Richard and Brett were ordered to help push, but the car wouldn't budge. The two were ordered to lie face down on the ground while Davids and Marlie wedged a board under the wheels for traction. Davids gave the pistol to Marlie and told him to shoot if either of them moved.

Somebody, either Richard or Brett, screamed.

'The shots were fired from behind,' the statements read. 'Both deceased had two entrance wounds at the back of their heads and two exit wounds at the front of their heads.'

CHAPTER 4

Straight from Black to Blue

IN EARLY FEBRUARY 2002, Timothy Maurice Webster, an African American from the small town of Madison in North Carolina, boarded a 747 out of JFK. There were, including himself, only twelve passengers on the flight. As the aircraft gained altitude and turned south-east over the Atlantic, Timothy climbed the stairs to the top-floor cabin and occupied a row of seats near the cockpit. He stretched out and fell asleep. When he awoke, the small icon on the digital map was approaching the coast of Africa. He raised the blind and stared into the darkness.

In less than seven hours, Timothy thought, he would land in an alien and hopelessly backward place. He knew – because he had seen it with his own eyes on television – that South Africa was a land of disaffected poor people with a president who denied that HIV causes Aids. But Timothy closed the blind and reminded himself that the country's problems were no concern of his. His girlfriend, a Swazi princess, was the sole reason for the trip. They would visit a game park and they would learn how to be intimate again after more than a year apart; and then, when he asked her, she would agree to return with him to the United States.

The flight arrived in Johannesburg on schedule. The young American, fresh and refined in a tailored sports jacket and Abercrombie & Fitch jeans, wheeled his trolley out into the arrivals terminal. A tall black man was holding a banner bearing his name. He shook the man's hand. Timothy was told that his girlfriend couldn't be there – her presence, said the man, was required at a reed dance festival in Swaziland.

Timothy masked his disappointment behind a barrage of small talk.

He followed the man into the parking lot, detailing for him the in-flight service and the height of the snow back in New York. He noticed, as he walked, that the parking lot was filled with German suvs and luxury se-dans. The man stopped beside a late model c-class Mercedes. 'Damn, guys are ballin' in South Africa!' Timothy said.

His observation was not without irony. The American was sure the cars were a quirk, an exception to the endemic poverty waiting right outside. But nothing on the road into town confirmed his belief: not the flawless six-lane highway nor the enormous billboards; not the furniture showrooms nor the light-fitting stores nor the giant depots for Japanese technology firms.

The Mercedes turned into the driveway of a two-storey townhouse in a quiet suburb. The place belonged, said the man, to a sister of Timothy's girlfriend. She too was out of town and this was where he'd be staying. Timothy let himself in and dropped his bags beside a potted palm. He looked around.

Mirrors covered the walls. A leather lounge suite was arranged in a wide half-circle around a home theatre system. In the garden was a mar-ble fountain. The bed in the main upstairs bedroom was king-sized and pristine white: Timothy hurled himself across it and inhaled the fresh smell of fabric and smiled.

The following morning a young woman named Ayanda arrived. She had wide-set eyes and wore an expensive dress; she carried herself like a ramp model. She said it was her job to show Timothy around.

Ayanda took Timothy to a party where beautiful black people stood around a large swimming pool and listened to hip-hop. She took him to a mall where Italian and French labels lined the shelves of *à la mode* boutiques. Timothy the image consultant – the fashion prodigy, the man being groomed for an executive position in North America's largest menswear chain – saw an alternative version of his future. Someone like him could really boom in South Africa, he thought.

At the end of his first week in the country Timothy travelled to a resort in the bush to meet his girlfriend. It took only a day together for the re-lationship to be rekindled. One afternoon, together with another couple, Timothy and his girlfriend went river rafting. They had been in the river almost an hour when they came to a rapid. They dragged the raft to the shore and clambered onto a boulder and looked down into the torrent. Timothy decided he was going to swim through.

He plunged into the cool water. As he tumbled downstream he could hear muffled clapping. They were clapping for his bravery, he realised; they didn't see that he was drowning.

———

A weekday morning in June 2007. I'm heading north on the N1 highway out of Johannesburg. I've got the radio on, Redi Direko's talk show on 702. The caller is angry.

'Our government is corrupt, Redi. The people deserve better.'

The country, I'm thinking, as Redi cuts to commercials, is preoccupied with this thing called *the people*. It's always been like this, even if the level of obsession waxes and wanes with the historic moment.

Once they were known as *die volk*, but now history has translated them back into English. It's a casual kind of English, though. Imprecise. *The people*, when invoked in the country's imagination, are tolerant and noble and covered with dust – calloused men and women who stand outside their mud huts, shading their eyes from the sun, waiting for the day when they will be given a house made of bricks.

But then, just before noon, driving through downtown Pretoria, I see a plausible picture of *the people*. They are marching up Paul Kruger Street, from Church Square. They are coming straight for the Alfa. They are wearing red and yellow T-shirts with socialist symbols and they have some banners that demand a twelve per cent pay rise and other banners that heap insults on cabinet ministers. They are singing in tones at once mournful and threatening, and they are whistling through their teeth, shaking traditional sticks, blowing vuvuzelas. The police are following in brand-new Ford four-by-fours.

———

Close to exhaustion, Timothy washed up into the shallows at a bend in the river. He took in a lungful of air and dragged himself onto the bank.

With his legs dangling in the current and his arms spread out before him, he coughed up into the mud the water he'd swallowed. He waited until his breathing had normalised. He stood, and was overcome by a profound sense of wellbeing. He headed upriver, to where he had last seen the others. On the way, brushing aside branches and scrambling over rocks, he made his decision. He would come to live in South Africa.

Timothy did not read a magazine or a book on the return flight to New York. He didn't watch the in-flight movie. Instead, his seat in the upright position, he stared out the window and considered his difficulty – how was he going to explain this to his colleagues, his mother, his boss?

At twenty-eight, Timothy had his own office at company headquarters in mid-town Manhattan. Every week he'd travel to another destination in the north-east United States, where he'd stand before a packed hall and make poignant statements about clothes and status and power. He was so good at his job – local sales of suits and ties always seemed to spike after his presentations – that his employers had allowed him to start his own consultancy on the side. Already he could count as his clients a dozen influential city types, brokers and bankers who wouldn't make a fashion move without him. The financial rewards had been prodigious – the previous year he'd cleared seventy thousand dollars, this year was destined to be his first above six figures.

And now, at thirty-seven thousand feet, staring down on the dark steel surface of the Atlantic, he searched for the words that would explain to everyone why he was moving to Africa.

He didn't find them. Not during the flight and not after he landed. But that winter was the coldest on record in New York and Timothy dreamed of the faraway sun and went ahead with his plans. He called up his boss to resign, and was met with an interminable pause. He sold his Range Rover at a punishing loss. He took a trip to the family farm in Madison, where his mother and uncles give him their blessing but swore they didn't understand.

By September the following year Timothy was back in Johannesburg. He lived, with his girlfriend, in a small cottage in the front garden of a property in the new northern suburbs. There was no ADSL line in the cottage, no way of conducting business from home, but in the beginning he was patient.

Every day he got up early and put on his jeans and a clean French-cuff shirt. He walked from the cottage, along a busy main road, to a nearby shopping centre. At first he enjoyed the heat, the novelty of his situation, the distinction of being the only boy from Madison ever to have walked the route. And then the weeks passed, and his questions began to mount.

Why was there no sidewalk? This was supposed to be a nice neighbourhood; they should have a sidewalk.

September became October. The temperature rose. It now felt to Timothy as if he were carrying the sun on his back. Once the brightest symbol of his move, the African sun beating down on him as he walked became the weight of his move. And the grass reached up to his waist. Were they ever going to cut the grass?

At night he would ask his girlfriend, 'Why don't they cut the grass?'

Her response, mostly, was to laugh.

Timothy walked back and forth. In the shopping centre was a courier franchise, where he could go online and quietly service the few clients he'd retained in New York. But the young white girls who worked in the franchise began to show an unfortunate interest in his accent. 'Have you ever been in a movie?' they'd ask. 'Do you know Jennifer Lopez?'

He tried to concentrate on his work. He tried to stifle his irritation at the ridiculous Internet fees and the connection that cut out half the time. Every afternoon, when he got back to the cottage, he'd call the telecom company to check up on the progress of his line.

'What percentage of your growth is ADSL?' he'd ask the service consultant.

'I don't know.'

'You telling me it takes this long to get to somebody's house?'

Timothy's Internet problem spilled over into a relationship problem. He promised himself that he'd stop complaining to his girlfriend about the telecom company, but it was a promise he couldn't keep. It was apparent to him that South Africa wasn't a Western country at all. What he'd seen on his first visit had been a façade, a brittle veneer. A mantra was playing loudly in his head. 'The grass hasn't been cut, there's no Internet, nobody has answers for anything.'

His routine assumed a relentless monotony. Each day, when he returned from the courier franchise (after he'd called the telecom company), he'd sit motionless for hours on the edge of the bed. There was no couch in the cottage and no radio, and he refused to watch daytime TV. He simply stared out the bedroom window at the walls, wondering why they were so high. An ice-cream truck would come by in the late afternoon, always the same grating melody. Timothy would then stand up and go outside to ask the ice-cream vendor to turn down the noise, but he could never find the truck.

Sometimes, late at night, when she was in a gentle mood, Timothy's girlfriend would express concern at his state of mind. 'Why don't you just relax?' she'd ask. 'Take off three or four months.'

But Timothy would stubbornly shake his head. He'd speak about his grandfather, Thomas Webster, a man who worked half his life in a brickyard.

Thomas worked in the brickyard until he could afford to buy himself a hundred-acre farm, Timothy explained. 'He was a good man, straight and honest, a black landowner before America was desegregated. And he never took time off.'

———

The nationwide public service strikes of winter 2007 have been going on for over a week now. Queues form at government offices around the country and in the major cities the state machinery verges on complete shutdown. The media choose to focus on the teachers and nurses, who are amongst the worst paid government employees and whose demands for a twelve per cent pay rise elicit much public sympathy. The catch, of course, is that while teachers and nurses strike, pupils go untaught in schools and patients go untreated in hospitals.

This afternoon I am covering a very different story – although one that is not wholly unrelated. Together with a handful of journalists and a co-terie of food and wine buffs, I have been invited to a whisky tasting at The Grace hotel in Rosebank. An 'ultra deluxe' new version of Johnnie Walker Blue Label is to be launched in South Africa before any other market, a whisky that will retail at four thousand five hundred rand a bottle. In The

Grace's carpeted elevator a colleague from a Sunday newspaper offers a comment on the price: slightly less than the average monthly salary of a graduate teacher, equal to the average monthly salary of a staff nurse.

The elevator deposits us on the fourth floor. We pad through to the private dining room, where a thick mahogany table is laid out for fourteen people. We take our places and introduce ourselves, and soon a bottle of regular Blue Label is being passed from hand to hand. A lantern-jawed man in his mid-forties, face shining and flawlessly shaved, takes charge of proceedings. 'It's quite smoky for a blend,' he says. 'The smokiness carries forward in the taste.'

We follow his lead and take a sip. We let the amber liquid play over our tongues. When we're done we look up and smile. The man – Jonathan Driver, who flew in from Johnnie Walker's UK headquarters for the event – smiles back. He learns something new at every tasting, he says. Today it's 'the cedar aroma, the surprising taste of cake'.

We nod.

Now for the preliminaries: the facts and statistics, the stuff of our news reports. The public relations women, who occupy three seats to Driver's immediate right, hand out fourteen royal blue folders, each containing a pair of press releases. The youngest of the women guides us through the relevant parts. Johnnie Walker's new product is coming to South Africa first, she says, because the country has one of the fastest-growing markets for premium whisky on the planet. In volume terms, she continues, the premium whisky category in South Africa has grown by 28.8 per cent in the last year alone. Within this category, the woman concludes, sales of Johnnie Walker Blue Label are up 45.9 per cent.

Driver thanks the woman and suggests that we move a bit quicker through the regular Blue Label – retail price, twelve hundred rand a bottle – so that he can unveil the belle of the ball, the Johnnie Walker Blue Label King George V. 'First just sample,' he says, 'what this whisky does with a small dash of water.'

We lift our jugs to our tumblers and pour. We sample.

'See how all that complexity inside the glass is released?'

We nod.

The reason for the regular Blue Label, Driver explains, is that introducing a new blend to an audience without 'some terms of reference' is inadvisable.

We nod again.

Driver asks to be excused; it's time, he says, to prepare for the King George V. A waitress in a spotless uniform moves around the table, placing before each of us a fresh crystal tumbler embossed with a portrait of the dead monarch. A conversation ensues in whispers. People compare their whisky collections: some prefer single malt, Glenmorangie or Glengarry, and some swear by the top Johnnie Walker blends. 'Why don't we get Johnnie Walker Premier in South Africa?' a one-time nightclub manager (turned producer of a TV chat show) asks.

Before he gets his answer, Driver returns with a royal blue box the size of a 1980s hi-fi speaker. He places it gingerly on the table. All talking stops and we lean forward in our chairs.

There is a Russian-doll intricacy to the casing. Driver removes the top layer with the practised theatricality of a magician about to uncover his rabbit. The final layer is a pair of doors, which Driver opens slowly, from behind, with the thumb and forefinger of each hand.

And there it is. A crystal decanter in a bed of silk. Liquid as rare as gold and almost as expensive: forty-five rand a sip for a hundred sips (add around eighty per cent if you're drinking in a northern Johannesburg cigar bar).

As the waitress circles once more, pouring a sliver of the decanter's contents into each tumbler, Driver holds forth on the rarity of the blend. King George V is made from a stock of whiskies that date back to the early twentieth century, he says, many from distilleries that no longer exist.

We are encouraged to sniff the glass, to try and locate the 'delicate balance between the peatiness of the West Coast and the lighter aromatic qualities of Speyside'.

We locate the balance. We think about the balance. We look up at Driver, who now wears the expression of a gameshow host on final-four night. He pauses, like he's about to cut to commercials. Then, almost imperceptibly, he dips his head.

We take the cue.

We drink.

It tastes remarkably, uncannily, like … well, like Johnnie Walker Black. I don't get the chance to offer that opinion, though.

'I think it's a more modern taste,' says a middle-aged white man at the far end of the table, a *bon vivant* type with a turquoise pullover and a neat white beard. 'The Port Ellen comes through strongly in the glass.'

Another man – black, shaved head, in a finely cut suit – says, 'I'll be honest with you. I thought, when I heard about this, that it was just a marketing exercise. But it's totally different. Totally different.'

Over three thousand rand different, I'm thinking, if your standard drink is Johnnie Walker Blue. If you're a single malt fan, you'll be averaging an extra four thousand per bottle. Of course, it is the price of King George V, its conferred mark of success, of having 'arrived', that is bound to ensure its triumph in contemporary high-life South Africa.

The company has chosen the country, Driver reiterates, because of the 'confidence and experimentation' brought on by our buoyant economy.

'Johnnie Walker offers a ladder. You can go from Red to Black to Green to Gold to Blue.'

The former nightclub manager, who's lost more than two hundred pounds in weight in the last year – 'I have no trouble saying that' – jumps in. 'We do something funny here,' he says. 'We go straight from Black to Blue.'

———

I meet Timothy Maurice Webster for breakfast at the Mugg & Bean coffee shop in the Killarney Mall. Through the wide bay window that looks south onto the ridge and east across the suburbs, I can almost make out the traffic island at the corner of the MI on-ramp and Houghton Drive. Because it seems relevant to our conversation – to how whites in suburbia experience one South Africa, *the people* in the townships and rural areas another – I tell Timothy about the attempted smash-and-grab of the previous week (the incident happened, I tell him, within hours of an über-deluxe whisky tasting).

'No way,' Timothy says. 'You're kidding.'

He is droll, impassive, politely unimpressed.

Timothy has been living and working in Johannesburg for four years now. In that time, he has not witnessed a hijacking or a serious assault; the crime stats, for him, are over-hyped. Then there is what Timothy does. His personal website (www.timothymaurice.com) labels him a brand philosopher, designer, author, speaker and mentor. He is not a man who responds well to the idea of oppression of the privileged.

Neither, apparently, is he a man who neglects his image. He is dressed this morning in a charcoal pinstriped suit, a gunmetal-grey tie, a shirt fastened at the wrists with platinum cufflinks. A carefully folded silk handkerchief peeks out of his breast pocket.

As I would learn in the weeks and months ahead, Timothy did not sit for long on the bed in his girlfriend's cottage, staring at the high walls, getting wound up by the ice-cream truck.

By December 2003, he had discovered Sandton City, one of the largest malls in the southern hemisphere. Specifically, he had discovered the Sandton City branch of Exclusive Books. There he would station himself, six to seven hours a day, five days a week. He would occupy a corner table – drinking lattes, reading magazines – and he would scan the store for business. His strategy was to approach people sitting alone, on the far side of the cafeteria, and compliment them on their dress. 'Seems there's nowhere to sit,' he would say, 'do you mind if I join you?' Because the people he approached always looked as if they could afford an image consultant, because Timothy had learned the art of salesmanship from a North American retail chain, within six months he had amassed twenty clients: each paying four thousand five hundred rand a month.

It was, according to Timothy, the memory of his grandfather, Thomas Webster, that inspired him to get off his butt and build a new clientele; just as it was the memory of his grandfather that inspired him to write and teach and do some good for the legions of poor in South Africa.

But this morning, in the Killarney Mall, facing him over coffee and orange juice and poached eggs, I know nothing of his history or motivations. Almost everything I know about the suave American I gather from the conversation, which is still more or less on theme: how whites in suburbia experience one South Africa, *the people* in the townships and rural areas another.

'The next revolution is a race-brand revolution,' Timothy says, pushing a napkin into his collar and spreading it over his tie. 'White is still the strongest brand in the world.'

Timothy talks about his forthcoming book, provisionally entitled *The Last Chance for the Brand Black Man*. 'It's about shock and awe tactics, extreme demonstrations of excellence. The reality is that blacks are trying to get as comfortable as whites. You as a white man living in your suburbs are complicit.'

This comes more as a statement of fact than an accusation. It is delivered evenly, purposefully, with a wide and authentic smile.

'Luxury gives whites a position of equity. There's a default value in there that says *you're the shit*. We don't have anything like that.'

I want to react, but have no base from which to argue. He continues, filling in the outlines of his theory.

'If you are black and you go into a white workplace, immediately you are at a disadvantage. Your equity goes down. So I say dress better than they do. Be proactive when they're not expecting it. I teach my students to build a portfolio of evidence around their brand.'

The one thing I do already know about Timothy is that his students are undergraduates at an institution called CIDA, a university in downtown Johannesburg that provides a subsidised tertiary education to the brightest matriculants from the country's poorest schools. Timothy has read a feature I wrote about the university for *Maverick*, which is why we're having breakfast today – he thinks there's a lot I left out of the piece.

After a particularly cogent line – 'There's a knee-jerk reaction to whiteness that I don't think white people can afford' – he invites me to join him at the end of the month when next he takes a group of his students to mentor Aids orphans in Soweto. 'We meet on Saturday morning at CIDA and go from there. Before we leave we try to get our game face on. Extreme things are happening, it can be overwhelming.'

I'm a little insulted. I'm a journalist in this country, I'm thinking, I'm supposed to be familiar with the story. Still, I know enough to know how thin my knowledge is. So I ask myself the question: Does this warrant a trip to Soweto? Visiting a township as a white South African, even in 2007, even one as reputedly tame as Soweto, is always a statement. Look here, you're saying, I'm progressive; I'm not like the others. And sometimes (often) this statement isn't appreciated. Sometimes what you need is a reason.

But there is a reason to go with Timothy. Two, in fact. First, it's a chance to see Soweto through the eyes of a black foreigner – he might show me things about my country that I'm historically conditioned to ignore. Second, Timothy's route into South Africa's most famous township begins in Johannesburg's malls and suburbs – we share a vantage point.

———

I am sitting in the passenger seat of Timothy's metallic blue hardtop BMW z3. We are on our way to Soweto, and we are talking about the country's new rich. The discussion is framed by the Gini coefficient: whether people's crassness gives it extra bite. The consensus, in the absence of any hard data – aside from the Gini score itself, which at 0.685 places South Africa amongst the world's most unequal societies – is an unremarkable 'Yes'.

So, no measure for crassness – how do you weigh up greed, compulsive consumption, bad taste? – but the inequality can always be probed and unpacked.

Like the fact that, as of 2007, South Africa is the planet's fourth most efficient producer of dollar millionaires, minting them at a rate of around seven thousand a year, and climbing, while unemployment stands at forty per cent and the number of people living on less than a dollar a day is more than twice what it was in 1996. Over forty thousand dollar millionaires; over four million people living on less than a dollar a day.

The country's rich, I inform Timothy, could double the income of the country's poor if they each donated about thirty-six thousand dollars a year; the price, at current exchange rates, of an entry-level BMW.

'Wow!' he says.

We have left the motorway and are driving west now on Kumalo Street. Soweto presents itself in its perennial colours. The auburn dust, the pale blue winter sky. The red face-brick and the product signs – Omo, Iwisa, Mageu – painted in thick enamel on grey concrete walls.

And the new colours. High-gloss black and gold and silver; everywhere the luxury cars.

As we enter the outskirts of Orlando West, Timothy speaks about what we've come for. 'I've been to four funerals my whole life,' he says. 'My wife, being married to her ... she's in Swaziland every other week for a funeral. I can't take it.'

'What?' I ask. 'What can't you take?'

He is pensive. 'My first Christmas here we visited an Aids orphanage in Swaziland. There was one girl who wouldn't smile. Her brothers and sisters were having a good time and she was just sitting alone. I tried to find out what was wrong. I'm just off the plane from America, not really aware of the challenges and what's happening and shit. Two weeks later I heard she had died. I couldn't deal with it.'

The z3 turns onto a gravel road. I'm thinking about the way Timothy frames his stories: the self-deprecation, the candour about his vanities and blindspots. Sure, there's the air of the preacher, the strong hint of caricature, but he does come from Southern Baptist stock. His grandfather, Timothy told me, once threatened to shoot the Madison reverend – for using the parish's charity box as pocket money. There's something wholesome in that, steadfast. Something that explains how Timothy comes to be in Orlando West every second weekend, driving his flash ride up this dirt track, fully convinced of the righteousness of his mission.

We pass through an open gate. The bus carrying the CIDA students is following behind. Timothy stops and shuts off the engine.

He has to arrange the day's activities, he says. In the meantime, he suggests I interview Carol Dyantyi, the director and founder of the orphanage.

Ikageng Itereleng Aids Ministry: a single-storey prefabricated house no bigger than my apartment. It's set on the northern end of a dusty field, on the same grounds as an apartheid-era male hostel and some buildings belonging to the Department of Social Development. Soweto's major train line runs along the western perimeter.

I wait on the porch. Carol comes to the door, a middle-aged lady in a beret and jeans and green socks. 'Us Africans, we don't wear shoes,' she says.

She explains the set-up.

'Ikageng Itereleng, it means *to do for yourself*. This house is our head office. From here we handle the referrals from the churches and hospitals. We provide food parcels at the end of each month to many households, almost three hundred, because the kids they must eat. But there are also many more than that. Right now, we have two thousand kids in four hundred and seventy-one households.'

The children range in age from newborns to eighteen-year-olds, Carol says. They are taken in by volunteer 'mothers' in Orlando West and the nearby Soweto districts. All of the children, I'm told, have lost or are soon to lose their natural guardians to Aids.

'How many children are infected?' I ask.

'Forty-seven that we know about. The problem is we want to do an HIV test on the children, but we cannot force them. Everything must be confidential. Even if they have HIV, they can withhold from us.'

'What do you think is the real number?'

'Two hundred, maybe. I can see the signs. It's the weight loss, the shingles, the swollen glands. Sometimes we ask them to go for a test and they come back and tell you stories.'

The phone rings in the office, Carol steps inside and invites me to follow.

The room is compact, almost half its space taken up by a cluttered desk. On the far side is a small glass cabinet, displaying trophies and pictures of smiling kids with medals around their necks. Next to the cabinet, tacked to a board on a yellowing sheet of A4 paper, is a gentle prompt:

'ALWAYS REMEMBER
HAPPY MOMENTS
PRAISE GOD
DIFFICULT MOMENTS
SEEK GOD
QUIET MOMENTS
WORSHIP GOD
PAINFUL MOMENTS
TRUST GOD
EVERY MOMENT
THANK GOD'

Another A4 sheet is tacked to its left. I read the large serif print, an invitation to the staff and children of Ikageng to 'attend the unveiling of a tombstone for the late Thulisile Baloyi'. Below is a further invitation to an unveiling, this for a half-dozen members of the Shozi family – Alina, George, Michale, Mondla, Johannes and Sydwell.

Just a few names, I'm thinking, that speak of what is left behind: around 1.8 million orphans in South Africa, around four per cent of the population.

Outside, Timothy calls.

'Okay, so plan *A* hasn't worked,' he says, businesslike. 'We were going to get the kids to come here, but that's not gonna happen. So it's back to plan *B*. The CIDA students will go out to the homes.'

I stand on the fringes as Timothy gathers the students in a circle. Eleven have volunteered today, eight of whom are female, all aged twenty-two or under.

Timothy's in the centre, vital and strong in his trainers and white Italian football jersey. 'You guys have to make them feel that you're regular people. You can't intimidate them, okay?'

He's talking loudly and rubbing his hands together. 'We all know about the teachers' strike, right? Find out what the weaknesses are in the education areas so that you can help out. Anybody have any innovative ideas?'

Nobody.

Timothy loosens them up with a well-worn joke. 'The men at CIDA don't seem to be as strong as the women at mentoring. Do you think it has something to do with the emotional content?'

'Yeah, guys don't want to get emotional,' a girl in dreadlocks says.

'Is it a Zulu manhood thing?'

'Ag, the Xhosas are worse.'

Before we visit the houses, Carol wants a word. She wants to apologise to me for the children's absence. 'Sometimes I get embarrassed, you know. *Yoh!* Even at the winter school we got six to go out of fifty-five. And I told the kids. I said, "You need it!"'

Timothy explains, as we walk out the gate, that the children are reluctant because they've been let down so often. Western charities and non-governmental organisations come through Ikageng all the time – European volunteers with their clipboards and cameras, their insistence that everybody speak English. They will connect with a child for a week-end, they will be moved to tears by the experience, they will write a letter when they get back home.

What the child *needs*, he says, is follow-through – which is most likely to come from someone who speaks the same language, someone with a similar background.

'The goal is that these could be kids that would enrol at CIDA. Our students grew up like them.'

In ten minutes we're on Vilakazi Street, the corner in Orlando West where Hector Pieterson was shot. There's a small memorial plaque, slate stone and rusted metal. A black tour guide stands before a white family – father, mother, yawning daughter – and tells the story. 'Hector Pieterson was twelve years old when he was killed by apartheid police on June 16th 1976,' he says. 'He was the one who came to symbolise the resistance of our nation.'

Whose nation? I'm wondering. I can't get away from my whiteness on these streets; there's nowhere to put it. Does this nation belong to the yawning daughter and her middle-aged parents, a family still living off the fruits of entrenched privilege? Does this tour to the township prove that they're a deserving white family? Is that what I'm proving?

Or did the tour guide intend something less accommodating by *our*, something more in tune with the country's history?

We come to a house opposite a school. A wire-mesh fence, unpainted brick, on the front façade an old (intentionally depersonalising) apartheid address: number 11527A. The CIDA students stand in a circle in the yard. Through the open door I see a cracked linoleum floor, patches of carpet, a coal stove in the kitchen.

This house has taken in two Aids orphans in the last year. The older one, a girl, loses her shyness as the students break into song. The mother here is a large woman; she wears a blue jersey and a huge orange T-shirt that bears the slogan: 'The greatest mom in the world'.

I'm watching, not understanding a word. I'm trying to imbibe the scene through the expressions on the kids' faces. Time passes; I'm still on the fringes. And then Timothy taps me on the shoulder; an urgent call, he says, we need to leave. 'You'll come back with me tomorrow, right?'

The next morning we are in a classroom on the western end of the Ikageng field, near the railway tracks. Timothy is giving a presentation. He is showing the CIDA students and the ministry children, fifteen of whom have come through today, slides of himself at the *Bucega* ceremony, from the time he was initiated as a Swazi warrior. There is a slide of Timothy in the deep bush, his shirt off, sweating; there is a slide of Timothy carrying a leaking bucket of water up a steep hill; there is a slide of Timothy surrounded by men in traditional Swazi dress, an expression of profound satisfaction on his face.

'The name they gave me,' he says, 'is Kancane-Kancane. It means "slowly but surely".'

It may be the slides of Timothy in his warrior skins juxtaposed against the high-style zip-up jacket he is now wearing, it may be the way his southern-fried American accent swirls around the intricate clicks and consonants of the Swazi language, but everyone – every mentor and Aids orphan and observer in the room – is laughing. Which, I guess, is just as he wants it.

'When I came to Joburg I had no clients; it seemed like the worst move,' he says. 'I realised I was an ignorant American who needed to learn a lot of stuff.'

He stops to let the class quieten down. 'Okay, how many of you guys are struggling because of the strike in schools?'

Ten hands go up.

'Good, we'll focus on that.'

We leave the classroom and the students pair up into their mentoring groups. I speak to Thabang, a matric pupil who complains about his maths teacher. He goes to school in Everton, he says, south of Johannesburg, and his teacher 'doesn't know anything, even when she does come'.

Thabang's mentor today is Lucky Madonsela, a second-year finance major from the East Rand township of Duduza. Lucky is one of CIDA's top students – his aim when he graduates, he says, is to work at JP Morgan or Goldman Sachs. The way he announces this, the note of conviction he achieves, suggests that either firm would be *lucky* to get him.

Thabang and Lucky, together with another dozen pairs, head off to where they'll be working today: kitchen tables and small studies and front rooms in houses around Orlando West. I watch them go and wait for

Timothy. We join two Ikageng volunteers and a group of ministry children who don't have mentors (there aren't enough CIDA students here
this morning; Carol has been more successful in her efforts to corral the
orphans) and we walk out the gate. The plan, Timothy says, is the same as
yesterday – to visit as many of the houses as possible.

But, like yesterday, the plan is scuppered. On Vilakazi Street, just beyond the Pieterson memorial plaque, we are accosted by the neighbourhood urchins, five miniature *tsotsis*, pint-sized gangsters in training. They
are far too small to pose a threat and yet there is no way past them. They
are abrasive and curious, and their story demands attention.

The oldest boy, we learn, is a 'trainrider': an adept at the new sport for
the intrepid (and bored and faithless) Soweto adolescent. He sniffs glue,
he tells us, and he's quit school. His sport, says the boy, is sometimes called
'tomb-rider' and sometimes 'm'rider'.

'Sometimes just *spara-para*.'

Timothy asks the boy a question. 'What do you do when you get on
top of the train?'

'Ya, I dance *skanda*, like this,' he says. He sends his four limbs into a
controlled robotic spasm. The other boys howl and screech and clap.

'What else?' I ask.

'We hang on the side of the train.' He puts his left arm in the air and
shakes his body and turns his eyeballs up in his head.

A younger boy introduces himself. 'Me, I am Mfundo,' he says. He's
about ten years old, wide-eyed and barefoot, in a dirty peak hat and an old
brown jersey three sizes too big. He stands on his tiptoes and whispers in
my ear, 'He's telling you he only sniffs glue, but he's a drug dealer.'

'Okay,' I smile.

The boys urgently need to know about Timothy's digital video camera.
How much does it cost? How does it work? Timothy says it costs plenty.
He shows them the record button and how to frame a shot. Then, with an
instinct for the footage it could provide, he hands the camera over. As we
all move again up the street, the trainrider – blue tracksuit, shaved head, a
deep scar on his chin – is interviewed by Mfundo, *Hard Talk* style.

'Why do you do it?' Mfundo shouts, holding the camera six inches
from the subject's face.

'I don't know – 'cos I like it.'

'Ay, if the cable takes you, they leave you there!'

The trainrider shrugs.

'Where did you get this scar?' Mfundo asks, taking his right hand off the camera and touching the trainrider's chin. 'Don't lie!'

'I don't know.'

'When do you do m'rider? Before you go to school?'

'In the morning.'

'How old are you?'

'Fourteen.'

'You're too small. You can kill yourself.'

We walk past a church, an Apostolic Faith Mission with a full carpark – it's Sunday, I'm reminded – and a cavernous main hall. A melodic bass escapes from the open windows. When we have passed I turn back to the boys and see that the roles have been reversed. Interviewer has become interviewee. Mfundo is now in front of the camera, and the trainrider is interrogating him about stealing.

'Why do you steal?'

'Ay, you, you taught me how to steal. Because you, you say we must get in this way.'

'Which way?'

'This way. Around these security guards, through this fence.' Mfundo points and gestures, evoking the scene of the crime.

'But then you ran away from the security.'

'No, I never ran away.'

'Why did you steal? You were hungry?'

'No.'

'You were hungry for a chocolate,' the trainrider says, mocking.

'Why do you steal?' the other boys ask, giggling. 'Why do you steal? You know stealing is bad. If they caught you, you go to jail.'

Mfundo is annoyed. 'They don't want to give me a key.'

'Who's they?'

There's more laughing. We move on up the street. Timothy takes his camera back now. He turns it on the smallest boy – no more than six or seven – and asks him his name.

'Thumi,' the little man announces proudly.

'This boy is very wild,' offers Mfundo.

'Are you wild, Thumi?'

'No, it is Mfundo.'

Timothy tries to get more out of Mfundo, who's emerging as the ring-leader; maybe not the strongest boy, but easily the smartest, the most charismatic. 'So Mfundo, sometimes you get hungry and you have to steal, huh?'

Mfundo puts on a hurt face. 'No, I'm no more stealing.'

'You've stopped stealing, that's good. When you used to steal, before, what happened?'

'Nothing. They once caught me.'

'They caught you. And what happened?'

He evades, makes up a story, something about 'this one and his brother and that other one'.

'*Hamba*, Mfundo,' a boy laughs.

We walk down a hill, around a corner, the huge painted smokestacks of Soweto's mothballed power station coming into view.

Timothy points the camera at the trainrider. 'You, have you ever stolen before?'

'Yes.'

'You have stolen?'

'Yes.'

'Where?'

The trainrider grins.

'Do you steal in Soweto or only in the suburbs?'

He grins some more. Mfundo helps out. 'Here.'

'Only in Soweto?'

'Yes.'

'Why don't you steal in the suburbs?'

'I'm afraid to steal in the suburbs. There's a lot of sos.'

'There's a lot of security?'

'They're going to beat him up,' says Mfundo.

'Oh, so he gets beat up in the suburbs, but not here?'

'Here you are risking,' a boy says. 'Someone could just come and get you.'

Mfundo explains. 'Out there, by the hostel. They hit you with *mvubu*.' He jerks his arm, as if cracking a whip.

'*Mvubu*. What's *mvubu*?'

'It's like a big cane,' says a boy. Mfundo says, 'This thing they are beating cows with.'

Timothy stops and turns around. The Ikageng group is a few paces behind. In an effort to engage them, he asks, jokingly, 'So you guys are also stealing?'

'No.'

Mfundo cuts in. 'Ya, they are stealing. They are stealing pens, in my class.'

An Ikageng girl is scandalised. 'No, he's lying! How can you trust this guy? He's lying!'

'She likes the boys so very much,' says Mfundo. 'So very much.'

We pass a mongrel dog, mustard yellow, lying on its outstretched forepaws; an old leather car seat placed like a deck-chair under a corrugated iron shed; a cracked plastic washbasin discarded in the street. And around the next corner the bigger boys (Mfundo and his crew in ten years, maybe) standing around a marine blue BMW M3. They're dressed in expensive labels, thick sunglasses, kwaito blaring from the speakers. Our entire posse stops talking.

When they're out of view I am the first to speak. I ask Mfundo, 'What do you think about white people?'

'Uh?'

'White people. What do you think about them?'

'Ah, white people. They're nice.'

'They're nice?'

'Ya.'

'Why do you think that?'

'Because sometimes they adopt us, you see. And then we have a nice family, you see.'

'And the blacks with money?' asks Timothy. 'They don't adopt you?'

'Ah, they do. Some of them. But, ay, they beat you up.'

'They beat you up?'

'Ay, the *magogos*. Yoh! They hit you with slippers. The morning shoes.'

Mfundo gets bored with the discussion. He points to a wall on the left. 'There's June 16!' he says. 'There's June 16!'

I look. On a white wall, below the date 'June 16, 1976', are words spray-painted in blue and orange: 'Every revolution beginz at the Street Khona La. Toyi-toyi 25 hours.'

Mfundo displays his reading skills. 'This means,' he says, 'toyi-toyi 25 hours.' He repeats the claim three times. 'And the *magogos* say, "Viva! Viva! Viva!"' Everybody laughs.

'So when you think of June 16,' Timothy asks, 'what do you think about?'

Mfundo ignores the question. He goes over to the wall and touches another symbol painted there; the raised fist of Black Consciousness. He raises his own fist but this time doesn't raise a laugh.

Timothy asks again, 'What do you think about when you think about June 16?'

Mfundo leans into the camera. 'I wish I was not born then.'

Thumi, the little one, mimics him. 'I wish I was not born then.'

'June 16 was hard,' says Mfundo.

'If you could talk to Hector Pieterson now,' says Timothy, 'and you told him you were stealing, what do you think he'd say?'

'I won't tell him. 'Cos he would say, why are you doing those things?'

'So you would be afraid to tell Hector Pieterson?'

'Mm.'

'Hector Pieterson fought for freedom. Do you think you are free now?'

'Not too much,' says Mfundo. 'Not too much.'

'Not too much. Why?'

''Cos, 'cos, they are still killing some blacks in the farms. And there's lots of gangsters here.'

'So when you guys get older, do you think you're gonna be gangsters?'

'No, we're not,' says Mfundo.

'But you guys have already been practising.'

A boy says, 'I'm going to finish my school first. I'm going to have my house and my car.'

'You want a car?'

'Ya, a Lamborghini.'

'But me, I don't like Lamborghini,' says Mfundo, 'I like Hummer H-3.' He lifts up three fingers. Thumi, who hasn't left Mfundo's side, repeats the mantra, 'Hummer H-3.'

———

Later, one by one, Mfundo and his crew peel off in search of lunch. We visit three houses. The last house is on the outer fringes of Orlando West; the mother is a wrinkled woman in a *kopdoek* and a bright yellow skirt that touches her ankles. The Aids orphans line up to greet her. I wait my turn in the queue behind Timothy. '*Sawubona mama*,' I say. She offers a limp hand and stares at a spot behind my left shoulder.

I move to the back of her yard and resume my conversation with a young man whose name means 'prayer'.

Thapelo Leeuw is twenty-five years old and unemployed. He is a volunteer at Ikageng, he explains, because the alternatives hold no appeal. 'I thought to myself, no, I'm not here to steal, to be a drug idiot, to be a drunkard.' He tells me that most of the people he grew up with are in jail or dead. Then he talks about his mother.

'She spoke at the last minute, and now it's very bad because the nurses are not working. The strike, you know.' His face collapses. 'She started taking ARVs but it's too late.'

He gathers himself and changes the subject. 'How long will you be in the country?' he asks.

'I'm South African,' I say. 'I live maybe fifteen kilometres from here.'

———

At the end of June the strikers sign a deal with government. Zwelinzima Vavi, head of the Congress of South African Trade Unions, accepts a civil servant wage increase of 7.5 per cent; not quite the 12 per cent he was asking for, but an acceptable compromise nonetheless. Economists and commentators are asked to assess the damage.

The longest public service strike in South Africa's history has cost the country 11.5 million working days, significantly more than the 9 million days lost in the industrial action of 1987 (when the dissatisfaction was directed at white capital and the PW Botha regime). The link between the casualty rate in hospitals and the absence of nursing staff, say the experts, is impossible to calculate. The effect on the education system, they add, can only be determined after the full year's matric results are in.

Once again, the rage of *the people* has been confined to their own areas. Amongst the stories that make it into the press is an item out of Lakeview, Soweto: an 'angry mob' of striking teachers – wielding sticks, knives, rocks and guns – has assaulted scabs and wrecked property at a primary school; the principal has to be rescued by police. Similar reports of intimidation involving healthcare workers emerge from public hospitals around the country.

Such stories provoke (and fail to provoke) the elite in expected ways. Some in the suburbs express shock at the 'destructive' and 'irresponsible' behaviour of the strikers; mostly, though, apathy prevails.

As for me, while I'd like to say that my decision to dump the Alfa the week the strike ends is informed by a keen awareness of class injustice, the argument doesn't hold. Fact is, the Alfa's performance has become too erratic, its service and upkeep too expensive. Within days of the truce, I trade in the car for less than a quarter of what I paid – the Selespeed boasts one of the worst resale values in the book – and make a deposit on a 2004 diesel-engine Golf.

But it does feel good, right even, to travel unnoticed on South Africa's roads. Instead of silver spoilers and two-tone leather seats, instead of the unfailing attention of the traffic-light hawkers – 'Ya, Mr Alfa Ro-*may*-o' – the Golf's ubiquitous lines and colour (white) come standard with a welcome anonymity.

At lunchtime on a Tuesday in September, when I park the car outside Timothy's new apartment on Pritchard Street in downtown Johannesburg, I am free to watch without being watched.

I am ten minutes early. I roll down the window and look up at the glass and steel façade of The Franklin, the former headquarters of accounting firm Ernst & Young, now converted into residential units by the same company that failed in its plans for Penmor Tower, the invisible skyscraper in Rissik Street. In The Franklin's marble front entrance stands a large black man in bowler hat and coat-tails, the building's concierge. Occupying the loading zone is a delivery van from *The Star* newspaper, whose offices are next door.

A white man in a dark suit emerges from The Franklin's lobby. He has blonde stubble on his sunburned pate, mirror sunglasses, a wide and flexed back. He strides up to the delivery van and bangs on the passenger window. There is no movement from inside the vehicle. He makes as if he's going to shatter the window with his fist, but thinks better of it. He jerks open the door.

'Hey you, I've told you before! If you don't get your van out of my loading zone I'm calling the police!'

A short black man in a T-shirt and 'sporty' (the headwear of the township wag) gets out the driver's side and walks around to the pavement. He's at least thirty kilograms lighter than his adversary.

'You better call the police then,' he says.

'Get your fucking van out of here!'

The black man laughs. The white man turns on his heel and storms back into the lobby, swearing.

My cellphone beeps. An sms from Timothy. 'Come up to 1503.' I lock the Golf and wait at the entrance. The big black man in the bowler, clearly no ordinary concierge, has taken up where his boss left off; he is arguing with the driver in Zulu. I touch him on the shoulder. He turns around and smiles and hands me his book to sign. As I head for the lifts, I hear him start up again on the driver.

This country is crazy, I'm thinking, unfathomable. '*Race*, man,' I say to Timothy, as I step inside his apartment. 'We like to tell ourselves it's about class, but we're still totally obsessed with race.'

———

Timothy doesn't disagree. Our final interview returns to where we started in the Killarney Mall back in June: the non-existent brand equity of young blacks in a white workplace, the tactics the new recruits must adopt to compete.

Timothy talks about the students in his 'personal branding' class at CIDA. 'They have zero idea in terms of poise,' he says. 'When they see a white professional, they crumble. I call it the remnants of a hurricane. It's a disaster.'

But, he says, at one of South Africa's big-four banks, which takes on final-year CIDA students as interns, they're beginning to understand. 'The executives know that they need to start the students with a black manager, because then they do much better. They are much more confident.'

The man from Madison goes over to his fridge to prepare drinks. I look around the apartment. Marble tiles, suede couches, a flat-screen TV. On the kitchen counter is a twelve-year-old bottle of scotch and a filter coffee machine.

Timothy brings two juices and a bowl of biltong and sits on a neon-green barstool opposite me. He is silhouetted by the view west over the city, by stained mine dumps and railway tracks and electricity pylons that stand on the horizon like reluctant sentries.

We pick up the thread. 'It's a struggle between value and what the market perceives of you,' says Timothy. 'Black South Africans must ask themselves some tough questions. The international community has said, "We're not interested in your culture, except for your entertainment." There is a need to survive, and survival means new ways. Some people see this, they tell themselves, "I got to be Western, I got to run away from my diseased family."'

The fifteenth storey window is open. I hear a muezzin call from the Kerk Street Mosque. Something troubling is emerging in Timothy's philosophy, I'm thinking, something deeply uncomfortable for the South African liberal. It's a taint in this country, a badge nobody wants, but if you're white and affluent and you believe vaguely in equality – and you say things, when confronted with inequality, like, 'ah shame' – you are, like me, a liberal. There are two ways to avoid the label, to sidestep the inconsequence of your pity: one, admit you're a racist; two, dedicate your life and income to closing the inequality gap. So most of us are liberals: ethical, detached, blameless. And most of us don't know how to take it when a black man tells us that South Africa would not be where it is if not for its whites.

'I think this country is different to the rest of Africa,' says Timothy. 'I think the only thing that makes it different is the number of white people who are here.'

'Are you sure you want to say that?' I ask, shifting in my seat. My pen is ready to scratch a large OTR over the sentence.

'Yes I am. In the white community you have a lot of skills. What the whites represent to the rest of the world is confidence. Confidence in the economy, which will help people the most. Frankly, I don't give a shit who is uncomfortable with that.'

I take a handful of biltong. I choose not to segue into the liberalist line about vast natural resources and cheap migrant labour and institutional-ised exploitation. Timothy, I know by now, is either bored or witheringly amused by the obvious. So I ask instead for more detail: what else does he do in his personal branding class that helps black students compete?

'I try to get them to see how what they're feeling, in terms of being labelled and talked down to, can be managed. White people are talking down to them because they look like the person who came and hijacked them. We get them to do research on their own personal brand, come up with a strategy. Like, if you approach a woman in a bar, and you try to get her number, you want to position yourself in a favourable way. They need to go in and get the number.'

'Get the number, right. For example?'

'For example, a student walks into a big white bank to do an internship. They recognise immediately that there's a deficit. To get them out of a de-ficiency, to a place where they can say, "I've got a chance", you've got to do some work. You've got to go on the offensive. Take ten words from your language that are difficult to pronounce, and important to the company culture, and get the white managers to pronounce them.'

I take another handful of biltong. Not bad, I'm thinking. The managers, whoever they are, must be from the liberal school – or at least, for the sake of their jobs, must pretend to be. Force someone like me to click, to get my tongue behind my teeth and properly articulate a Swazi or a Xhosa word, and you've got my full attention. Not bad at all.

But there's one more thing I want to ask. Black kids *look like* the people who come and hijack us? *That's* why we talk down to them? I see an image of my aunt and uncle the day they are told about the men who murdered their son, the day they know for certain that this country is not and never has been a place for them.

'What if,' I say to Timothy, 'because you haven't experienced a serious crime since you got here, you have no idea how bad it really is out there? What if you have no idea how battered some of us are by the pandemic?'

Timothy is aware of the circumstances of my cousin's murder, he accepts this part of my question. 'But let me tell you something,' he says. 'Often I'm in Sandton with a group of my wife's friends, who come from the top families … Hanis, Sisulus, Mandelas. They're sitting there and having drinks and usually it's very fine wine. I sit and I listen a lot. I listen to their laughter about white people who complain about crime. They hear it so much they become numb to it.'

———

Before I leave his apartment, Timothy hands me a mini-DVD. I play it as soon as I get home.

The scene is the yard of Ikageng on a winter morning. Timothy has his video camera pointed at a seventeen-year-old youth with earrings in each ear and short dreadlocks dyed blonde at the tips. The youth, determined to assert his manhood, has a neatly cropped moustache. A white woollen beanie, recently washed and gleaming in the winter sun, perches at the back of his head. He has a black-and-white bead necklace, and the collar of his red tracksuit top is turned up.

'How you doin' today?' Timothy asks.

The youth turns away from the camera and looks at the ground. He rocks back on his sneakers. 'Ya,' he says. 'Fine.'

'Yeah. You seem to be unique. Some of the students here, they all look alike. But there's something about you that seems special. Tell me why.'

The youth turns to the camera and smiles. 'I'm not shy.'

'You're not shy? You're willing to talk to people?'

The youth nods.

'And, uh, what do you like about school?'

'Studying.'

'Studying. You like to study. What's your favourite subject?'

'Accounts.'

Timothy compliments the youth on his choice. Then he asks him what he finds difficult about school. The youth says, 'Eish, to wake up in the morning.'

Timothy laughs. He says sometimes he also doesn't like to wake up in the morning.

'So, where do you live? Orlando West?'

'Orlando East.'

'What's the most difficult thing about living in Orlando East?'

The youth looks down at the ground again. He shakes his head. He mumbles an answer that ends with the word 'society'.

'A what kind of society?'

'A fucked up society.'

'The society is messed up?'

'Ya.'

'How?'

'Crime.'

'The crime. Have you seen crime before?'

'Ya,' the youth says. His tone suggests the answer is obvious.

'What kind of crime have you seen?'

'Robbery. Robbery and housebreaking.'

'You've seen this before?'

'Ya.'

'Do you have friends who have done this thing before?'

'Ya, they were doing it. But now they are not doing it.'

'They've stopped now?'

'Ya.'

'Why did they stop?'

The youth looks behind him and then at his shoes. 'Ay, because they see, if you keep on doing crime you will die or get arrested.'

'Have you had friends who died?'

'Ya,' the youth says. He expands, mumbling.

'What happened?'

'He was on top of the train, yesterday.'

'Yesterday?'

The youth corrects himself. 'Ay, last week. Uh, Saturday.'

'Did he fall off?'

'The cable beat him. Then he died.'

'Your friend? What was his name?'

'Tsepho.'

'And. And, um, how long did you know Tsepho?'

'Ay, we grew up together.'

'And was it hard for you to deal with?'

'Ay, it was hard, even now. I don't believe even now.'

'This happened last week?'

'Ya, last week Saturday. There by Orlando station.'

'And, has he, has he had his funeral yet?'

'Ya. It was yesterday.'

'Did you go?'

The youth nods.

'And did you know his family also?'

'Ya.'

'So what can you do to help his family?'

The youth is silent.

'Maybe if you go to school and you make good grades you can help them in Tsepho's memory. Right?'

The youth nods.

'That's good. And … And how old was he?'

'He was seventeen.'

'He was seventeen. And he was riding the train. Have you ever ridden the train before?'

'I'm going with the train to school. I'm using it.'

'But do you ever ride on top of it?'

The youth shakes his head. 'Me, I don't do that thing.'

'Never?'

'Never.'

'So why did he do it?'

'Ay, he was trying to impress … to impress the girls.'

'He was trying to impress the girls. And he died.'

The youth nods. There are now tears in his eyes.

'When, um, when … did the girls see him die?'

'Ya, they seen him.'

'How did they feel?'

'Ay, they feel sorry for him. But you know, ay, what happened it happened. You can't do nothing.'

'And. And, um, how many friends do you have that have died?'

The youth looks away and thinks. 'Now,' he says, holding up his fingers, 'three.'

'Three?'

'Ya, the other one he was beaten by the schoolchildren. By bricks. He was making housebreaking.'

'He was beaten by more students?'

'Ya, the students there by Diepkloof. They killed him with bricks.'

'With bricks? Damn! And you didn't see this, did you?'

The youth shakes his head.

'You heard about it?'

'Ya, they even show it in the *Sowetan*.'

'In the newspaper?'

'Ya.'

Timothy shakes his head, takes a breath. 'So are you learning anything from this programme?'

'Ya. I'm learning.'

'And is it helping you some?'

The youth nods.

'Who is your mentor here?'

'Lerato.'

'Lerato. Is it a guy or a girl?'

'A guy.' The youth flares out his shoulders. 'The big one.'

'The big guy. And, um, what have you learned from Lerato?'

'I learn many things. Like you mustn't, you mustn't give up.'

'So make sure you don't give up, alright?'

The youth nods.

'Cheers.'

DIE ON ROPE FOR BLOODY CRIME

THE LAST JUDICIAL HANGING in South Africa occurred on November 14th 1989. Up until that date, the country had frequently ranked amongst the world's top three in terms of annual executions. Throughout the 1980s, South African gallows put people to death at an average rate of over one hundred per year.

These are some of the facts I come across in the months after the sentencing of my cousin's killers. In late 2007, I read whatever I can about the death penalty. I read essays and articles, court transcripts and judgments, detailed opinion pieces that argue both for and against. From a personal standpoint, though, the most helpful thing I read is Truman Capote's *In Cold Blood*, which famously ends with the death by hanging of Perry Edward Smith and Richard Eugene Hickock.

'Well, what's there to say about capital punishment?' Hickock wonders, a few years before he is executed by the state of Kansas. 'Revenge is all it is, but what's wrong with revenge? It's very important.'

Hickock, as Capote shows, knew what the public wanted. On the day in 1965 that he and Smith took their 'ride on the Big Swing', the front page of the Kansas City *Star* rang triumphant: 'Die on Rope for Bloody Crime'.

The passages, when I read them, help formulate my questions. Would my uncle and aunt have liked to see a similar headline in, say, a Cape Town newspaper? Would this have satisfied their anger, their desire for revenge? Were such feelings more 'important' to them, more instilled, than the aching and ever-present reality that nothing could bring Richard back?

I know better than to ask them directly. Still, it's plain where the answer lies. By forgoing the trial and accepting the plea bargain, my uncle and aunt were putting vengeance aside. After endless months spent waiting, deliberating, mourning, their anger had gradually faded. At some point, it had been replaced by something else.

And yet what's so incredibly strange about this, I'm thinking, is that my uncle and aunt are almost certainly in the minority. Ever since the death penalty was abolished by the Constitutional Court in 1995, polls have shown that somewhere between seventy and eighty-five per cent of South Africans want it reinstated. If a survey were held tomorrow to establish whether people think Shavaan Marlie and Clinton Davids should be executed for the murders of Brett Goldin and Richard Bloom, it's more than likely that three out of four respondents would answer 'yes'. Because it's not just anger or the desire for revenge that drives support for capital punishment in South Africa, it's also faith in the deterrence factor – the presumption that potential murderers will think twice if they know that they too might pay with their lives.

The presumption is, of course, wrong. In South Africa, as elsewhere, most convicted murderers do not plan to go out and kill. They do not weigh up the pros and cons of what they are about to do before they do it. They are simply drunk, or jealous, or consumed by rage, or – as in the case of Marlie and Davids – whacked out on tik and looking to maybe scare some white boys and steal a car. And they lose control.

This raises the issue of punishment, of just retribution. In the landmark judgment that removed South Africa from the company of China, India and the United States (where capital punishment is still practised) and placed it in the company of Australia, Canada and the European Union (where it isn't), the point was made that 'a living being held for years in prison is punished; a corpse cannot be punished, only mutilated'.

But what the Constitutional Court judges didn't know, couldn't know, is that in the case of Marlie and Davids prison might not be much of a punishment either. The prisons of the Cape are run by the 'Numbers' gangs, the so-called 26s, 27s and 28s, each with affiliate gangs on the outside. The outside affiliate of the 26s is the Americans, whose alleged leader is Igshaan Davids, older brother of Clinton. With a connection like that, with the automatic respect that comes on the inside from having killed two *lanies* (white men), it's highly improbable that Marlie and Davids began their terms at the bottom of the prison hierarchy. More likely is that they entered with rank, that they have already established their authority, and that when they return to society – somewhere in their mid- to late forties – they'll be seasoned and ruthless gang generals.

So the concerned South African citizen, I'm thinking, sometimes requires what the poet John Keats called 'negative capability': the ability to sustain paradoxes, to live in uncertainty 'without any irritable reaching after fact and reason'.

Maybe it's this quality, in slightly altered form, which our politicians display when talking about things like the death penalty. Maybe, when applied to politicians, a better name for it is expediency – but in November 2007, a month before he is set to challenge Thabo Mbeki for the ruling party's top spot, Jacob Zuma is poignantly uncertain about capital punishment.

'The people themselves must voice their views about the matter,' he says, at an anti-crime rally in Mitchell's Plain, the very heart of the Cape ganglands. 'If the population is not happy, then let the population tell us what needs to be done.'

The less-than-hidden subtext: Zuma may one day be in a position to offer *the people* a referendum.

CHAPTER 5

Gedleyihlekisa

'POH-LOKS,' SAYS BRANKO BRKIĆ.

I reach over and turn down the volume on the car stereo. I look at him.

'Poh-loks,' says Branko. 'This came to me last night. This is what we are going to call the trip.'

I still don't get the reference. I have learned, though, not to ask my editor and friend to repeat himself twice: his accent is a source of some concern to him. I have learned, too, that if I mentally recast the vowels, Branko's references become clear on their own. This one does now.

'Good,' I say. 'I like it. Rhymes with bollocks.'

Branko laughs. The joke conforms to his opinion of South African politics, which he now compares (no joke at all) to his homeland during the rise of Milošević. He sips on his coffee and with one hand on the wheel pilots the gold Audi A6 down the hill. At the traffic light at the corner of the MI on-ramp and Houghton Drive, he turns left. Three hundred kilometres to the north lies the capital city of Limpopo province, an old Voortrekker town recently renamed *Polokwane*.

Poh-loks.

We have been planning the trip for a month, almost. Our excitement has built as the date has approached. We have booked three rooms in a guesthouse on the far side of Tzaneen. We have submitted our credentials to the party's media liaison office. A few days ago, when we knew that Sally would not be joining us, Branko bought a camera, a Panasonic Lumix with a Leica lens and a powerful optical zoom.

And now the day has arrived, December 15th 2007. Registration day of the fifty-second national conference of the African National Congress.

Destined to be, as far as we can tell, amongst the country's largest international media events since Winnie Madikizela-Mandela appeared before a special session of the Truth and Reconciliation Commission to respond to allegations that in the late 1980s she had murdered a fourteen-year-old boy.

That event, which happened at a venue outside Johannesburg in 1997, attracted two hundred journalists from sixteen countries. Ten years and one month later, at the national conference that will elect a new ANC leadership, seven hundred journalists are expected.

Where these two events coincide, we agree, is in the narrative of the populist demagogue. Their lure for an international audience lies in a recurrent question: is post-apartheid South Africa an exception to history, or is history in the country still waiting to happen?

———

In 1982 in Yugoslavia it became possible to publish books that had been translated into Serbo-Croatian from a foreign language. Before 1982, unless one practised *samizdat*, it had been possible only to publish books in the languages in which they had been written, but now the languages of the West were open to publishers too.

In 1984 Branko Brkić, age twenty-two, published the first Serbo-Croatian translation of *Do Androids Dream of Electric Sheep?* Branko spoke no English, but he had seen *Blade Runner* – the cinematic adaptation of Philip K Dick's sci-fi masterpiece – and despite his reliance on the subtitles he had fallen in love.

So Branko hired a pool of translators. From Dick he branched out into the work of Isaac Asimov, William Gibson, Douglas Adams and Walter Miller. After a year he extended the scope of his publishing interests beyond sci-fi. In 1987 he embarked on a Serbo-Croatian translation of the *Complete Greek Tragedies*.

This was not a small undertaking; it required long hours and much expertise. In the cafés and bars of Belgrade, people predicted the demise of Branko and his business. It took eighteen months for the last critic to be cowed.

When the *Complete Greek Tragedies* was published in 1988, Branko was twenty-six and his partner, Veljko Topalović, twenty-two. It was the first time in history that the *Tragedies* had been published in Serbo-Croatian in a single volume. The book turned a small profit.

But Branko and Veljko believed they should have turned a big profit. At the time in Serbia there were 116 libraries. If you were a government-sponsored publisher, all of these libraries were required to buy three copies of your book. If you were an independent publisher, you were deemed to be an anti-socialist and the libraries did not have to buy any copies. Branko and Veljko were independent publishers.

Still, enough library officials could see they had no choice but to carry the world's only single-volume version of the *Complete Greek Tragedies* in the national language. So the decision was made to buy one copy instead of three. The explanation given was that the book's text was Latin and not Cyrillic, but the message (as ever) was plain: excellence is one thing, what you really need to be is a Party man.

Unrehabilitated, in 1989 Branko and Veljko began translating the *Complete Shakespeare* into Serbo-Croatian. Like the *Tragedies*, it was to be the first in a single volume. And then 1989 turned out also to be the year of the ascension to power of Ante Marković. As the new prime minister of the Socialist Federal Republic of Yugoslavia, Marković implemented reforms like stabilisation of the currency and privatisation.

The reforms reduced inflation and the general standard of living rose. Progressives in Belgrade started to feel good about themselves. Branko and Veljko became local celebrities and appeared frequently on radio and television. Their office became a gathering place for members of the political opposition.

In 1990 Branko and Veljko published *Tito: The Technology of Power*, a book whose author was Kosta Cavoski, an opposition leader.

One afternoon Branko was in his office with Kosta, going over final changes to the layout. 'We should do a book called *Milošević: The Technology of Power*,' he suggested.

'Nah, he's not going to win one free election,' said Kosta.

'You know what Kosta? I'll make you a bet. If Milošević wins, you write a book. If he loses, don't worry, there's no point.'

'Fine,' said Kosta.

———

'What you need to see,' says Branko, 'it's happening the same way here. The negative selection. Is that an English term? Because we call it *negativ selektzia*.'

'It's an English term,' I say.

We have picked up Phillip de Wet and we have not yet reached the outskirts of Pretoria and already we are baiting one another. Phillip's response, from the back seat of the Audi, is to talk about a murder. The scenery has reminded him of a long-running story that has just landed again on the front pages.

The day before, says Phillip, in the Pretoria High Court, two teenage black boys were found guilty of the murder of an Afrikaans girl by the name of Samantha Uys. The boys, he says, were friends of Uys; one night in 2005 they all went to a bar, and later, after picking up Uys's mother's car, they stopped on a bridge to smoke a zol. It was there that one of the boys strangled Uys while the other boy held her arms down. They then dragged her to the riverbank and stabbed her three times in the neck. They kicked her and threw a rock on her head to make sure she was dead. They folded her body into the car and drove away and dumped it next to a squatter camp outside Mamelodi. They did all this, apparently, because they wanted to sell the car; they needed more money for drugs and alcohol.

'Uys was at the same school as one of them,' says Phillip, 'which is why the press are so fascinated by it. Think about it. Not so long ago that was a whites-only school.'

I look past Branko, out the driver's window, at a spotless suburb on a hill. Mamelodi, I know from a feature I wrote a few months back, is fifteen kilometres to the east of that hill.

A fact, I'm suddenly thinking, that could have fuck-all to do with the murder of Samantha Uys. Just like the distance from the Cape Flats to Bakoven could have fuck-all to do with the murder of Richard Bloom.

Today, on the road to Polokwane, the old (the obvious) explanations seem irrelevant, empty.

Irritating.

And I don't want to think about why. What I do want to think about: Phillip has baited us and must be baited back. I take up the theme. Lawlessness, decay, collapse.

'We haven't had water at my place for two days,' I say, pivoting in my seat. 'The mains burst in Killarney on Thursday. The family came for *shabbos* last night and we had to ask them to bring as many bottles as they could carry.'

'How do you shower?' asks Phillip.

'I swim.'

'This place is falling apart,' says Branko.

We have left Pretoria; we're on the open stretch where the N1 straightens out towards Bela Bela – the new name for the old white spa town of Warmbaths. We pass the Zambesi, Pumulani and Walmannsthal off-ramps. Again it's Branko's turn.

'Yesterday I heard on 702 that Joburg Gen has twenty-three lifts. Guess how many are working?'

'Three,' offers Phillip.

'Four,' says Branko. 'On the ninth floor there were bodies that they couldn't transport to the mortuary.'

We listen to the radio; stop talking for a while.

Until Branko shares his thoughts. 'I told you, many times. It's exactly what is going to happen in South Africa. The Yugoslavian economy was destroyed by incompetence, corruption and political correctness.'

Bela Bela, say the signs, is almost upon us now. Branko suggests we stop for lunch at the casino just before the town.

'It will be the perfect way to begin,' he says. 'You know, fear and loathing in Polokwane.'

We laugh. Branko has an abiding love of sixties counter-culture, which he badly wants us to articulate in the piece. With Hunter S Thompson, we're thinking, he may be on to something.

And then it occurs to me that nobody has yet brought up the second-biggest news item of the week.

Four days ago, eleven men were killed in what the press dubbed 'The Battle of Bela Bela'. The victims were cash-in-transit robbers. They were fleeing Bela Bela in a convoy of three vehicles, including the hijacked van holding the money, when they ran into an ambush. A crack police squad opened fire and made almost every bullet count. National police commissioner Jackie Selebi (in a rare moment of personal and professional triumph) said he had received word that the criminals wanted to set the van alight with the kidnapped guards still inside.

I remind Branko and Phillip of the incident.

'Ya-ya, they were on their way from the casino,' says Branko. 'Are you still cool to go there?'

'What, lightning strikes twice?'

'Not even here,' says Phillip.

We have entered acacia country. On either side of us, scattered amongst the dense umbrella thorn, are tin and chipboard shacks: in their yards are chicken coops and mealie stalks and dogs. A giant thunderhead looms on the horizon. I open the window an inch; the air is warm and thick.

Branko points the A6 at the next off-ramp. 'Let's go eat boys!'

This is good, I'm thinking. Mid-December in South Africa is a good time to be on the road. When I was a boy, December 15th was the day my father would pack us in the car and drive us to the coast. Every year the same day, the same time. Four in the morning – to be in Durban by ten-thirty.

Poh-loks, I'm thinking, is turning out to be a peerless mid-December road-trip.

As Branko hoped it might be, the sight of the Carousel Casino and Entertainment World rising above the Limpopo plain is an inspiration. The three-storey walls a deafening shade of pink, the roof a brazen super-green. The theme tied together by domes, by a large carousel over the entrance, by pagodas.

Inside there is more on the theme. Gold-plated umbrellas, their rods bare, hover above us like tropical sea creatures; a fountain reaches up in tiers towards the ceiling.

Underfoot are green and pink tiles, the route to the restaurant flanked by bruised peach faux-marble columns. The carnival excitement of bells, the thrill of money falling into buckets.

And then, like a cowpat on a marble floor, the restaurant: a musty, cavernous steakhouse in the Wild West motif – cowboy hats and leather saddles and dark walnut wood. 'It can take sometimes five hundred people,' says the waiter.

But on this Saturday afternoon, going on 1.15pm, we are the only customers. And there's a problem with the grill, so no steak.

Fifteen years ago, before a handful of similar casinos were built much closer to Johannesburg, this steakhouse was famous. 'The jalapeño steaks,' says Branko, 'I promise you.'

Waiting for our meal, we discuss the weirdness of gambling during apartheid – how casinos like the Carousel had to be out in the veld, out in the distant and dusty homelands. 'More weird than having them twenty minutes from home?' asks Phillip.

It must be my notebook and pen, Phillip's flak jacket, the camera around Branko's neck. Either that – either we are too obviously what we are – or today everybody is asking everybody regardless. After lunch, on our way out of the casino, the security guard asks, 'Who do you think is going to win?'

———

Kosta Cavoski made good on his bet. The manuscript of *Milošević: The Technology of Power* was delivered to Branko and Veljko in June 1991.

But there were problems.

The economy had gone into freefall. Spurred on by the nationalist rhetoric of Slobodan Milošević, each republic in the former federation of Yugoslavia had held elections, and each incumbent, to pay for his campaign, had taken control of state finances. The republics now had the right to issue their own money. In the Serbian republic, to secure mass support, Milošević paid every state worker two salaries.

The Serbian book publishing industry was an early casualty of the collapse. The government-sponsored publishers owned all the bookstores, and in the monetary squeeze the decision was made not to pay the independents. The cashflow crisis forced Branko and Veljko to postpone publication of *Milošević: The Technology of Power*.

With the office quiet, in August 1991 Branko went on holiday to the mountains of Montenegro. One night, as he and his friends were enjoying dinner in the hotel restaurant, a shootout erupted. Everybody ran for the doors; Branko remained to finish his soup.

His bravado notwithstanding, it was the first time he thought about having to leave his country.

A few weeks later, as he walked down the Boulevard of the Revolution in Belgrade, he noticed that instead of the intellectuals and artists he was accustomed to greeting on the street there appeared a wide variety of lowlifes.

It occurred to Branko then that Milošević's reign was destined to reflect the man's own understanding of the world. Milošević's ascension to power brought lowlifes to the Boulevard of the Revolution, he realised, because people who thought like Milošević would now establish the measurement system for what was acceptable.

People like Arkan, owner of Redstar Belgrade, the football team whose fans had developed a sideline in ethnic cleansing.

Branko sank into a mild depression.

It was October already when Branko and Veljko had enough money to publish the book. *Milošević: The Technology of Power* appeared in stores in mid-October. Within a few days Branko got a call from his 'former' landlady to say that the military police had been looking for him. He had been drafted to go to Vukovar.

Branko had not been drafted since he'd completed his national service in 1982, and so the message was clear. His choices, he knew, were simple.

He could stay in Belgrade and hide, but he was reasonably high-profile so that would be difficult. He could go to Vukovar, where it was more than likely he'd be killed. He could skip the country.

As the CEO of a publishing company, Branko was able to send himself to a non-existent print fair in Munich. He managed through connections to secure a pass. On November 9th 1991, he said goodbye to his parents and boarded a bus.

He stayed in Stuttgart with a friend for two weeks. Then, with another friend, he travelled to Réunion Island, where he waited for eighteen days. The plan was to fly to the first country – any country – that would grant him a visa.

Branko arrived in South Africa on Friday, December 13th 1991. He had two thousand five hundred rand in his pocket, no English, and a broken heart.

He also had the telephone number of a woman who told him to go to a hotel near a place called Hillbrow. The Cronia Hotel, 45 O'Reilly Street. He would find other Serbs there, the woman on the phone said.

Branko took a bus to the Rotunda and then a taxi. He arrived at the hotel at 1pm. He found a Serb who needed a roommate. At 4pm, from his bed in the small room, he said to the man, 'You know what? I don't know where I am. I was dropped here from the air. Let's have a walk.'

'I don't think we should go for a walk now,' the man replied. 'It will be dark in two hours.'

———

Tacked to a pole on a traffic island, as the N1 abruptly deposits us in the industrial outskirts of Polokwane, is a message from the Limpopo police. On first reading, the message is a simple warning: do not venture out onto these streets after dark. But there is something there that invites another look, something in the word choice that makes it appear more human and sympathetic than is normal for an object of its ilk.

Before the Audi speeds past, I read the message again: 'Lonely night walk can be dangerous.'

I alert Branko and Phillip to the significance.

'Did you see that? You don't want to be lonely out here. If anything happened, who would you call?'

'Ya-ya,' says Branko.

'And who would remember you?' says Phillip.

We let it go; there is a lot to distract us. A speeding Range Rover and a pimped-up Chrysler and a maroon Mercedes E500 with the plates 'Red Fox' up ahead. A half-dozen metro cops at every intersection. In the air, circling low above the traffic, three police helicopters.

Then Branko sees a sign of his own. Through central Polokwane, on the N1 route out of the city and on to the border with Zimbabwe, are a series of posters pointing the way to the airport, where registration is taking place. The posters prominently display the ANC colours – green, yellow and black – and they prominently display, too, a sponsor called 'Datamaster Polokwane'.

Branko instructs us to make a note. 'Wouldn't it be funny,' he says, 'if the sponsor were tendering for a government contract.'

Sirens. A motorcade has descended on us from behind. We swerve into the slow lane. Two black sedans, two black BMW X5s, two black Mercedes Vitos shunt past in a display of flashing blue lights and imperious force.

The motorcade, already half a kilometre ahead of us, veers sharply onto the access road to the airport. We guess that it is carrying a cabinet minister: it is too small to be carrying ANC deputy president Jacob Zuma, who has secured an entourage of twelve cars for the event, and it is certainly too small to be carrying President Thabo Mbeki, who is anyway expected to arrive in the state jet.

We follow the motorcade onto the access road and are confronted immediately by the other face of South Africa's ruling party.

Rank-and-file delegates from the provinces, ANC members from the Free State and Eastern Cape and Mpumalanga, people eating and talking and dancing amongst rows and rows of buses. Not coaches, not air-conditioned liners with on-board toilet and TV, just buses. Torn seats and undercarriages stained by decades of belching diesel fumes.

'What are they dancing for?' I ask, reflexively, because I want to be sure that what I am witnessing is a bona fide display of party factionalism. I don't need to wait for an answer. There, worn by every member of a crowd of at least three dozen delegates, are the '100% Zuma' T-shirts.

And there, after we park the Audi and proceed down to the registration venue, is the other side.

'Viva, Thabo Mbeki, Viva!'

'Viva!'

'*Amandla!*'

'*Ngawethu!*'

We push through the throng. In his right hand, high in the air, Branko is holding his new camera. He is taking ten shots a minute. He is smiling, as are Phillip and I, who are shouting our observations at one another and scratching furiously in our notebooks.

Time to register. The registration hall is a hot gaping hangar enclosed at the front by a wire mesh fence. The marshals at the gate are not letting us through. I find myself at the wrong end of a large group of impatient delegates. My face grinds against the fence. But soon the marshals relent, and I breathe, and walk to the back of the hall, where I almost collide with Jackie Selebi.

Above a pair of baggy board-shorts, covering his paunch, is a canary yellow T-shirt. On his head is a blue baseball cap, on his feet a pair of open-toed sandals. Belying his laid-back outfit, though, his face is drawn, his complexion ashen; he looks harassed. He steps around me and walks out the hangar, ignoring my request for an interview.

With good reason, I'm thinking. Selebi – not only South Africa's top cop, but, as head of Interpol, effectively the world's – is waiting to hear whether the National Prosecuting Authority will be allowed by the minister of justice to lay a charge of corruption against him. It does not look good for the man who has admitted a close personal relationship with organised crime boss Glenn 'The Landlord' Agliotti.

If Mbeki loses to Zuma, say the pundits, the NPA will be permitted to proceed with its case against Selebi. And given what we have already heard, given what we are seeing in the hangar, Mbeki *will* lose.

Phillip and I have deciphered the hand gestures. Three fingers in the air means 'third term': these are the Mbeki supporters. Rolling one hand over the other in quick succession, as per the signal for a substitution in a soccer match, means 'change': these are the Zuma supporters. As raindrops start to fall on the corrugated iron roof, as the thunderhead we saw hours earlier fulfils its promise and turns the hangar into a giant *hammam*, the group with the rolling hands swells in number and pushes its opponents to the far side of the mesh fence. Their small victory thus secured, the Zuma supporters march the length of the concrete floor and chant in a deep and resonant bass:

'Wena u lawula ka thathu

Awu sitshele

Ukuthi uZuma wenzeni'

I find a young journalist to translate this for me. They are singing, he says, 'You heading for the third term, tell us what Zuma has done.'

The question these delegates want answered is one that interests most South Africans. For them, the answer is plain: Zuma has done nothing; he is a victim of a conspiracy; Mbeki fired him as deputy president of the country for selfish and devious reasons. For many others, however, the answer is less plain: even if Zuma has not done everything he has been accused of doing, he has clearly done something, and that would make him a problematic choice for the next head of state.

What message, this group asks, would a Zuma presidency send to the rest of the world?

We get our registration cards and head back outside. We find two journalists from *Le Monde* and ask them about their angle for the following day's edition. 'We don't know yet,' the older journalist says. 'Most of the people in France think Nelson Mandela is still the president.'

———

Seven months earlier; midday on a quiet suburban street.

There are six of them. They are wearing black suits. They leer down at us from behind folded arms. They are spread out amongst the cars: a black s-class Mercedes, a black 5-series BMW sedan, a white Mercedes E320 and a black BMW x5 with a blue light on the roof.

The other vehicle here today is a silver mountain-bike that belongs to a policeman in standard SAPS uniform. He is smaller than the other men, and friendlier, and he invites us into a wooden hut to record our details.

Phillip and I wait on the slasto path. We take note of the hydrangeas and palms. A bald and thickset bodyguard – the largest of the men in the suits – is not happy.

'What are you writing?' he asks.

'We're journalists,' I say. 'We're, uh, writing what's in the garden.'

He shakes his head. 'Ay, you, you write everything.'

Maybe so. Still, I'm thinking, such details can be revealing.

Jacob Gedleyihlekisa Zuma might live in the upmarket Johannesburg suburb of Forest Town, with ground ivy on his pavement and a mani-cured lawn, but this home could just as easily belong to a senior manager at an insurance firm. Maybe, I write, Zuma's relatively modest style of living – 'discounting security detail: outsized, mystifying' – lends credence to his standing as man of the people.

And then he opens the door. In his house clothes, with his hand outstretched in greeting and a broad grin, Zuma is personable, gracious, disarming.

We quickly forget the recent history of the man: the corruption trial and the rape trial and the story he told the court (during the latter) about the shower he took to cleanse himself of Aids. We forget, too, the meaning of the Zulu name.

Gedleyihlekisa. He-who-smiles-at-you-while-he-messes-you-up.

What we remember, what's foremost in our minds, is a shrill and nasal chorus: 'If that Zuma becomes president …'

Here, in the TV room of Zuma's home, it clings to us like a stain, a blemish we can't remove but can perhaps render less noticeable by acknowledging. Our first question after the pleasantries: Why do you think you are feared by large groups of white people?

'I don't know. It is an invention of the media, I don't know.'

We hear him, and we want very much to believe what we hear.

We hear Jacob G Zuma describe his relationship with whites in general and Afrikaners in particular the same way he describes his relationship with the Inkatha Freedom Party: as good, perhaps even great.

We hear him defend white rightwingers who protest the name-changes of streets and towns, saying their views must be considered.

We hear him define the controversial song 'De la Rey' – which has more than once been called a declaration of racial war by Afrikaners – as a celebration of history akin to a Zulu praise hymn.

We even hear him upbraid the now-defunct National Party for 'failing to take the Afrikaners on board at the given time when the reconciliation was done'.

For two hours, there we sit: an Afrikaner and a Jew.

Speaking not to the potential leader of a delayed revolution, speaking to a mild-mannered politician in brown slacks and an open-necked shirt. Speaking not to a revenge-hungry demagogue, speaking to a middle-aged man in an armchair, a man at peace with himself and the world.

In late September 2006, after he had been in the country almost fifteen years, Branko Brkić, now the publisher and editor of South Africa's most irreverent business magazine, wrote an opinion piece for a popular local website:

> Eventually the day came when the man, known up to then mostly as the loyal lieutenant of the president, decided that it was his turn to run the country. So he surrounded himself with a motley crew of people who had nothing in common ideologically but shared his lust for power. Together they hatched a plan to seize control of the ruling party.
>
> That was almost twenty years ago. The president was Ivan Stambolić. The party was the Serbian Communist Party, and the plot was put into action at its August 1987 congress. The shadowy character didn't remain so for long; he became one of the world's most maligned villains after bringing untold misery and grief to the Balkans. He was Slobodan Milošević ...
>
> The grey majority of delegates to the Communist Party congress didn't give a fig about Milošević. At least not until they woke up one morning to find a fight brewing, a fight in which Milošević somehow seemed the stronger. Most decided to help (or save) their careers by declaring themselves for Milošević early enough to give the appearance of having been on his side all along. Some of the more prudent set off for the meeting with a speech in each pocket, one pro and one anti ...
>
> Two decades later I have the strange feeling of watching the same movie with different actors. Every day I see more and more ANC members waking up to the fact that Jacob Zuma could be the next president and adjusting their positions accordingly. The movement shows every sign of [the] snowballing grey majority, and once it becomes big enough there is no stopping it ...
>
> The Cosatu congress and Zuma's legal reprieve yesterday helps speed things along. Even the guys with the pro-Mbeki speech in one pocket and the pro-Zuma speech in the other will have to discard one soon, to save what is left of their careers ...

Where will that take South Africa? I don't know, and I don't think anybody else does either …

———

The University of Limpopo, Turfloop campus; the main marquee on the morning of the opening day of the Polokwane conference.

I am on the carpet next to Branko, my knees folded up against my shoulders, straining for a position from which I can get my pen at my notebook. A few places to my left I see John Simpson, veteran BBC journalist and presenter of *Simpson's World*, doing the same. Branko taps me on the shoulder and points up at the stage. Less than ten metres from us, looking relaxed and confident in semi-formal attire, are ANC national executive committee members Charles Nqakula and Manto Tshabalala-Msimang.

'Ya-ya,' says Branko.

I get the inference. In the last few years, as the cabinet ministers directly responsible (respectively) for the safety and health of all South African citizens, Nqakula and Tshabalala-Msimang have demonstrated a consistent inability to do anything constructive about crime and Aids in the country. Given the subtext here this morning, given their firm position in the Mbeki camp, they appear too smug.

I have found that I can get my pen at my notebook if I use the open space under my right leg. How bad can a Zuma victory be, I write, if it brings with it a new NEC and therefore a new government executive?

And then on the stage appears another NEC member: minister of finance Trevor Manuel, a man courted by the world's top financiers and central bankers, a Mbeki man whose replacement by someone less capable would result in the very real prospect of disinvestment and capital flight.

As it has recently become with the ANC, the symbols here are vivid and incongruous – a fact further confirmed by the sudden arrival of the marshals. Looming above us now, spread at close intervals along the small strip of carpet directly beneath the stage, are twenty-five men and women in the uniform of Umkhonto we Sizwe.

Those are the leather boots and khaki fatigues and Fidel-like hats of the liberation movement's old armed wing. Those are the men and women whose job it is to keep us in check, the footsoldiers who have been ordered not to brook any dissent, the loyal cadres whose indignant expressions suggest that we (the journalists) are guests here and that our continued presence is not, in fact, guaranteed.

The counter-reaction is subtle but swift. Bheki Khumalo, Mbeki's former spokesman, easily recognised by his strong jaw and sunken eyes, strides down the unoccupied strip of carpet and demands that a group of standing photographers make way. A tall unshaven lensman from a local daily says, 'Bheki, anything for you, my brother! Anything for you!'

He continues to take his shots. The footsoldiers step forward, but, perhaps sensing the headline, Bheki signals for them to back down. He smiles at the tall photographer, who returns the smile, takes a bow and steps out of the way.

The stand-off between the media and the party will be revisited, in greater intensity, in the days ahead. It won't become nearly as intense, however, or as meaningful, as the stand-off between the party and itself.

A chant begins at the back of the tent. Within seconds there are thousands of delegates on their feet, on their chairs and tables, swaying to a slow and hypnotic refrain. 'We-eh *Zu*-maah. We-eh *Zu*-maah.'

The chanting continues, insistent and rhythmic and a little menacing. Then, on the two projection screens as big as sails that flank the stage, on the three screens of equal size that run along the tent's three-storey-high spine, appears a close-up image of a portly and bespectacled woman. The chanting stops. Now, as one, the delegates boo.

The woman behind me rises onto her haunches, inadvertently digging her knees into my back, and asks in an urgent whisper, 'Who are they booing?'

I turn around. Her nametag says she works for a British current affairs programme. 'They're booing Nkosazana,' I say.

'Wow!' the woman says to her assistant. 'They're booing Nkosazana. Did you get that? Write that down. They're booing Nkosazana!'

Ja, I'm thinking, it's a poignant scene, an irony a British audience might relish: Nkosazana Dlamini-Zuma, minister of foreign affairs in Mbeki's cabinet, booed by her ex-husband's wild supporters.

The chanting starts again. 'We-eh *Zu*-maah.' A delegate sitting in the first row of seats is belting it out louder than his comrades. The British producer, like most of the people here, is losing her poise. 'Get his name!' she says to her flustered young assistant. 'We must interview him! Get his name!'

More NEC members and dignitaries enter the tent. Patrice Motsepe, the third wealthiest man in South Africa (personal net worth, as per the *Sunday Times* Rich List: R13.5 billion), walks by in a peach suit. He stops, bends down and pecks Charlayne Hunter-Gault, former CNN bureau chief, on the cheek.

Mandla Langa, former head of the communications regulator (and working novelist once again), walks by in a more muted outfit.

The chief rabbi walks by in black suit and tie.

With the rabbi are a priest and an imam.

'A rabbi, a priest and an imam walk into an ANC conference,' I say to Branko.

'Ya-ya,' he says, laughing.

I'm still thinking up a punchline when the party's national chairperson, Mosiuoa 'Terror' Lekota, approaches the dais, leans into the mike and looks worriedly out into the hall. The booing is deafening and immediate: Lekota has made the mistake of publicly denouncing Zuma; he must now be humiliated.

'*Amandla!*' shouts Lekota, his fist raised in the liberation salute.

No answer.

'Long live the ANC, long live!'

A lame and subdued 'long live' from the middle of the tent.

Lekota, observing protocol, goes through the list of long lives: for the South African Communist Party, for the Congress of South African Trade Unions, for the ANC Women's League, for the ANC Youth League.

There is a commotion at the door and the marshals move forward. The photographers jump up and surge towards the stage. Mbeki and Zuma have entered the tent, they are walking up the ramp together.

'*Umshini Wam*', the call to arms of the Zuma supporters, spontaneously erupts. Bring me my machine gun. Lekota shouts in vain for order.

There is no let-up for fifteen minutes. '*Hlala phansi!*' Lekota says, again and again. It's the religious leaders who finally restore calm. There are prayers from the rabbi and the imam; there is a Hindu blessing. The priest recites a version of the prayer of St Francis: 'God, grant us the wisdom ... to defeat corruption by being good, to defeat lies by being honest, to conquer oppression by recognising that this is the day of reconciliation.'

December 16th, we're reminded. It used to be the *Day of the Covenant*, the day devout Afrikaners gave thanks for their victory over the Zulus at the Battle of Blood River.

The new ANC government could have scrapped the day. Keeping it a national holiday and renaming it the *Day of Reconciliation*, I'm thinking, has got to be one of the most remarkable statements a liberation movement has ever made.

———

The world's seminal book on African liberation movements is not simply *unintended for* white people; it's a book that writes past white people, around them, regardless of them.

I am reading Frantz Fanon's *The Wretched of the Earth* because it is famous for speaking deep racial truths, and because it is long past time that I do so, and because – when I flip through a copy in the bookstore at the Rosebank Mall – I see the following in the preface by Jean-Paul Sartre: 'Read Fanon: you will learn how, in the period of their helplessness, their mad impulse to murder is the expression of the natives' collective unconscious.'

A book first published in 1961, in French, holds out the promise of context, of a framework.

This near the beginning: 'To break up the colonial world does not mean that after the frontiers have been abolished lines of communication will be set up between the two zones. The destruction of the colonial world is no more and no less than the abolition of one zone, its burial in the depths of the earth or its expulsion from the country.'

This in the middle: 'For the propaganda of nationalist parties always finds an echo in the heart of the peasantry.'

This a few pages later: 'These men get used to talking to the peasants.

They discover that the mass of the country people have never ceased to think of the problem of their liberation except in terms of violence, in terms of taking back the land from the foreigners, in terms of national struggle, and of armed insurrection. It is all very simple.'

———

At 9.30pm on day two of the Polokwane conference, after more than ten hours of press conferences and interviews with party delegates, we leave the University of Limpopo campus. The Audi is parked just outside the main gate, in the commercial centre of the surrounding township, and as we get to the car we hear singing.

Around the first corner, in an open parking lot, we see the source: a group of fifty or so young people, dancing as a tight heaving unit, draped in Zuma flags and wearing '100% Zuma' T-shirts.

'Should we stop?' asks Branko.

A little reluctant, I say, 'Let's stop.'

We cross the road. We tell the young men at the edge of the circle that we are journalists. Can we ask a few questions?

One young man nods and steps forward.

Why, I ask, are you wearing the paraphernalia that has just been banned by the ANC leadership? Hasn't the NEC told delegates that wearing those things shows that the ANC is not united?

'It has nothing to do with any form of intimidation,' says the young man. 'It is to pledge solidarity with Comrade Jacob Zuma. We believe delegates from all provinces will join us. We are going to grow. We are expecting thousands.'

The young man says he is a member of the Turfloop branch of the ANC Youth League. He is a student on this campus and his name is Jacquaslatin. It's not a name that we've heard before, we don't know whether it's a first or a last name, and he won't tell us because first he wants to warn us about something.

'You people. You must maintain the code of good conduct of journalism. The media says many things that are wrong. We are tired of that.'

Jacquaslatin's friend intervenes. He has booze on his breath and a beer bottle in his hand. 'You must write this,' he says. 'You must write that the current guys are promising jobs and money. But people have been suffering.'

This new young man says his name is Percy.

'People tend to be power drunk,' says Percy. 'They tend to misuse their power. But the ANC is a caring organisation for the people. These tendencies were never there when Oliver Tambo was leader.'

More young people break away from the singing and dancing circle. They come to talk to us, to make their points.

'There is an abuse of state organs!' 'Enough is enough!' 'We want to take the ANC back to its original purpose!'

'So the ANC hasn't delivered?' I ask.

Says Jacquaslatin: 'The ANC has delivered. But the leadership style of Thabo Mbeki has not delivered. The style of Thabo Mbeki is one of a dictator.'

Says Percy: 'It's high time he left. The majority of people want Zuma. People have been killed for this democracy.'

Percy takes a big pull from his bottle and raises his voice. 'The other thing,' he says, pointing his finger at us, 'please don't misquote. Some people, we are saying that the leadership of Thabo Mbeki never took us seriously.'

Someone shouts from the crowd, 'Ya! A vote for Jacob Zuma is a vote for poor people.'

We are surrounded now. The smell of booze is powerful.

Then: 'They think we don't know, but we know. Ask Comrade Thabo, where is Chris Hani? What happened to Chris Hani?'

I look at Phillip and raise an eyebrow. Hani, the revered former head of Umkhonto we Sizwe, was gunned down by a white rightwinger in 1993; to announce that the current president was somehow involved in the murder is a wild and serious accusation, a statement indicative of deep mistrust.

We make a note and move on. Somebody from the middle of the throng says, 'The succession race is between us, we come on buses, and the people who come in MLs and Hummers.'

Another voice: 'The people here, we know what the conditions are that we need. We know we need streets, we know we need houses.'

'This one is worth noting too,' we hear. 'Write this down! Why are we here? We are here from the rural areas. We are representing the poor. JZ is for the poor and the working class. Mbeki is for Gordon Brown.'

The shouting rises in pitch, people all want to speak at once. We're being pushed and jostled. The singing and dancing has stopped, everyone has gathered around us. Jacquaslatin and Percy say they want to see where the article we are going to write will appear.

We don't have a *Maverick* with us, so we give them a current issue of our media and culture magazine, *Empire*. They look through it and stop on the page where David Bullard has written a column under the header, 'C'mon JZ, show me what ya got!'

Bullard is one of a handful of commentators who has been sued by Zuma for defamation; the column is a challenge to the ANC deputy president to prove his case, and the pull-quote in bold on the right-hand page reads: 'If Zuma imagined he would scare the hell out of journalists and cartoonists by threatening legal action then he was either badly advised or is even more stupid than I suggested in my original article.'

We say our goodbyes and get in the car and leave. On the way back to Tzaneen, Phillip and I insist that Branko (a teetotaller) parks the Audi at a roadside pub; our nerves begin to settle on the second drink.

May 2007. Together with Sally, who's scheduled today to take profile shots for the cover, Phillip and I return to Jacob Zuma's Forest Town home for a second interview.

It's a Tuesday, rubbish collection day in these suburbs, and four black bins have been left outside on the pavement. The sky is a bleached and cloudless blue. A piet-my-vrou calls its name against the distant hum of the highway.

Up the street a man in an overall lies in the shade of a conifer. A late-model Mercedes eases up to a driveway; an electric gate slides open; a pine cone drops from a branch and rattles in a gutter.

No clue here, I'm thinking, that the ANC deputy president was recently the target of an alleged assassination attempt.

Even if a Sunday newspaper identified the 'assassin' as a hobo, even if the pundits are correct and the affair was no more than a ploy to divert Zuma from his preparations for the December conference, security today is lax. There are just two policemen and one bodyguard: the batteries in both metal detectors have run flat and they wave us through the system and into the house in minutes.

Zuma is at a table in a nook under the stairs. He is reading a newspaper and scooping cereal into his mouth. His assistant asks us to wait and directs us to a couch in the centre of the atrium. When she leaves we reach for our notebooks.

On the east and west walls of the upstairs gallery, facing one another, are two portraits. One informal, Zuma in a relaxed pose, stretched out on a sofa; the other an oil painting on goatskin, a replica of the official photograph from the office of the presidency: Zuma in a jacket and tie with the red ribbon of Aids awareness fastened to his lapel.

Phillip whispers, 'How close do you think that picture is to the Aids shower, the original?'

I look to where I think the main bedroom must be. 'Can't be more than a couple of metres,' I say.

A *maskanda* bass blares from a radio somewhere in the house.

A woman in her twenties, perhaps one of Zuma's daughters, emerges from an upstairs bedroom, rubs the sleep from her eyes and makes for the bathroom.

I point out to Phillip the rising damp on a downstairs wall.

Then, from the far corner of the atrium, Zuma approaches. We stand. He's unshaven, in loose-fitting jeans and a long-sleeved white vest, his eyes bloodshot. He smiles and shakes hands with us and says that it's good to see us again. We tell him that we are ready to begin as soon as he is ready, but he says, 'No, we finished our talk.'

He's still smiling. We smile too – at what we hope is a joke.

'No, that was a fullstop. That was where we ended the interview. Today is just for the photos.'

That's it then. Zuma goes to his bedroom to change for the shoot. I follow Sally upstairs and watch as she prepares her tripod and film. I decide in my disappointment to search for more colour for the story.

In an anteroom off the upstairs corridor I find it: surrounded by board games – Monopoly, Twister, 30 Seconds – an object almost, but not quite, discarded.

A souvenir. A silver desk tag emblazoned with the words 'Deputy President, JG Zuma', which must have sat at one time in a large, wood-panelled office. What grabs my attention is the autograph at the base of the tag. From where I'm standing, it looks to be the autograph of Thabo Mbeki.

If it is, I'm thinking, it poses some profound questions. Did Zuma ask Mbeki to sign the tag on the day he was dismissed from office? Is this a statement about the brotherhood of former freedom fighters? Is it a deliberately ironic expression of the principle that in the ANC, no matter what, loyalty amongst comrades endures?

I move in to get a closer look. But Zuma appears now in the corridor; he has on a jacket and an open-necked shirt. I put my notebook back in my pocket and retreat.

Zuma works easily with the camera, obliging Sally like a pro. After twenty minutes he says, 'I must go and argue with these guys now.'

'These guys', it occurs to me, means us. We're on again, but with conditions. Our subject informs us he won't talk specifics.

We go downstairs, into the same room as last time, the TV room, where the radio is tuned to Ukhozi FM. Zuma sits in the same armchair and we sit on the same couch. He reaches for a remote and turns down the volume. The first no-go area he outlines is his old comrade.

'As I'm telling you, I don't want people to say I am talking against certain people.'

We nod.

Then he says, 'It is the wrong time. My time is coming at the conference.'

———

Day three of the Polokwane conference. D-Day. The day – this phrase has been in circulation for months already – that four thousand South Africans get to decide the fate of forty-six million.

At 10.30am we are outside the voting station designated for the elite amongst the four thousand: the sixty members of the NEC. It is cold and grey and a light rain falls. We take shelter under an oak tree. With us under the tree is Greg Marinovich, one of the two surviving members of the Bang-Bang Club.

Marinovich, I'm thinking, has seen about as much as a person can see of this construct called the New South Africa. During the violence of the early nineties his photographs from the frontlines appeared in newspapers across the globe; he watched his colleague Ken Oosterbroek die of a gunshot wound on a township street; he won a Pulitzer Prize and went on to write, with fellow Bang-Bang Club member Joao Silva, the eponymous book that became the statement of an era.

Marinovich, as *The Bang-Bang Club* reveals, also has a Yugoslavian background. Since yesterday he and Branko have been comparing notes; they have much to say to each other about the old country.

Now, though, it's time to focus on the country at hand. Marinovich lifts his camera and trains it on a crowd of delegates that has gathered in the open courtyard before us.

The crowd dances and whistles and sings '*Isondo liya jika jika*'. The chorus has a staccato, popping beat, not unlike rifle fire, and it means, a delegate tells me, 'the wheel will keep on turning'.

The song goes on for ten minutes. Then, as soon as an NEC member with perceived Mbeki sympathies emerges from the voting booths, it stops.

There is a brief silence. The crowd converges on the NEC member and shouts 'Change! Change!' and shows him the rolling hands gesture.

The NEC member, I realise, is Mbhazima Shilowa, current premier of Gauteng province and former boss of the trade union movement.

As Shilowa puts on a brave smile and quickens his step, a lady standing near me, a middle-aged woman whose badge says she is from the Department of Health, laments the scene. 'It means they don't read. They don't know what the constitution of the ANC is saying. Mbhazima is a principled comrade.' Her face is a picture of pain.

I'm contemplative; I'm digesting the fact that the split in the party is a source of real anguish to some, when Branko calls me aside and points at the woman's handbag. I look. I see that it is placed upright against the bark of the oak, and that it isn't one handbag but two, a Louis Vuitton high-end model concealed within a caramel-brown no-namer.

While the woman watches Shilowa leave, Branko leans over and takes a photograph of the item.

Next to emerge from the booths is Tony Yengeni: convicted fraudster, known to the press as the 'Armani'd One', an anti-Mbeki campaigner whose star appears to be back in the ascendant.

The crowd claps and cheers. The woman with the hidden handbag shouts, 'No accountability!'

At 10.45am Trevor Manuel comes out. He is under an umbrella. His smile is more confident than Shilowa's, but still a group of fifteen or so breaks away from the main crowd to taunt him. Manuel is angered. He thrusts his umbrella at a photographer's intruding lens.

Closely following Manuel is Essop Pahad, minister in the presidency, Mbeki's loyal strong-arm. The jeering is the loudest yet. 'Change! Change! Change! Change!'

Pahad is a tall man and he gets to a waiting car in a few loping strides.

I stand next to Marinovich as the car pulls away. 'Carnage,' I say.

Says Marinovich: 'This morning when I came in I saw a woman with a Mbeki scarf over her head. Her eyes were closed and she was on her knees, praying.'

We move back towards the oak, to get out of the rain, which has started to fall in heavy drops. Marinovich tells me about a rumour he heard earlier: the Reuters guys have run the numbers, he says, and according to them Mbeki could still take it.

Impossible, I'm thinking. No way. In flagrant disregard of the NEC's ruling, the Zuma T-shirts are out now, and with them the banners that read: 'Zuma my president!'

I try the Reuters theory on a pair of international journalists standing close by. Their reaction, while sceptical, is that maybe the firebrands have alienated the swing votes. 'Maybe the Zuma people have annoyed the delegates who came to the conference without a favourite?'

The crowd of Zuma supporters gets bigger. Shortly after 11am, they perform the liberation movement's most militant dance, the war dance that terrified legions of apartheid's riot police.

'Oes … oes-oes! Oes … oes-oes!'

Marinovich is next to me, crouching, his camera shutter working fast. 'This is the *toyi-toyi*,' he whispers. 'The original. The exact one Umkhonto brought back from exile.'

He stands up. 'You can't not dance,' he says, following the beat from one leg to the other.

A young photographer approaches. 'Greg, you think you are still in Tembisa?'

Marinovich laughs.

'It's our time now,' the photographer says. 'We have read about those days in your book, and now it is our time.'

'No,' says Marinovich. 'The dance was nice, but not the other stuff. Go do it in Zimbabwe, not here.'

———

At 3pm we are called to a news conference in the media briefing room. Kgalema Motlanthe, current ANC secretary-general and a good bet for deputy president of the party when the new 'top six' is announced tonight, will be taking questions.

Motlanthe, a Robben Island veteran and former head of the mineworkers' union, is known as an independent thinker, a careful strategist, a dedicated and learned cadre: all reasons he is likely to be the only member of Mbeki's leadership team to survive a Zuma purge.

We take our seats and Phillip hooks up his laptop. We discover that the words 'Zuma' and 'Polokwane' are now the top two search items on Google news, which means – if you believe in the supremacy of the Google idiom – that this conference is now the top news story on the planet.

At 3.30pm Motlanthe seats himself behind the central microphone. Impassive in khaki hat and Abraham Lincoln beard, he clears his throat to speak.

He opens with a statement about the calibre of ANC leaders elected during the struggle: they didn't look for material rewards, he says. 'Now people are always willing to offer you gifts of one kind or another. From gifts to outright bribes is a very short distance.'

He says that division in the ANC is not a new thing: he recalls an incident from the 1970s involving the so-called 'Group of Eight', a faction that pursued its own political agenda.

He talks about the need to resist the urge to act against popular leaders, and cites the example of Winnie Madikizela-Mandela: the danger of acting against a popular leader, he says, is that people might leave the party with them.

Then it is question time. Amongst the first issues Motlanthe is asked to address is the issue of ill-discipline. What action will be taken against the cadres who have shown their support for Jacob Zuma in inappropriate ways?

'If this malaise is not corrected,' says Motlanthe, 'in 2009 we could very well be faced with an untenable situation.' Offenders will be dealt with after the conference, he says, 'when they have an ability to self-critique'.

Some minutes later, when he invokes Nelson Mandela in response to a similar question, the subtleties of Motlanthe's approach become more apparent.

'When Madiba was young he liked to disrupt meetings of the Communist Party,' he says. 'He would make sure to disrupt them. The leader at the time, Moses Kotane, tried to secure a meeting with him, but he always ducked and dived. Until one day Madiba came home and found Moses Kotane waiting for him. The old man had made arrangements to sleep there that night. He stayed up and engaged him for hours. Madiba says that was a pivotal moment in his life. It changed him.'

The story's message, I write in my notebook, is plain: we do such things in our youth, that is who we are, but it is better to educate and instruct than to rashly punish and thereby risk the loss of valuable talent.

On the most important question, the question that has been asked countless times these last few months by local and international journalists in this venue and many others, Motlanthe's words are again well measured; even if – as some will say afterwards – they verge here on the disingenuous.

'Now, I once worked in the mineworkers' union. In 1987, Anglo American dismissed thirty thousand of our members, including the union president. At some point we took a decision that leaders could be full-time employees of the union. Had we not taken that step, it would mean that the union would be at the mercy of employers. So the issue of the stability or otherwise of Jacob Zuma is assessed in that context. If they elect him, we have to live with that. And if he's charged, we have to live with that. In fact, that is why, I suppose, when the police arrest people in a cash-in-transit heist, they never reveal identities. It's done to protect those people. If prosecutors announce ahead of time, they put people and their families in a very difficult position.'

Motlanthe pauses for a moment, looks from under his cap at the journalist who brought up the matter. Then: 'But I agree with you. We need leaders of a calibre that can always say, "I've got nothing to hide."'

———

Four hours later, outside the main marquee.

Much pushing and shoving. Mud. Rainwater spilling off the roof. A marshal shouting: 'The media must move to the entrance at the far side!'

Pushing and shoving and sweating.

8.15pm, ushered through the door. Four thousand delegates on the chairs and tables. Vuvuzelas blowing hard; atmosphere like a cup final. Delegates doing the *toyi-toyi*. A woman in the aisles dressed as a sangoma. The hat and robes and stick of the traditional healer, a sangoma in ANC colours.

8.25pm. Thabo Mbeki and Jacob Zuma walking side by side onto the stage. Ear-splitting. A woman on the left of the stage, an NEC member, quietly crying. Looks like Brigitte Mabandla. Mbeki's minister of justice, crying.

The chairperson of the electoral commission, Bertha Gxowa, voice cracking into the microphone: 'We are going to ask the present officials and the present NEC to leave the stage.'

Whistles, drumbeats.

Exit the old guard. The new country, come good or ill, to be a different country.

Exit the members of the electoral commission.

One woman, a white woman, owner of the company contracted to manage the voting, alone on the giant stage.

'Good evening, comrades. It's been a long day. Thank you all for your extraordinary discipline. Comrades, 3 983 ballot papers were issued to registered voters.'

The woman lists the spoiled votes, the abstentions, each of the candidates as they appear on the ballot paper. She asks the comrades to hold their applause until the end.

'Now for the position of president.'

Heart rate lurches.

'Comrade Thabo Mbeki …'

Ululating, eruption.

'Please comrades, discipline!'

Waits.

'The number of votes for Comrade Thabo Mbeki … one thousand three hundred and …'

Pandemonium. Minutes to settle down.

'The number of votes for Comrade Jacob Zuma, two thou …'

———

An albino delegate, overweight, hysterical, on the stage and running for Zuma and being sideswiped by the marshals, tackled, wrestled to the ground.

———

9.30pm. Singing to Zuma, hymns of praise. Pointing, bowing. Zuma in the chair occupied an hour ago by Mbeki. Unmoving, regal.

The sangoma in a trance, walking the aisles. More singing. A delegate behind me answering his cellphone: 'Zuma for president, hello?'

———

11pm. Back at the Audi. Overwhelmed, silent as we leave the township. Phillip the first to talk. 'Let's compare notes.'

We check to see we have the same numbers.

Kgalema Motlanthe, deputy president, 2 346 votes; Baleka Mbete, national chair, 2 326 votes; Gwede Mantashe, secretary-general, 2 378 votes; Thandi Modise, deputy secretary-general, 2 304 votes; Mathews Phosa, treasurer-general, 2 328 votes.

'I have Zuma on 2 329,' says Phillip. 'You?'

'Same.'

'These numbers are too close to one another; they voted how they were told.'

'Exactly. Zuma's top six.'

At the crossroads onto the highway Branko turns right towards central Polokwane, the direction away from our guesthouse in Tzaneen. He closes his Nokia and gives us a triumphant grin. He has secured us access, he says, through a friend who heads up a private bank, to a post-results event at a club downtown.

At midnight we arrive at 64 Jorrissen Street, a converted house just off Thabo Mbeki Street. It's a house with gables, a gazebo, a three-metre-tall statue set in a fountain – the facial features of the statue half-Caucasian, half-Negroid; the chest bare; the loins covered by a warrior skirt; the left hand holding a shield and the right hand a spear.

Branko and Phillip wait by the fountain and I go to the bar to order a beer. I am the only white person in the room. I find an open space next to a bald man in a cream suit and a black silk shirt. The bald man is upbraiding the barman.

'Let me tell you something, my brother. You never put ice in cognac.'

The barman takes fifteen minutes to acknowledge me. He looks my way and says I'm next. But then another man in a cotton suit slides in on my right. The barman smiles at the man. 'You're not next any more,' he says to me. 'You're after him.'

———

Frantz Fanon, *The Wretched of the Earth*: 'In fact, the bourgeois phase in the history of under-developed countries is a completely useless phase. When this caste has vanished, devoured by its own contradictions, it will be seen that nothing new has happened since independence was proclaimed, and that everything must be started again from scratch. The change-over will not take place at the level of the structures set up by the bourgeoisie during its reign, since that caste has done nothing more than take over unchanged the legacy of the economy, the thought and the institutions left by the colonialists.'

———

At 1pm the next day I am sitting beside Branko in the media briefing room.

A thickset man in his thirties talks into the central microphone.

'The ANC Youth League believes the election results are a true reflection and expression of the will of the people. We salute these warriors, delegates of our glorious movement. We salute the gallant fighters of the ANC Youth League ...'

The man is Fikile Mbalula, head of the Youth League, a leftist firebrand whose stature in the party is now fully confirmed. Mbalula is not – as Churchill would have it – magnanimous in victory.

There are rallying cries, demands. There is talk about the ultimate triumph of the national democratic revolution; talk about the party as a central authority; talk about the integration of the Scorpions – an independent crime-fighting unit handling the corruption case against Zuma – into the structures of the South African police.

'You must know that President Mbeki was made by the Youth League and was removed by the Youth League,' says Mbalula.

Branko leans in to tell me something. I tilt my head to listen. He tells me he thinks Mbalula has the makings of a first-rate populist.

'He'll be your president one day.'

I look at Branko. I don't know what to answer. I shrug.

And then I hear Mbalula issue a series of threats – in a manner that may or may not be construed as joking – to all anti-Zuma campaigners.

'Ha-ha, you enter this zone at your own risk ... As the ANC, we take no responsibility for what may happen to you ...'

Later in the briefing Mbalula eases off, treads with a measure of discretion.

In response to a question about the style of leadership he expects from the new top six, he says, 'Selfless. They must act in a manner that reaffirms the interests of the poorest of the poor. We expect a leadership that is not going to be feared, to be vindictive. We will not run around the country seeking revenge. The Youth League will oppose any tendency that seeks to undermine the African National Congress.'

But the moment of discretion is short-lived.

As the news briefing draws to a close, Mbalula compares himself to General Zhukov, the man who liberated the Soviet Union from Nazi occupation, the military commander who advanced through Eastern Europe and conquered Berlin.

Says Mbalula: 'We have had to fight and win every battle, and we have fought and won. The last was for Zuma to be elected as president. That was the war. Like Zhukov, we won the war against fascism and installed the communist system.'

I look to my left. 'Zhukov,' says Branko.

Mbalula's final words are directed to the members of the press. As far as he is concerned, we have exposed ourselves, all of us, as Mbeki supporters.

'You failed! You have made us strong! We are like a rose that grew from the concrete because of you …'

———

Late the following night. In the gold Audi, heading south on the N1 back to Johannesburg.

The radio is tuned to 702, Tom London's late-night talk show. The subject of the show: Zuma's inaugural speech as president of the ANC, a speech we have recently witnessed live in the main marquee.

On air is a middle-aged white woman from a working class suburb on Johannesburg's fringes.

'Tom, he stopped like that 'cos he can't read, you know. He's only got a standard three or something.'

Tom cuts to the next caller.

I take out my notebook and record the statement.

Three weeks later, when we reconvene in the magazine offices to prepare for February's cover story, it's these two sentences – from amongst almost thirty thousand words of transcribed notes – that lay claim to our attention.

The white woman's statement becomes, for what it encompasses and for what it excludes, the focal point around which Phillip and I make sense of the conference.

While Branko remains convinced that Polokwane should be read in the context of a contemporary populism, of a type of nationalism that can morph easily into ethnic chauvinism and state-sanctioned violence, Phillip and I want to cast the story in more local terms. We argue, given the confusion and contradictions of the conference itself, that *Maverick*'s readers – affluent, economically conservative, seventy per cent white – will best be served by a piece that concentrates on what is unique to South Africa.

Our editor concedes. We agree that the title of the piece should still be 'Fear and Loathing in Polokwane', but it will be a title that subverts and probes, a title that exposes, rather than a title that describes and explains.

Phillip and I begin drafting. We open the story with a scene from Zuma's inaugural speech as president of the party; the scene where – before five global news networks, dozens of wire services, the world's most influential newspapers – Zuma stalls.

We cite the collective intake of breath, the tension in the marquee, as Zuma stares for fifteen interminable seconds at the page in front of him.

We quote the line that comes before the long pause: 'It is a counter-revolutionary force which needs to be eliminated ...'

We quote the statement of the white woman on 702 later that night: '... he stopped like that 'cos he can't read, you know ...'

We quote the line that comes after the pause: '... Our strategy and tactics addresses organised crime as a threat to our democratic order.'

We ask the reader our question: What if Zuma 'stopped like that' because he saw in the words on the page the enormity of his task? What if, his goal now achieved, he was suddenly visited by a vision of the job's complexity?

Aside from asking him directly, we write, there is no way of knowing for sure.

And then we posit our thesis. Wherever it was that Zuma went in those fifteen fraught seconds, we write, what's clear is that when he emerged he articulated a solution to the crime problem that was more elegant in its conception than anything President Mbeki had recently offered on the matter.

'I therefore call on all ANC branches to actively lead, champion and facilitate crime prevention strategies. We had street committees before. If we were able to defeat vigilantism and the apartheid system, what can stop us from defeating this ugly factor that has tainted our democracy?'

The piece is edited and ready for print on the night of deadline. It is agreed that on the front cover of *Maverick*'s February issue, in a bold blue font on a black background, will be two words:

Apocalypse Not.

Branko, never one to impose his views, signs off on the issue with reluctance.

It Hasn't Turned out that Way

LAURIE AND I FINALLY GET around to watching the documentary. We had meant to watch it sooner, but as always happens towards the end of the year, Laurie's calendar had filled up and most nights she was either rehearsing or performing – or, if at home at all, fast asleep by 9pm. Still, even at this late date, *Murder Most Foul*, which premiered on Britain's Channel 4 and South Africa's M-Net in September, remains the subject of enduring controversy.

Not that we've been drawn to the documentary by the hype. We are watching, rather, because its central narrative is the double murder of Richard Bloom and Brett Goldin. The fact that many critics are saying it's an irresponsible take on the country's crime problem, that it tells the South African story in a limited and blinkered way, is mildly interesting but of secondary importance.

Our stake is personal, and as I hit the 'play' button there's really just one thing we want to know: how director Jon Blair, South Africa's first Oscar winner, and presenter Antony Sher, Cape Town's famous export to the Royal Shakespeare Company, have handled in film the night of our cousins' murder.

My uncle and aunt have declined to be interviewed, but Laurie's cousins are a prominent part of the storyline. Early on, Brett's parents, Denise and Peter, and his sister, Samantha, appear sequentially and individually on screen, and detail for the viewers the events of Sunday, April 16th 2006 – how they reacted, what they did, when it became apparent that Brett had been missing far too long for something terrible not to have happened.

Laurie and I are lying together on the big upholstered couch, and when the segment is over she turns to me and asks if I know what she's thinking.

'Help me out.'

'Richard and Brett, imagine they heard we got engaged.'

I laugh. I do know what she's thinking. They were inseparable friends. They would have been jumping around, calling each other 'cousin', telling each other they were now practically related.

———

It's clear that Blair and Sher have respect for the families. They're attuned to the sensitivities of their subject matter; charges of garishness are not going to apply. I relax, and concentrate on the themes.

The list of commentators is impressive. It includes Archbishop Emeritus Desmond Tutu, whose face appears in wrinkled and shadowed close-up.

'Archbishop, help me with my critics,' says Sher. 'They say that we shouldn't be focusing on the murder of two white guys when, obviously, the majority of murder victims in this country are black.'

Tutu's lyrical way of speaking, his familiar cadences, are flatter than usual. 'You are not saying you are doing this just for them,' he sighs. 'You are saying, this is the country you love, and you were proud when we overcame apartheid, and you were amongst those who were longing, hoping to see a South Africa where everybody would feel safe and secure, enjoying themselves. It hasn't turned out that way. And if you are able to use this means to highlight a particular situation, then for goodness sake go on and do it.'

———

If there is one 'particular situation' that the documentary highlights best, I'm thinking, it's the growing anger of the disempowered at the elite. As the film progresses, Blair and Sher paint a persuasive picture of two interconnected yet hostile worlds. Their underlying message seems to be that bloodshed in South Africa is inescapable.

And while I'm focused on this interpretation as a good thing, as a statement that's both necessary and bold, whatever it is about the angle that's also begun to irritate me remains in the background, shapeless and undefined.

Because, by now, the parts of the film that resonate most are no longer the interviews with Brett's family, or the photographs of Richard, or the visits to the crime scene. The most powerful segments are now those about Cape gang culture – and specifically the segment on Igshaan Davids, aka Sanie the American, alleged boss of the largest gang on the Flats and older brother of the convicted co-murderer of Richard and Brett.

Pearlie Joubert, an experienced local journalist, assists in these scenes with access to Igshaan and with information on his background.

'I think in a different world Igshaan might have been, I dunno, a schoolteacher, a lawyer,' says Pearlie. 'He's not stupid. He grew up in a very violent place. He grew up in a place where scores get settled. If you piss me off, I stab you, with a knife. The world where you come from, you have no idea where he lives. Most of the people living in Camps Bay have never crossed that bridge at Salt River to go into the Flats. They think the whole world is this blue sky, lovely mountain, lovely ocean, girls-with-big-tits thing.'

During the following scene, in the car on the way to visit Igshaan, Sher tells Blair that he still has serious doubts, that the previous night he almost called him up to say, 'I actually don't give a fuck about the other side of this story.'

Says Sher: 'I've spent my career playing monsters. Richard the Third, Hitler, Macbeth, whatever. And I've heard myself over the years saying, monsters are human beings, you know, you've got to see a rounded picture of them, see the world from their point of view. In this case, I just don't give a fuck about seeing the world from their point of view … As far as I'm concerned, two good bright lives were wiped out for fuck-all reason …'

Pearlie, who is sitting in the back seat, responds, 'Do you know what I thought last night, after I spoke to you? Because I wasn't eloquent about why you should meet these people. I thought, the only way I can explain this is: to live here we have to understand. We have to understand that we kind of rub off on each other … We're living in the hangover of an incredibly violent history, and to make sense of living in this place we have to be able to understand.'

As it pans out, however, Sher does not get to meet Igshaan. The camera shows Pearlie knocking on a door, and a man answering, and Pearlie apologising and saying in Afrikaans that the crew has been driving around and around looking for number fourteen, and the man replying, also in Afrikaans, 'Didn't Sanie phone you? He said he's fasting and he's busy.'

While Pearlie remonstrates with the man, I turn to Laurie and point at the house in the frame. 'That's got to be the house that David rents to him.'

David: a close friend, a real estate agent and budding landlord in a predominantly coloured area of Cape Town called Maitland.

'David says Sanie is a model tenant,' I tell Laurie. 'Always pays his rent on time.'

———

The degrees of separation in this story, in this country, are of course even less than that; the ties are closer even than my relationship to Richard.

An acoustic guitar on the soundtrack plays a familiar riff. When the first verse begins, I recognise the voice of my fiancée. And then I hear the chorus, the Patty Griffin-type spareness of the title line, 'What else is there?' This is the song that Laurie composed on the bed in our apartment after the back-to-back funerals of Brett and Richard.

She played the song for Brett's mother, who played the song for Jon Blair, who then met her in the Killarney Mall in early 2007 to discuss his intention to buy the rights. Her impression of Blair, she reminds me, was of a man sure of his achievements, a man with few doubts.

The credits are rolling and I am about to switch off the TV when the man himself appears again on screen, this time on the set of a well-known local studio. Blair has agreed to answer a series of questions about his work.

I sit back down. The first question, the toughest one, is also the most predictable. 'Watching the film, aren't you just joining a chorus of ex-South Africans who continue to be negative about the country? I mean, isn't it a betrayal of the country, in a sense, to tell the story?'

Blair calmly nods. In his answer he appeals to a quote of Martin Luther King. 'We will remember not the words of our enemies, but the silence of our friends.'

I now understand what's been irritating me all along. 'His approach is too glib,' I say.

In the months to come I watch the film another four or five times. At each viewing my sense of its surface smoothness, its too-easy fluency, is confirmed. The question of the critics becomes my question too.

How does one leave a country, miss out on the nuances of its development, miss out on the daily intricacies of its effort to remake itself, and then have the temerity to suggest (during a visit of a few short weeks) that this country one has left can be divided into plainly identifiable halves; us and them, victim and killer, civilised and depraved?

Murder Most Foul, given what would happen in South Africa during the winter of 2008, seems in hindsight almost one-dimensional, naive.

CHAPTER 6

Ways of Leaving

Part I

IN EARLY JANUARY 2001, shortly before the death of Laurent Désiré Kabila, president of the Democratic Republic of Congo, Tony Muderhwa, age twenty-five, was a content and well-integrated inhabitant of the city of Kinshasa, a rambling metropolis on the lower banks of the Congo River and capital of this the second largest nation in Africa. Tony worked in civil intelligence, in a job arranged for him by his uncle. The firm for which Tony and his uncle worked was a semi-secret entity with an important mission: it was a firm under contract to provide information on matters of internal security to the president himself.

On January 16th 2001 Laurent Kabila was shot and killed while at home in the presidential palace. The assassin was identified as one of the president's bodyguards, and the Congolese people were informed that their leader had been the victim of a premeditated plot. Joseph Kabila, Laurent's son, chief of staff of the country's armed forces, installed himself immediately at the head of an interim government. Amongst Joseph's first executive actions was the launch of a full-scale investigation into the circumstances surrounding his father's death. Many security officers were arrested, including members of the firm for which Tony Muderhwa worked.

To be *arrested*, Tony soon discovered, often meant you did not return: you disappeared; you were not heard from again. Tony prepared to flee Kinshasa for his hometown of Bukavu, a city in the east of the country under the control of anti-government rebels. In the east, Tony assumed, he and his family would be safe.

It is three thousand kilometres from Kinshasa to Bukavu. But there are few roads through the jungles of the vast interior; those that do exist were subject at the time to frequent roadblocks, and there was no direct flight linking the two cities because to operate such a route would be to invite attack by a rebel missile.

So Tony and his wife, Claudia, and two young sons had to go the long way around. They crossed over the river to Congo-Brazzaville; from there boarded an aeroplane to Nairobi; from Nairobi took a bus through Tanzania and Rwanda – and only then re-entered the DRC through Kivu province on the eastern border.

It was a journey that took the better part of a week, a journey that appeared at first to be worth the effort: for the following two years, the family lived in relative peace. Then, in 2003, after the ratification of a peace agreement between the DRC government and the Ugandan- and Rwandan-backed rebels in the east – an agreement based on talks held in Sun City, South Africa – the country was reunited under the stewardship of Joseph Kabila. Travel between the provinces of the west and the east became possible again, and government forces could resume their search for the exiled intelligence officers.

Soon a former colleague of Tony's was arrested. The man's family and friends – including Tony – visited the police station and the army base and the prison, but he was nowhere to be found in Bukavu. The man's wife travelled to Kisangani, six hundred kilometres away, to see if perhaps her husband was in prison there. In Kisangani she was told her husband was being held in the province of Kasai. She travelled to Kasai, but nobody she met had heard of her husband. She returned to Bukavu, and said to Tony, 'Maybe my husband does not exist.'

Tony grew increasingly fearful for his own life. His fears proved justified. There was a man in Bukavu with a name very similar to his: *Anthony* Muderhwa, instead of Tony. The man was arrested and killed.

Tony knew he must not stay in one place for too long. He changed his address every two months. Then, in March 2005, at a house he had occupied for a few weeks, he heard knocking at the gate. He heard a man say, 'Open, or we come by force.' It was early evening, and Tony switched off all the lights. He heard shouting, people jumping over the fence. He heard shooting.

Tony ordered Claudia and the boys to lie down. He lay beside his family as the bullets passed overhead. Suddenly Bonheur, the younger boy, the four-year-old, stood up. Bonheur was shot in the head. Claudia rushed to help him. She was shot in the stomach.

Tony made a quick decision. He decided it would be better for Claudia and Lionel, the older boy, if he were not found in the house when the soldiers broke in. He opened a window and jumped into the street. He ran to a friend's house and explained what had happened. The next day his friend helped him to get to Uvira, a town on the shores of Lake Tanganyika.

In Uvira Tony boarded a ferry. He disembarked at Mpulungu, on the far southern end of the lake. He was now in Zambia.

On a highway in Zambia, Tony found a truck driver heading south. He offered the driver one hundred US dollars to take him to South Africa.

———

Monday morning, May 19th 2008. The news-stand at the convenience store at the Killarney petrol station has me transfixed. On the front page of the newspaper on the middle shelf is an image that has not been seen in local media in fifteen years.

Captured by a Reuters photographer, the image shows a heavyset white policeman in a bulletproof vest standing above a thin black man on his knees. The policeman is holding a fire extinguisher, and he is covering the black man in a cloud of foam. The snow-like substance envelops the kneeling man, spreads out on the ground around him, floats in the air above him: it is clear from the man's charred head and frayed clothes that moments before the picture was taken, he was on fire.

It is also clear, from the burnt tyre around his neck, that the man has been necklaced. This technique once used by ANC cadres in the townships – the rubber tyre doused in petrol and set alight; the punishment meted out to informers during the final years of apartheid – is, with a single image, plucked from collective memory and deposited in the consciousness of the present.

I pick up the newspaper and scan the caption: '… believed to be linked to xenophobia … foreigners took refuge in police stations and churches as the week-old violence against them spread …'

———

Before he reached the border post on the Limpopo River that separates Zimbabwe from South Africa, the truck driver adjusted the position of his seat and told Tony to hide himself in the gap. The truck crossed the border without incident.

Within hours of arriving in Johannesburg, Tony had found the Congolese expatriate community in the suburb of Bertrams. He was fed and given a place to sleep. Soon he secured a job as a cellphone technician – a skill he had learned in the DRC during his studies for a diploma in general electronics – and he began to earn the not insignificant sum of three hundred rand a day.

Tony quickly discovered, through the Congolese expatriate network, that Claudia and Lionel were alive. He managed to get hold of Claudia on the phone, but he had some trouble convincing her that it was him. Eventually Claudia accepted that her husband had survived, and she agreed to join him in Johannesburg. Tony sent her five hundred US dollars for the journey.

Claudia left Lionel in Bukavu, at the house of a friend. It was a difficult thing for her as a mother to do, but Tony had warned her that without entry visas the trip to South Africa would be too dangerous for a young boy. 'We can fetch him when we are legal,' he said.

A few weeks later, Tony and Claudia met on the streets of Johannesburg. It was a reunion filled with joyful tears. The couple walked arm-in-arm back to Tony's room in Bertrams. They sat together on the bed, and Claudia explained to her husband everything that had happened after he fled from the house in Bukavu.

The soldiers, she said, broke the door and came inside. But the noise must have alerted the army captain who lived on the street, because he also came to the house. From the bedroom, Claudia said, she heard the captain ask the soldiers what they were doing. Somebody told him that they were looking for a man who was wanted by the government of Kabila. The captain then came into the bedroom. He found her lying on the bed, bleeding from her stomach, and next to her Bonheur, who was dead, and hiding under the bed Lionel, who was very afraid. The other soldiers followed.

'Where is your husband?' they asked.

'I don't have a husband,' she told them.

The soldiers asked again and again, even though she was bleeding and the boy was dead.

'I don't know this Tony person,' she insisted.

Eventually the captain raised his voice to the soldiers. 'You see, you have killed for nothing! You are supposed to ask first!'

Claudia told her husband that she wasn't able to give Bonheur a proper burial. She was in hospital, she said, and there was no mortuary to keep the body while she recovered. 'I was not there when they buried him.'

Tony and Claudia sat for many minutes on the bed, crying quietly. Then Tony stood, and with the back of his hand he wiped his eyes. 'There is no recourse,' he said. 'We must accept. That is all.'

Tony continued to work as a cellphone technician. He made extra money after hours by repairing televisions. After a few months, Tony and Claudia moved into a small house in the inner city suburb of Malvern.

In May 2006 Claudia fell pregnant. It was also around this time that the couple began to overhear – in taxis, in buses, in the hospital where Claudia went for her check-ups – a word that suggested their presence in South Africa was not wanted.

It was a word, they knew, that parodied the sound of a foreign African language to local ears. *amaKwerekwere* – the people who say, '*kwere-kwere*'.

———

Half a day after the photograph that would come to be known as the 'burning man' has been picked up and published by news editors from New York to Sydney, I am waiting in the Golf on a side street in Sandhurst Extension. I am early for my appointment, and the radio is tuned as usual to 702: reporters in the studio and out in the field are updating listeners on the unfolding situation.

'... the United Nations has deplored the violence ... Nosiviwe Mapisa-Nqakula, minister of home affairs, says we cannot be seen to be attacking these people ... Winnie Madikizela-Mandela says the government should be held accountable ... police are patrolling the area ... this is Gia Nikolaides, live from the Ramaphosa informal settlement ...'

I turn off the radio, drive up to the gate and ring the bell.

From the outside the home is modest and inviting. Abundant flower-beds line the driveway, a whitewashed brick façade displays red shutters on black window-frames.

Professor Alan Paterson, the father of the household, has called to say he will be fifteen minutes late – the traffic back from his daughter Jamie's school is impossible; I should wait in the living room and talk to Angus, his son.

Again I ring the bell. The domestic opens the electric gate and unbolts the front door. She ushers me inside. The interior of the home confirms what the exterior implies: fresh fragrances from the kitchen, lived in furniture, photographs of a smiling and close-knit family.

Angus is sitting cross-legged at a coffee table in a room awash with late afternoon light. He is tapping with his index finger on a laptop.

I sit down and ask the boy what he's working on. A review for a book, he says, the *Spiderweb Chronicles*. 'It's only due on Monday, but I type very slowly.'

He resumes his tapping. After ten letters or so, he says, 'My mother's gone to gym; it's the only thing she ever does for herself, is go to gym.'

I nod, and add a line to my notes. I write: Probably better not to get A's v/point on the incident … boy seems too small, fragile …

Angus is now speaking softly to his laptop, chiding it. 'I have not finished with that word. Do not do that to me.'

The house smells of air freshener, lilac. There is a DVD of the *Golden Compass* on the armrest of the couch.

'Are you a fan of fantasy, Angus?' I ask.

He nods.

'Harry Potter?'

'Yes, a very big Harry Potter fan.'

Angus tells me about the world of the *Spiderweb Chronicles*, a world of magic and trolls and fairies. The family dog, a tiny terrier that has until now been hiding under the coffee table, gathers the courage to come and smell my hand. Angus interrupts his story to tell me that the dog's name is Pippin.

And then Angus's father comes home. I stand, but Alan Paterson waves at me from across the room and says he must go out again – to take the domestic to the taxi rank. With a gesture part resignation part disgust, he drops the afternoon edition of *The Star* on the rug.

'Country's gone nuts, huh?'

'Jeez,' says Alan. Then: 'You can speak to Jamie; I'll be back in five.'

I sit down again. Jamie walks into the room. A striking young woman in school uniform, long dark hair tied in a ponytail, wide and candid eyes; the same young woman who, months earlier, appeared on the current affairs programme *Carte Blanche* to share her ordeal with a television audience of thousands.

'I'm just thinking …' she says, after I introduce myself.

'That's a first,' says Angus.

Jamie smiles at her brother.

'I'm just thinking we should talk outside.'

We go into the back garden: a lush lawn, more flowerbeds, a swimming pool. I tell Jamie about the work I am doing, why I think her experience is relevant. I tell her that the kind of writing I do is usually more intimate than television, that in the pages of a book – no matter how many broadcast or print journalists she has shared it with – her story might appear more immediate; that my approach might seem more intrusive, though hopefully not. I tell her that if she accepts this and if she agrees, my intention is to schedule a number of interviews over a period of months.

Jamie says she will think about it. I finish the cigarette I've been smoking and wait for Alan in the living room. When he arrives and takes his seat, I repeat my motivations. I mention the murder of my cousin, and say that I am interested in the ways that the victims of violent crime – or, in the worst-case scenario, those they leave behind – choose to carry on.

Says Alan: 'That's what the kids did, you know. This happened on a Tuesday night and on Thursday morning the kids were back at school.'

He gets up to fetch a beer. 'I've had a hard day and I deserve it,' he says.

He re-emerges from the kitchen with his beer in a glass. I reframe my last statement, casting it in terms of the choice of whether to emigrate or not.

Says Alan: 'My immediate response when I managed to untie myself was, I intend to get the hell out of this place. That feeling didn't change, so now we're leaving. You know, I've always been a committed South African. It's something that's only been exploded in the last six months.'

———

The sense of safety – of hope and possibility – that Tony and Claudia Muderhwa had felt upon first arriving in South Africa gradually faded, and by February 2007 had all but disappeared.

Claudia had been due to give birth at the end of January, but it was only on February 13th that she felt the pains that told her the baby was coming. Tony phoned a taxi service and accompanied his wife to the hospital. In the hospital reception he spoke to a nurse.

'Why are foreigners delivering babies in our country?' asked the nurse. 'Why is it only foreigners who are pregnant? Foreigners don't have rights; only citizens have rights.'

Tony did not respond. He sat down next to Claudia and squeezed her hand. Later he said politely to a different nurse, 'But my wife, you know, she's ready to deliver.'

This nurse was equally rude. 'If you keep on talking,' she said, 'you can help your wife yourself.'

Tony stopped talking. Claudia cried throughout the day. The dayshift staff knocked off and a new rotation arrived for nightshift. Tony overheard a dayshift nurse say to her incoming colleague, 'You see these? These are *kwerekwere*.'

The nurses said many things to one another that Tony chose to ignore.

Then, when it got dark outside, Tony could keep silent no longer. He decided to take action. To the next nurse that passed, he said, 'I will give you one thousand rand if you help my wife.'

'Okay,' said the nurse. 'Wait here.'

But the nurse failed to return. Tony didn't know what else to do. He sat and waited. From his seat beside his wife he overheard the nurses repeat the same line to each other, over and over. 'Why are foreigners always pregnant?' they said, and then they laughed.

Some time in the early morning a nurse came to put Claudia in a bed.

She told Claudia to push. 'If you don't push,' she said, 'this baby will die inside your stomach. If it dies, it will kill even you.'

Claudia tried to push. She screamed in pain. The nurse prodded Claudia with a stick. 'Sorry,' said Tony. 'Sorry, sorry.'

'Sorry for what?' asked the nurse.

In the hour before dawn, Tony spoke to a doctor. The doctor was also a foreigner from Africa. The doctor examined Claudia and asked Tony how long they had been waiting. When Tony told him, the doctor became agitated. He said that it was unlikely the baby was still alive. The doctor shouted at a group of nurses who were standing nearby, saying they must bring Claudia to the operating theatre. Tony signed the release forms for the procedure. The doctor did some tests and found that the baby had a heartbeat. He performed a Caesarian section. At 5.25am on February 14th the baby was born. The doctor said to Tony, 'You should give thanks to God for this baby.'

Tony and Claudia named the baby Plamedi, a shortened form of the French phrase '*Plan merveilleux de dieu*'. Wonderful plan of God.

———

In May 2008 I receive via email a copy of an extensive report entitled 'The Haemorrhage of Health Professionals from South Africa: Medical Opinions'. The report is sent to me by a doctor I have recently interviewed on the subject; the same man who put me in touch with the Paterson family.

On page twenty-two of the report I come across the following:

> Male health professionals have given emigration more serious consideration than females (53% vs 41%); whites have given it marginally more serious consideration than blacks (45% vs 41%); although both have given it less consideration than Indian or coloured professionals ...
>
> [But] seriously considering emigration is not the same thing as actually leaving. Around half of the respondents (52%) said it was likely they would leave in the next five years, 25% within two years and 8% in the next six months. In other words,

government and employers have a very brief 'grace period' in which to act to improve the situation and address the factors that make health professionals so disgruntled ...

Amongst the health professionals that government does not – in its 'grace period' – attempt to make less disgruntled is Professor Alan Paterson, head of the department of anatomical pathology at Wits University and chief pathologist at the National Health Laboratory Service.

In the living room of his home, between sips of his beer, Alan tells me that in the first four months of 2008 he saw seven consultants to the NHLS resign. He also says he will be the latest on a long list of faculty members at the Wits University medical school to emigrate.

'I am the last primary liver pathologist left in South Africa,' Alan says.

I consider the implications of this. I ask Alan which country will now get the benefit of his skills. He takes me through the options he has considered.

'The Australian offer was really one of conveyor belt pathology,' he says. 'Private practice pathology. I wasn't keen.'

To compete in the United States, he continues, you have to be a world expert. 'I couldn't see myself going backwards, or studying again.'

On Canada, he says, 'I can get in tomorrow. But you end up in Saskatchewan or somewhere.'

He says he also received two job offers in the United Kingdom, one in London and one in Newcastle. He decided finally on the latter. 'It was simple arithmetic. London is too expensive for me.'

I ask Alan when the family is leaving.

'My last day in the office is July 31st. I plan to fly to Newcastle ahead of the family, to set up a base. That should be in late September. But we've got a lot of issues. My wife doesn't want to go to the frozen north.'

Jamie, who has been sitting with us in the living room, talks for the first time in almost an hour. 'My mom doesn't really want to go anywhere.'

Says Alan: 'Bronwyn has recovered from the trauma of our incident, you know. She has her friends. She wants to stay. But I don't want to stay. I can't stay. Medicine is on a slippery slope. Dozens of doctors are going every month. They're going because they can.'

'Is the situation really that bad?' I ask.

'I don't know how intense the slope is, but it's coming. Private medicine continues to be excellent. As good as it is anywhere in the world. But if you go to private clinics like Milpark, Linksfield or Rosebank, you see a lot of specialists my age ... I'm fifty-seven. What could happen is that eventually the specialists will disappear. The young doctors, you know ...'

Alan says he had lunch recently with a guy, a top-rate specialist in his late thirties, who's on his way. 'He'll work nights when he gets there. He's prepared to do what he needs to do.'

'In the simplest terms,' I say, 'what does all this mean for our health system?'

'I don't know,' says Alan. But then he gives me an answer. 'I think it could degenerate to the level of Africa. If you're rich in Africa, you can still come down to South Africa and get attended to and go home again. I see a lot of patients from the Congo, Nigeria, Cameroon and so on. But if this exodus continues, the rich will have to go to Europe or America for treatment. And the rest will be left scrubbing in the dust.'

—

Plamedi Muderhwa, for the first six months of his life, was a happy and healthy child. He grew well, achieved all his milestones. He remained free of illness. So in August 2007, when Plamedi succumbed to a bad bout of flu and could not stop crying, his parents decided it would be better to take him to a clinic than to wait for him to recover at home.

The doctor at the clinic told Tony and Claudia there was no cause for alarm. He said that the child's chest was a bit heavy. He said, just to be on the safe side, that he wanted to keep Plamedi under observation for a few days.

On the day their son was due to be released, Tony and Claudia took a taxi to the clinic. They signed the papers and thanked the doctor and brought Plamedi back home. They sat the child on the floor in the front room. While Claudia prepared a meal, Tony fetched Plamedi's toys and knelt on the floor beside him. He saw now that something was still wrong. The child could no longer sit upright, as if the strength had left his body.

Tony did not understand. He told himself that maybe it was because of the medication. Then he noticed that Plamedi's head was swollen. 'There is a problem with his head!' he shouted through the house to Claudia. 'We must take him back to the clinic!'

Plamedi was sent for x-rays. The results were inconclusive. Plamedi was sent for physiotherapy. The physiotherapist said the baby must go for more tests. Tony returned to the first doctor, who transferred Plamedi to the Johannesburg General Hospital. The doctors at the hospital found that the child had a build-up of fluid in the brain cavities. They said he required an operation.

The date of the operation was postponed for three weeks, and then on the new date it was postponed again. Meanwhile, Plamedi could not stop crying. He ran a constant temperature. All Tony and Claudia could do was give him Panado syrup.

And still the doctors at the hospital did not operate. They kept sending Tony and Claudia back. The couple were sent to a hospital in Pretoria, but the doctors there also didn't operate.

When Plamedi was one year old his parents took him again for an appointment for an operation. The doctor did tests and found that there was damage to the brain. It was because of this, said the doctor, that the child had stopped growing.

Plamedi at one year weighed eight kilograms, the same weight he was when he got sick – if they were to operate now, said the doctor, it would make no difference. The prognosis was that Plamedi would never in his life be able to walk or talk.

Tony's grief soon turned to anger. He blamed the incompetence in the clinic and in the hospital. He blamed the South African healthcare workers, those who disliked foreigners. When Plamedi's head began to swell, Tony remembered, nobody had answers. People said maybe an antibiotic had caused the damage, maybe it was meningitis that wasn't treated, maybe there was a lack of oxygen – it all meant there was no precision. Tony also remembered what some people in the hospital would say when he showed them his identity card – they would say, 'But this is not a South African name!'

Tony spent a long time reliving these events, a long time feeling helpless and frustrated. Until one day he said to Claudia something he had said to her before. 'We must accept. That is all.'

Tony continued to work as a cellphone technician and to repair televisions after hours. Every month he provided for his wife and his hydrocephalic son. He lived quietly with his small family in the house in Malvern. Despite all that had happened, South Africa still seemed the best place in Africa for Tony and his family to be.

———

Seven weeks after it was first published, I am drawn again to the editorial written by Branko Brkić for the April 2008 issue of *Maverick* magazine. At the time, the response to this editorial had been one of unmitigated approbation – more readers' letters had been received about it than about any editorial previously, and the interest was such that the piece had been republished at extended length in a national newspaper.

But the sentiment it articulated now appears distant. Today, like yesterday and the day before, the South African press is filled with reports on the xenophobic violence; the front pages carry scenes of bloodshed and brutality, and the editorial seems in hindsight to reflect an almost trivial concern: the concern engendered when South Africans returned to work after the Christmas holidays to find an electricity grid that was no longer coping with its load.

I close the magazine and share my thoughts with Phillip, who's working at the desk opposite. His response is abrupt. For a country that sells itself as Africa's powerhouse, he says, there's nothing trivial about an electricity crisis. I tell Phillip that he's right, of course. And I don't acknowledge that this was not exactly what I meant.

What I meant exactly is vague to me. It has something to do with Branko's attendant angle on emigration, with the values (necessarily positive) that new immigrants tend to ascribe to their adopted country, with the ways in which the concept of nationhood has, in the weeks since Branko wrote his editorial, revealed the most malevolent of its flaws.

I read the piece one more time:

I watch the debate about people leaving this country with greater and greater dismay. More often than not, I am appalled by the laconic ease with which many of us approach the matter. I am also saddened by the dreadfully low level of brain usage being displayed.

I pretty much know that one day soon, as we look back to the crazy days of 2008, we will remember the debilitating costs of the Eskom crisis as one of the pivotal moments in our history, but I'm also convinced that we will remember them as the days when we simply couldn't avoid finally acknowledging another quiet tragedy unravelling in front of us. And let me not mince my words: the ever-growing river of people streaming out of this country, never to return, is nothing short of a national tragedy. These are the people who decided to stick with South Africa in many a turbulent moment in the past, who decided many times that their love for this country was stronger than the fear mongered by the messengers of doom.

At the same time, these are the people who *can* leave the country, people with means, skills, experience; people who know the world and could be crucially helpful in dragging this country out of the mess it has become. They have the capacity to live their lives in any country in the world and are welcomed by all sane governments. Their loss is pretty much impossible for this country to fix.

It is a tragedy. But I also feel another tragedy when I hear voices say: it's okay, let them leave, there are now simply more opportunities for the ones who stay.

Perhaps those brilliant minds should read macroeconomics 101. Then, just maybe in a moment of rare clarity, they might understand how empty that statement is. Cool sounding, but empty. And that is what really bugs me here: the sheer intellectual emptiness of the nay-sayers. They say good riddance, they don't deserve to live here. They say let them go, both our and the Aussie average IQ will increase. (All other countries only have sheep and boredom, you know?)

They say let them leave because they're cowards. Lovely. Just lovely …

It is not in human nature to want to leave the country you grew up in, the place that determined who you are, what you love and desire, what you value and care for. This is where your friends are, where your support networks are. This is the place you spent your whole life getting to know.

Yet, the people who leave feel they have no choice but to abandon it all …

Trust me, I know how it feels to lose all you have and be forced to start again from nothing. It is a traumatic experience in which you lose your friends and social status, and almost no one fully recovers from it. It is not a pleasure.

So … to all those leaving and reading their last issue of this publication, I say: we are very sorry you had to leave, friends.

We will miss you, terribly. We hope your new home brings the meaning and peace you lost here.

————

In the front room of his house in Malvern, in the third week of May 2008, Tony scans the newspapers and watches the television for updates on the attacks. The stories he reads and the images he sees convince him that it is best to stay close to home: he will leave Malvern again, he will return to work, when things have calmed down.

But even on his own street the atmosphere has changed. The couple next door, supposedly friends of Tony and Claudia, have stopped answering when they are greeted. Tony once fixed their television set, many times he has sorted out problems they have had with their cellphones, and now they don't want to say hello.

On the Thursday afternoon of that week, Tony confronts his neighbour and demands an explanation. The man looks down at his shoes. 'I don't talk to *kwerekwere*,' he says.

Then, on the morning of Sunday, May 18th, two Congolese friends of Tony and Claudia knock on the door. They are shaking and confused.

They say their house in Jeppestown has been set alight. They have come to seek safety in Malvern, they say. Tony and Claudia share a meal with their friends. They try to pretend it's a normal Sunday. But later in the day there is a strange noise outside. Tony and Claudia and their friends stop talking so that they can listen. They hear chanting in Zulu, the voices of many men. They go onto the street to look. They see a large crowd coming towards them. The crowd is armed with pangas and sjamboks and knobkerries.

Tony runs back into the house to call the police. 'Come quickly,' he says. 'We don't know what will happen if they catch us.'

The police vans arrive in minutes. The policemen instruct the crowd to disperse. The crowd taunts the police. They jeer and whistle. The police fire live rounds into the air and spray tear gas.

Tony and Claudia and their friends wait in the front room, watching through the curtains. A policeman bangs on the door. 'Come!' he says. 'Get your stuff and get in the van!'

Claudia lifts up Plamedi; she grabs the handbag in which she keeps his medical documents. Tony fetches the asylum papers. Everything else is left behind.

Out on the street, when the crowd sees them, people demand that the *kwerekwere* be handed over.

'Never!' says the police sergeant.

'*Fokken* police! *Fokken* police!'

The foreigners are hustled into the van and driven to the Cleveland Police Station. The police drop them off and go back to fetch more foreigners. The process is repeated many times. Later a mob arrives at the police station and tries to tear down the fence.

———

Phillip and I have come to the Central Methodist Church in Pritchard Street, downtown Johannesburg, to hear from the targets of the violence themselves about their predicament. In this week immediately following the worst of the attacks, the church – long a sanctuary for asylum seekers from north of the border – has taken in hundreds of additional foreign nationals. The church is presided over by Bishop Paul Verryn, an uncompromising figure whose recent interviews with the media have been laced with dark statements about 'co-ordination' and 'planning' – the clear implication being that a certain local faction has been orchestrating the violence all along.

Phillip and I want to see if we can learn more about this faction; or, failing that, at least approach the beginnings of some sort of context.

We enter the church through a broken door and are greeted straight away by Ephraim, a Zimbabwean who tells us he is part of the church's informal security.

He is glad to assist journalists, he says. He accompanies us up to the third floor, where the offices of the bishop are located.

The stairwells are unlit and smell of urine; empty cartons and cold-drink bottles lie underfoot. We are escorted past a queue of people waiting patiently in a narrow passage, and are introduced to a secretary who thanks us for coming. The secretary says the bishop will be back shortly. She writes out the bishop's cellphone number and says it is best to let him know that we are here.

Phillip dials the number and leaves a message on the bishop's voicemail. We wait in the passage, at the back of the queue. Ephraim waits with us. He wants to be the first to tell his story, he says. He stares hungrily at our notebooks until we begin to write.

Ephraim tells us he has been staying in the church for three months. He left Zimbabwe in February, he says. He has a wife and a five-year-old son who are still in Harare. He was working as a teacher back home and he also campaigned for the opposition party. Before the elections, he says, things became dangerous for him. 'Mugabe was against the teachers. He thinks they are contributing to his downfall.' Ephraim says he used 'some means' to get across the border; he paid a bribe to a truck driver and he hid amongst the cargo. When he arrived in Johannesburg he came straight to the church. He has applied for political asylum, he says, but so far he has not been successful. If he meets the police now he will be deported. He is living in fear every day.

When I have the story down, I ask Ephraim what he makes of the attacks on foreigners.

'It is not good for us,' he says. 'As Africans, it is for us to live together. But now love is no longer blind.'

'Can you tell me more about the people in the church? How many are fleeing the violence?'

'I can't give you the right numbers, maybe you must ask the bishop. But every day there are people who flood here because they think this is a better place.'

'Better how?'

'Many people come here who have been hurt. I have spoken to some of them. Those guys, they are so terrified. They have been beaten and threatened.'

A man who has been standing next to Ephraim now joins the conversation. He says his name is Langton and that he is also from Zimbabwe. He tells us that people don't stay at the church very long. 'A lot have left,' he says. 'They think that the attackers will follow them here.'

'And you guys,' asks Phillip. 'When will you leave?'

'We are praying that the opposition should win. After that we will go back home. But while Mugabe is still in power we wait for better jobs in South Africa and we live in the church.'

As Langton gives us his political background – he is a campaigner, like Ephraim, for Morgan Tsvangirai's Movement for Democratic Change – a young man walks into the passage with a look of abject fear on his face.

'Do you have a place to stay?' he whispers, his hands held together in supplication.

For some reason I assume that the young man is asking the question of me – as in, a place at my apartment.

'My brother, I'm sorry,' I stammer.

'No, he means at the church,' says Langton.

I smile, and force out a staccato chuckle, and Langton and Ephraim and the young man are kind enough to smile back, but of course the question hangs: Why *don't* I take him in?

Although an answer would be only to – and for – myself, I am saved from it by Ephraim, who feels an urgency to ply us with more information.

'Many families in Zimbabwe are living on one meal a day,' he says. 'You know, when a teacher is getting one hundred rand for a month, it's really bad.

That's why when we are here, we are all willing to work for little money.'

Adds Langton: 'That is the very thing. That is why the local people are starting the violence.'

We speak to Ephraim and Langton for another fifteen minutes, and then we head downstairs for a smoke. En route we pass a sign on a door. The sign is an advert, typed out in twenty-point bold on a white sheet of paper:

'Asylum Seekers
Passport-size photos while you wait!!!
Contact Alpha or William
Central Methodist Mission'

Outside, our cigarettes alight, we watch as a queue forms in two rapidly lengthening rows in front of us. People stream from the main entrance, there is much pushing and shoving. Langton has materialised beside the queue, he walks up and down wielding a truncheon; he too is obviously a member of church security.

'What are they queuing for?' I ask, when Langton returns to the head of the line, near where Phillip and I are smoking.

'Ah, for the parcels; for food and clothing.'

The church's main entrance opens onto the Smal Street Mall – a paved arcade notorious for its half-hourly muggings – and the building to the immediate west is the High Court. A white advocate in robes, holding a folder thick with documents, strides quickly past. He gives the queue barely a glance.

I am watching the advocate go, his tails billowing up behind him, and I am thinking (again) about the paradoxes thrown up by this strange city, when a tall African with a prophet's beard and crazed eyes appears improbably before me.

'Hello my brother, with my right information, I called to police, and did then call to the listeners. I've got the right information for the African people to be as one. Whatever professor you are, just come find me.'

Characters like this populate the world's major urban spaces; but in New York or Berlin or Buenos Aires, I'm thinking, the message is different. In those cities, the mad reflect a less marginalised discourse. The man says more about his 'right information' and I take down the words.

'I am the oldest black person to be here in Africa. And you were the second, the white one. The right information is very private and confidential, but anyone can share with me.'

Ephraim comes now to fetch us. He tells the mad man to go away. He has found two victims of the xenophobia, he says, who are willing to talk.

We push through the queue and head slowly back upstairs – there is a crush in the passages, people coming and going holding heavy bundles: boxes and dustbin bags filled with clothes and blankets and canned food.

Ephraim, after some minutes of halting progress, tells us to wait for him on the second-floor landing. He will go and fetch the men and he will bring them back down to us. He ducks under elbows and boxes and disappears into the throng.

When Ephraim returns Phillip and I speak to a man each. I speak to a Zimbabwean whose name is Forget.

'I was in Alex,' Forget begins, referring to the township – Alexandra – where the violence started. 'Maybe it was on ... I can't remember.

'They came where I was staying and they threatened me. "Why are you working for less money?" And they started beating us, and we ran away.

'They were planning. They were moving door by door. Some were in our place and some were in other houses.

'They beat me on the back and head. I didn't get injured very bad but I had some small injuries.

'Some of the people who were in our group, I heard that they passed away while I was here. Some were from Mozambique and some were from Zimbabwe.'

I ask Forget what his plans are now.

'I want to get some money so I can go back home and settle. I need money for nappies and clothes for my kids. I've got three kids; this one I'm expecting is my fourth one.'

'Why are you in South Africa?' I ask.

'Employment and the political situation.'

'And how did you get into the country?'

He says he came through Botswana and went straight to Alex. He plans to leave the church soon. 'My friend called me. He's left for Hillbrow, he is saying it is safe there. He is staying with his in-laws.'

I thank Forget for his time and wish him luck. While waiting for Phillip I look out the window, onto Pritchard Street. Tacked to the street poles are posters for today's *Star*: 'Help us to help the victims.'

Phillip, I see, is engaged in deep conversation. I join him and listen in. The man he is interviewing says that the Sunday after it started he was assaulted and mugged at Park Station, where he went for protection. 'But,' says the man, 'we are well secured here. The police have a look, they check in every hour. Let those other ones come if they want.'

The man is bitter. He feels keenly the irony that it is happening here, in South Africa, less than twenty years after his own country offered a safe haven to ANC freedom fighters.

'The officials of the so-called Azania, they were in Zimbabwe that time. Nobody assaulted them.'

He is also bitter that South Africa is going to be the host of the 2010 FIFA World Cup.

'This 2010. I don't know so much about this.'

Phillip carries on taking notes and I pull back to observe the surrounding activity. There is high-pitched shouting from around the corner. I find that an argument has broken out over a blanket. Two women are tugging at either end, exchanging insults.

Phillip is still busy when I return. I phone Laurie to tell her I'll be home late. While I am talking to her I notice, a few metres away from me, a tall man in a name-brand tracksuit and a baseball cap, his features more East African than the other men I have seen here today. He is also on a cell-phone. I say goodbye to Laurie in time to hear the man say into his own phone, '*Salaam aleikum.*'

The man catches me watching him and he comes over to talk.

'See what those guys can do, huh? All of a sudden they slaughter us.'

I'm taken aback by the bluntness of the statement, by the smooth and confident delivery. The man's name is Michael, he says, and he is from Kenya.

Michael has been in South Africa four years, he tells me. He owns pay-phone containers in the townships; he is a small business owner. He left home because there were problems in Kenya – 'tribal clashes', he calls them. He went first to Tanzania, then to Zambia and Zimbabwe, and now here.

His incident happened on Tuesday last week, he says. He explains the set-up.

'Alex is divided currently into nationalities. The Kenyans, Ugandans and Tanzanians are all in one place. We all speak Swahili. Three or four hours before it started we got information from the friendlies. So me and my buddies took everything we could and left. Some of us had just our pillows. The problem was coming here from Alex. We were around twenty guys, we couldn't all go in one taxi.'

I nod; he continues.

'One guy is missing. We tried to call him but his cellphone is off. So about him, we don't know. But all the other guys are safe.'

Michael tells me he is thirty-one years old.

I ask him, as I have asked the others, about his plans.

'Right now I don't think I have any plans. If this violence doesn't stop, maybe I will go to Mozambique. Because Mozambique is conducive for business. This thing doesn't happen there.'

'Botswana?'

'No,' he says. 'They don't show you, but it's inside.' He taps his chest with his palm. 'Here at least you know. They tell you to your face they don't like you.'

Phillip has ended his interview and is now next to me, listening. He asks Michael, 'Would you ever be comfortable staying in South Africa?'

'Never. Never. I am leaving as soon as I make a plan.'

The reputation of South Africa is ruined for other Africans, says Michael. 'This place is no good. Our own brothers. It's crazy. They are calling this thing an isolated case. I don't think so. It is something that is organised. In Alex there are unconfirmed reports that the first guys who raided are not from that area.'

Michael is convinced there is a political motive to the violence. 'Somebody wants to use this to gain something. It's very obvious. We all know. It's Zuma's thing. Everybody knows that. Ya, everybody knows.'

He has heard, Michael says, that Zuma has promised the Zulu attackers that as soon as he's in power they will all have jobs.

'You know what?' he adds. 'I'm not being selfish, but I think that these guys should lose the right to host the World Cup.

'Right now they are killing their black foreign brothers. What do you think they will do tomorrow? They will kill white South Africans. Then they will kill one another.'

———

We have not managed to speak to Bishop Verryn – we could not wait any longer; we wanted to be out of the church before nightfall – but we have heard that the next day there will be a 'Colloquium on Xenophobia and Violence' at Wits University, where the bishop will give the keynote address.

At 2pm on Wednesday, May 28th, I take my seat in the second row of the Senate Room on the university's east campus. The room is one of the institution's primary large-audience venues; it is where the governing body convenes to debate and ratify resolutions, and the decor is a suitable reflection of its prestige: a carpeted lobby with portraits on the wall of past vice-chancellors, two sets of heavy double doors opening onto a wood-panelled auditorium, ascending rows of leather fold-down chairs arranged in a semi-circle around a dais and a formidable rare-wood desk.

On the assumption that a four-hour academic colloquium is a waste of working time, Phillip has decided at the last moment not to join me. The absence in the venue of a recognisable media contingent has me concerned that his instinct may have been correct. Still, when the event starts, I know I'm where I should be: the welcome statement sets the tone for what promises to be an afternoon of exhaustive, no-sensitivities-spared analysis.

'One thinks of situations such as the Rwandan one where a relatively small degree of anger and resentment escalated and grew into a major genocide,' the deputy vice-chancellor, Professor Belinda Bozzoli, begins. 'And I'm not saying that *will* happen here. But when one sees the mobilisation, the spread, the contagion of this kind of hatred … it is certainly a risk.'

Following the preliminaries, the first hour of the session is dedicated to the insights of the social scientists. Their theses follow a similar line: the possibility, long latent, that the misery of South Africa's disempowered would some day boil over into mass aggression of this type.

There is talk of 'cultures of entitlement', 'relative deprivation' and the important difference, as far as uprisings go, between poverty and inequality – the latter always being the ingredient that fuels the conflagration. Statistics are quoted, such as the fact that the income ratio of South Africa's richest ten per cent to its poorest ten per cent is 255 to 1, placing the country amongst the most unequal societies in the world.

As the speakers acknowledge, there is nothing particularly new or groundbreaking in what they say. Inequality, usually measured by the Gini coefficient, has been cited time and again as a major contributing factor to the country's crime pandemic. But somehow today the well-worn theory takes on a fresh significance: there is a palpable sense of urgency in this auditorium, and statistics that were just last month stale and over-familiar have become shocking again, dire in their implications.

The last of the social scientists to speak is Daryl Glaser, from the Wits politics department. Aside from Glaser's line on the 'acquisitive individualism' of the elite, what he has to say *is* new – a response to the belief, dearly held by the refugees in the churches and police stations, that Zuma was behind the attacks.

'While it's true,' says Glaser, 'that there's been a desperate lack of political leadership in this country, it's also worth noting that there hasn't been a Le Pen or a Haider or a Pim Fortuyn, a populist leader who's actually mobilising anti-immigration sentiment. Not at the national level.'

Glaser goes on: 'I think it has to be said that Zuma himself is perfectly at ease with other Africans, for various reasons. He's played a mediation role elsewhere in Africa, and he's not mobilising this kind of xenophobia. But I think that obviously there is an overlap between his support base and some of the groups that are at the centre … And I think what this perhaps points to is some special responsibility that falls on Zuma's shoulders … I think there's a special responsibility that falls on Zuma's shoulders to address crowds in the vernacular and to make points about the importance of not engaging in this kind of violence …'

A brief scan of my notes reveals that Glaser has not dismissed outright the theory that someone is mobilising the violence, just the theory that it is someone 'at the national level'.

During the responses from the floor, a Jewish-looking man takes the microphone. (Is there such a thing? Am I, in the context of the stereotyping we seem to be discussing here today, a Jewish-looking man?) The man makes a simple observation that seems, to me at least, to lay bare the essence of the issue – an observation that echoes the final words of Michael the Kenyan in the church yesterday.

'This is really just a rhetorical question,' he says. 'I'm asking, how foreign is foreign? Coming back to the point that was raised earlier, I'm also the son of immigrants. And now we consider how tribal South Africa is. So technically, would a Zulu in Gauteng be considered foreign? Would a person from Limpopo in the Cape be considered foreign? How foreign is foreign? And how far will the mob, this mob that we've been talking about, how far will they want to go to get rid of foreign?'

A little later, Véronique Tadjo, head of the French department in the Wits school of literature and languages, provides something of an answer. Without deviating from her prepared speech, in a rich Francophone accent, articulating each syllable, she tells us the disheartening story of her homeland.

'As the world's largest producer of cocoa,' she begins, 'Côte d'Ivoire used to be West Africa's richest country in per capita terms. It was a magnet for millions of immigrants from poorer neighbouring countries like Burkina Faso and Mali. They came to work in the plantations. But by the 1990s the Ivorian model based on a liberal economy started to crumble and degenerate …

'After the death of Félix Houphouët-Boigny, in power for more than thirty years, the succession was difficult. The collapse of cocoa prices, the huge public debt, unemployment, poverty, widening inequalities between social classes, and the land scarcity, coupled with financial scandals at the top, brought social unrest and a mounting resentment against foreigners.

'It was then that former president Henri Konan Bédié, Houphouët-Boigny's successor, introduced the concept of "*Ivoirité*", or "Ivorian-ness". To sum it up, the concept of *Ivoirité* asked the question – who is an Ivorian and who is not? Self-affirmation became a way of defining and securing one ethnic group's position through the stigmatisation of the others. The government prevented opposition leader Alassane Ouattara, the former prime minister, from contesting presidential elections on the grounds that he had Burkinabé origins ...

'In 2002 the war broke out when a rebel group took over the north of the country. The rebel New Forces, as they are now called, have accused successive governments, including the present one, that of Laurent Gbagbo, of discriminating against northern Muslims and those of foreign origin. In spite of several past peace agreements, and the latest Ouagadougou Accord, Côte d'Ivoire remains in effect divided between north and south ...

'The concept of *Ivoirité* is at the heart of the crisis. It has undermined national unity, cost hundred of lives, displaced thousands of people, and further weakened the economy. Excluding foreigners is one of the main recurrent methods involved in strategies for the conquest or preservation of political power. Especially when the definition of the foreigner is ambiguous ...'

As she nears the end of her address, Tadjo explains how *Ivoirité* has evolved in recent years. The concept has become 'dual', she says. 'The *other* is not just the one who is not from the soil, or the national territory. The *other* is now also the one who is not from the local territory.'

Finally, while she is drawing an analogy between Côte d'Ivoire and the continent at large, she gets to the inevitable sentence. 'South Africa is no exception to the rule.'

The sentence hangs in the air long after she has collected her papers and returned to her seat.

In South Africa then, in May of 2008, with one eye on Tadjo's Ivorian warning, how foreign is foreign? Now that I'm looking for them, potential answers to the Jewish-looking man's rhetorical question appear everywhere.

Is 'white' foreign? In his address, Professor Loren Landau, director of the Wits forced migration studies programme, suggests that the recent attacks have exposed an underlying threat to white members of the middle class.

'The middle class in South Africa,' says Landau, 'as in many other wealthy countries, but specially here, can only ethically justify their continued position of privilege, positions often established during apartheid's dark days, if the state – if *their* state, *our* state – is actively promoting equity and fighting intolerance.'

Landau, a man whom local media have quoted on the attacks more frequently than any other academic, suggests that whites – and to some extent South African Indians – are understandably afraid.

'The kind of nativist rhetoric we've heard on the streets is an acute and direct threat, if not to our lives, then to our lifestyles, our privileged life-styles. And with Zimbabwe just up the road, there's a pointed reminder of what can happen if these sentiments move from the street into official government discourse.'

What *can* happen, I note. Whites, Landau implies, are of course not foreign yet. Indians are not yet foreign. Even the wealthy foreigners buying up sea-facing villas in Cape Town, the retired Brits and Germans living in Camps Bay and Clifton, are not – as a previous speaker, Pumla Gqola, has already observed – by the standards of the xenophobes, foreign.

But people from Cameroon, people with pitch-black skin who come to South Africa from the centre of the continent, from the rain forests up near the equator, they most definitely are.

When Achille Mbembe, Cameroonian-born research professor and award-winning author of *On the Postcolony*, appears at the dais, it is to wrap up proceedings before Bishop Paul Verryn gives the keynote address. Mbembe is one of the dark-skinned – one of the blackest men in the room – and he knows that under the circumstances there is no point in playing down this fact.

'I'm not a South African citizen,' Mbembe declares, his hands resting on the podium. 'My wife and my two children are South African citizens. So I guess I probably belong to that category of people who come here to steal jobs, but, even more terribly, to steal *our women*.'

On these last two words there is much appreciative laughter from the audience. Mbembe waits for it to subside. 'And even though we give back in return two children.' At which the audience laughs *and* claps.

'So I have been living here for eight years,' says Mbembe. 'I lived in

Cape Town for a year and I have lived in Johannesburg for seven. I have to say here today that I haven't been personally a victim either of racism or of incidents that I would qualify as xenophobic. Which says something about this country. Which doesn't say that racism and xenophobia do not exist, but which shows that, I mean, it's a very complex place.

'But I have to say that the recent events have disturbed me quite deeply. I was talking a moment ago, during the break, with Véronique, who spoke about Côte d'Ivoire. And it was quite amazing that we were feeling more or less the same thing.'

Mbembe names this feeling he shares with Véronique Tadjo; he is depressed, he says, saddened.

'Saddened not only for the thousands of people who have been displaced ... but also for those who overnight have decided that, after all, it's better to leave. Thousands of Mozambicans, Zimbabweans, and many others. And it's better to leave when faced with this terrible choice – either you go with your life, or we kill you here. We kill you after having burnt your property, having looted it, after having raped your wife and brutalised your children.'

And he is saddened for another reason, Mbembe says. He is saddened by the damage that has now been done to the *idea* of South Africa; the idea that is enshrined in its constitution, the idea that for once there could be a place in Africa where human dignity might be regarded as sacrosanct.

The recent violence, Mbembe says, renders a bit more complicated than before the continent's relationship to that idea.

'So I was asking myself, when we say South Africa, what does the *Africa* in the term South Africa stand for? When we say South Africa, what is it that the term *Africa* in South Africa is the name of?'

Mbembe says he has an explanation of his own to add to the many explanations that have been offered here today. He wonders, he says, whether there are limits to answers that are purely materialist; answers that look only at the social or political or economic conditions, however important these might be.

'When they are saying we are too dark, of course it has something to do with material interests,' Mbembe says. 'But it has something to do with something else.'

He pauses for a long time and looks up at the audience.

'It has something to do with self-hate.'

Every word is now underscored by his pumping right arm and his downward-pointed index finger.

'And we have to say it here.'

Pause.

'It has something to do with self-hate. Which is not inherited. Which is constructed over a long period of brutalisation. Of evictions, of non-respect for property, dispossession. All those things we know have been a huge part of the history of South Africa from the seventeenth century until now.'

A final long pause.

'That element of self-hate has also to do with the fact that today we live in a place where to be alive is not at all a guarantee for anybody. Because, you and I – township, informal settlement, suburbs, whatever – we can be killed tonight in our own home for no apparent reason. At any time. By whomever. That is the situation we are living under. But here we are. So, if that is the case, if death lives with us, then does it really matter that we kill fifty people who look darker than us? It becomes what is normal. And we have to denormalise it. If we do not denormalise it, South Africa will end in the same path, broken path, as many other countries in Africa.'

Mbembe returns to his seat in much the same way Tadjo did: the import of his words hanging in the auditorium air.

And then at the dais appears the man for whom we have all been waiting.

Bishop Paul Verryn has a warm, open countenance. He has a sandy-coloured beard. He wears a dark jacket and a stiff priest's collar and – mark of his rank – a lustrous purple shirt.

He gets immediately to his point.

'I've been asked to speak about xenophobia and ethics. Community ethics. As if there was such a thing. Aren't community ethics a little bit like looking for an honest politician?'

Laughter from the back of the auditorium.

Anyway, avers the bishop, his smile now disappearing, this ethical conundrum begins for him with the use of the term 'illegal alien'.

'It's as serious as calling people *kaffirs*,' he says. 'Forgive me saying that, but that is exactly what it's like. And it's particularly like that, I think, because they are so vulnerable. I mean, it's not as if we have a robust group of people climbing across the Limpopo River on a shopping spree. Which is how they have been described on more than one occasion.'

The bishop, like many of the speakers who came before him, is angry; unlike many of them, however, his anger is born of intimate experience – the experience of close daily contact with the hundreds of foreigners who seek refuge in his church; the experience of the attitude of the police to those foreigners.

'When you have a police force who are as rigorous, I mean, they really are amazingly rigorous, still they're rigorous about if they catch you without an asylum paper, what a joy to have you charged, criminalised … And so when one's talking about ethics, one has to understand that one is talking about a system of values in this instance that does not fit what our constitution says.'

The bishop cups his fist in his palm, clasps and unclasps his fingers.

'So let me then present to you my ethic. My community ethic.

'My community ethic is that we belong inextricably to one another on the African continent. And that some of our family are beginning to explore the rest of their family. And that therefore as an ethical statement the boundary, the border, between South Africa and Zimbabwe should be abolished. Comprehensively.'

A strange pronouncement, I'm thinking. Utopian and grandiose. But then I think again. Maybe a bishop, a man unencumbered by the rules that bind politicians and professors, can – *should* – express such thoughts.

Either way, buttressed by his mordant tone, the rest of the bishop's pronouncements are rooted firmly in reality.

'We kind of pacify the poor,' says the bishop, referring to the religious community. 'We give them analgesics every week, which make them feel valuable even though they really are rubbish. We are the ones who come with scriptures and tell them, "You are made in the image of God, even though you scratch for food out of a dustbin."'

The religious community, says Bishop Verryn, should therefore be held accountable to its own standards.

'We can't stand smug and say, Central Methodist ... I mean, it's very kind of you to recognise us, but the first xenophobic attack I experienced was in a little church just up the road here called the Braamfontein Methodist Church, where we had put up some of these "illegal aliens". And the vicious anger of the congregation that these people were messing up their church ... and they were, in a way. Eventually we actively had to get rid of almost every thread of evidence that there was ever a Zimbabwean in that building.'

At which, so quick and understated I almost miss it, comes the revelation: the reason behind the bishop's repeated allusions in the media to the planned nature of the May 2008 attacks.

'So it began three years ago in this country. Apparently four months ago Ronnie Kasrils knew about it. I've got a document that speaks of meetings that took place in Ulundi with some fairly senior cross-pollinated politicians and organs of state, which have brought ... which have made this thing happen.'

The bishop offers no more on the matter; this is all that is said. A reference to the prior knowledge of the minister of intelligence; to clandestine meetings in the traditional Zulu capital.

And as if it is unseemly for him to apportion blame in even this vague manner, the bishop closes on a caveat.

We have a responsibility to recognise, he says, that this stuff lies waiting to be born in each of us. We all have within us a profound capacity for violence and hatred of this kind.

They Cultivate Each Other's Fear

IN THE FEBRUARY 2008 issue of *The Believer* magazine, a literary journal based in San Francisco, a writer by the name of Eula Biss published an essay under the title 'No-Man's-Land: Fear, Racism, and the Historically Troubling Attitude of American Pioneers'. It's an essay that deals with the author's experiences of moving to a suburb of Chicago defined by white people as 'dangerous', a suburb inhabited by black 'gangs', a suburb where a white person ought to be fearful.

The essay is divided into eight sections, each with its own subtitle. In the third section, subtitled 'In the Imagination', Biss argues that while gangs are real they are also conceptual – that 'the word gang is frequently used to avoid using the word black in a way that might be offensive'.

Next, Biss introduces the reader to the example of South Africa, she writes about her cousin, who recently visited the country. Biss explains that while someone of her cousin's background would typically be considered neither white nor black, because of the lightness of her skin she is most often taken to be white, and that this is something to which she has become accustomed.

'But she was not prepared for what it meant to be white in South Africa,' writes Biss, 'which was to be reminded, at every possible opportunity, that she was not safe, and that she must be afraid. And she was not prepared for how seductive that fear would become, how omnipresent it would be, so that she spent most of her time there in taxis, and in hotels, and in "safe" places where she was surrounded by white people. When she returned home she told me, "I realised this is what white people do to each other – they cultivate each other's fear. It's very violent."'

On a Friday afternoon, I leave my fortnightly writing workshop at Wits University. It's been a good class and a long productive week, and I head to my local in Norwood for a beer with a friend. I park the Golf in the open lot below the bar just after 5pm. On the way up the stairs I call Laurie – today is two weeks and two days before our wedding – to tell her that I will meet her at home at around 7pm. After three rings the phone is answered.

The voice is not Laurie's.

It is the voice of a black man, backgrounded by hooting and traffic and crowds, and the language the man speaks is a local vernacular I don't understand.

'Who's this?'

The man hangs up.

I try the number again. My call is cut on the first ring.

I try the number a third time. The same man picks up and says something in the same vernacular.

'Who's this? Where's Laurie?'

He hangs up. I try a fourth, fifth, sixth time, but again the calls are cut on the first ring.

I am halfway up the stairs to the bar, leaning against the handrail. I turn and walk down the stairs and sit on a low wall outside the kosher restaurant on the ground floor.

'No,' I tell myself, 'this isn't happening.'

I run my hands through my hair and call the number again. The same man answers.

'Who the fuck is this?'

He hangs up.

I wait. I imagine for an involuntary instant the worst-case scenario. I push the image from my mind and try the number again.

'Hi, this is Laurie, I can't take your call right now ...'

The sound of her voice steels me. Must be a crossed line, a technical problem: a Friday afternoon city-wide rush on a network that can't cope with the load. I try the number again; again I get Laurie's voicemail. And twice more the voicemail.

And then: 'This number is no longer in use ...'

I call my home in a panic. Jane, our once-a-week domestic, is still at the apartment.

'Jane, it's Kevin. Is Laurie there?'

'No, she is out.'

'When did you last see her?'

'Ay, it was this morning already.'

I hang up. All the contact numbers of Laurie's family are on my old phone, which broke a month ago. I search through the messages on its cheap replacement for the number of Laurie's brother-in-law, who sent me a text earlier in the week. I find his message and dial the number.

'Johnny, it's Kevin. Listen, a strange voice is answering Laurie's cellphone. I haven't seen her since this morning. I'm a bit freaked out. Can you text me Tammy's number, and maybe Di's?'

Tammy, my fiancée's older sister, says she last heard from Laurie early in the morning. I consider for a moment sparing Tammy the news, but quickly realise I need her help. I tell her what's happened.

'Warren!' she screams through the house. 'Warren! Kevin says a strange voice is answering Laurie's phone! Warren! Was Laurie at work today?'

Warren, Tammy's husband, is also Laurie's part-time boss. He comes to the phone and says Laurie was still at work when he left, around mid-afternoon. I ask Warren to call around; tell him I'll do the same and check back in a few minutes.

When I hang up I see a missed call from Di, Laurie's mom, a number I recognise instantly. I call right back. It's Laurie. She's been crying.

'Love. Something's happened.'

'What? What's happened?'

'A man robbed me with a knife.' She sobs once, then, 'I'm fine, don't worry, I'll be fine.'

———

Laurie's parents' house is in the suburb next to Norwood. I get there in under five minutes. Laurie is sitting on the steps of the patio in the back garden. Warren and Tammy are there already, standing outside with Di and Laurie's father. They listen again as Laurie tells me the story.

Laurie left work at the start of rush hour. The Nelson Mandela bridge, her usual route home, was badly gridlocked so she continued on towards the Queen Elizabeth bridge, unconcerned that this was supposed to be a more dangerous route. Her window was open and she was listening to music. While she was waiting in the queue to turn onto the bridge, a man leaned through the window.

'Give me your phone,' he said. He reached into the car to rummage in the glove box.

'I don't have a phone,' Laurie said. The man took a large knife from his belt and held it at her chest.

'Give me the fucking phone, bitch.'

Laurie gave him the phone, which was lying on the passenger seat under a CD.

'Fucking white bitch,' the man said, as he walked (no running, no urgency) into the crowds.

An everyday Johannesburg story; its ending thankfully, mercifully, tame. 'At least you're all right,' we repeat, each of us in turn, like a mantra.

Except for Warren, who says, 'We all need to leave this place. Next time it will be worse. We need to start making plans, we all need to go.'

I am furious. I shout at Warren. I tell him that Laurie doesn't need to hear this right now. What she needs right now, I shout, is a little faith in humanity.

But the next morning I call to apologise. Unable to sleep, thinking about it all night, it occurs to me that my own anger, my own fear, comes from the same source.

———

Immediately following the paragraph on South Africa and the experiences of her cousin, Eula Biss brings her narrative back to America, and frames for the reader what appears to be a central thrust of her essay.

'We are afraid, my husband suggests, because we have guilty consciences. We secretly suspect that we might have more than we deserve. We know that white folks have reaped some ill-gotten gains in this country. And so, privately, quietly, as a result of our own complicated guilt, we believe that we deserve to be hated, to be hurt, and to be killed.'

I reread the essay a few days after Laurie's incident. I look hard at the passage above. In a South African context, I'm thinking, where (contrary to the experiences of Biss's cousin) whites are afraid for reasons as much real as they are imagined, the passage has the logic of a Zen koan.

Completely plausible and totally implausible all at once.

CHAPTER 7

Ways of Leaving

Part II

TWO DAYS AFTER THE Wits colloquium, I am waiting in the parking lot of St John's College for Jamie Paterson to finish her final lesson of the week. Although the façade of the school is visible from the pool area of my apartment block, I have not visited these grounds before, and up close there is much to admire.

The school building, a Herbert Baker design, is considered one of the finest architectural specimens in Johannesburg – a motif of dark stone, high arches and ivy. I watch pupils eat their lunch beside lush sports fields; I listen to bells chime in the chapel. I stand beneath a jacaranda tree and read a notice on a wall that advertises an upcoming performance of *Oedipus Rex*.

Long a school for the sons of South Africa's rich and powerful, St John's has only recently begun to accept girls into its post-matric class. Jamie completed high school at Roedean, the sister school across the road, and she has taken the extra year to get the A-levels that will facilitate her admission to a British university. As a female in what is essentially an all-male institution, she is required to wear the uniform of the boys: long grey trousers, white collared shirt, blue-and-maroon school tie.

It is in this uniform that Jamie gets into my car and drives with me to Norwood, where I know a quiet coffee shop that's perfect for interviews. We take a table outside and order two soft drinks. I tell Jamie, while lighting a cigarette, that last night I studied her family's police statements – the four given by her father, her mother, her brother and herself.

She doesn't remember much about it, she says; she wrote it in a fog.

'But then you went public with the story, you spoke openly to journalists. How come?'

'The first time I shared it with a journalist was three weeks later,' she says. 'A woman called from the *Sunday Times*, her name was Henriette … Henriette …'

'Geldenhuys?'

'Geldenhuys. Anyway, she called, and I thought, why should I keep it a secret?'

'Some people would say that what happened to you is a very personal thing.'

'It is. But it happened. And it happens to thousands of South African women. I thought, you know, these animals are not going to beat me. If I'm not able to talk about it, then maybe they've won.'

'Is that why you're sharing the story with me?'

'That. And because of what you told me about the other stories in your book.'

Jamie identifies to an extent with the foreigners, she says. She thinks they may be experiencing the same fear as she did, the same sense of being wrenched from an orbit. Since the xenophobic attacks started, Jamie says, she has been finding it difficult to get up in the mornings. She read a story about a foreigner who was gang-raped in her home, and she wondered whether that woman had any sort of support system.

'Everyone made such a fuss about us, you know. Within six hours there were people visiting. People with flowers, people with food. After it happened I had a bed to sleep in. It wasn't mine, but we had friends kind enough to take us in.'

And so lately, says Jamie, she's been thinking a lot about the foreigners.

I nod, extinguish my cigarette.

'I'm ready to begin when you are,' she says.

———

It's a red-letter day, the first Monday of October 2007, and in the car on the way to school Jamie Paterson is anxious. In a few hours she is to perform the practical component of her matric-final music exam, an exam for which she has been preparing for three weeks. The car arrives at the gate and Jamie grabs the handle of her flute case and kisses her father goodbye. She counts the minutes until the appointed time. On the strike of the hour she enters the recital hall and carefully takes out her instrument. She plays the selected pieces: a movement of a Mozart concerto in G Major, a Vivaldi concerto, a modern piece by Honegger, and *La Flute de Pan*.

The exam, Jamie knows, has gone well. Her mistakes have been minor and she has negotiated the transitions with skill. She is proud of herself, relieved, and she decides to remain behind after school to attend a lecture by her favourite English teacher – the subject this evening is classic British comedy, with a special focus on the series *Upstairs, Downstairs*.

On Monday night, when she gets into bed, life for Jamie is good.

She wakes on Tuesday in a room that still feels new. It's the room of her childhood, first bedroom on the right as you come down the passage, but redecorated for her seventeenth birthday in a tropical theme – a palm-tree mural, a green carpet and a hessian mat. Jamie swings her legs off the bunk and drops to the floor, landing amongst the folios of sheet-music she has yet to pack away. She remembers yesterday's success and opts to give herself the day off.

The morning is devoted to mooching. She doesn't change out of her pyjamas; she fools around for a while on the computer. Later she does some work on her history of music project. By late afternoon her mood has turned sour.

Jamie's parents are home on Tuesday night and the whole family eats together in the living room. After dinner she has a shower. She puts on her favourite sleeping shirt – the shirt with the picture of the kitten that says 'I don't do mornings' – and her Winnie the Pooh pyjama pants.

She returns to the living room and lies on the couch in front of the television. She wants to watch *24*, but she can't keep her eyes open. At 9.30pm she gets up from the couch and goes to bed. She falls asleep immediately.

She is woken at 10pm by men's voices and Pippin's barking.

'Shut your dog up and get your children,' Jamie hears.

She sits up. Immediately she knows what this is. Her heart thumps wildly in her chest. She thinks that maybe she should pretend to be asleep. Whoever they are, she thinks, she doesn't want them to assume that she's been listening – that she's called someone or done something.

Jamie lies back down and pulls the covers over her head and closes her eyes.

Soon the light in her room is switched on. Again Jamie sits up. A man is standing in the doorway. He looks as surprised to see her as she is to see him. The man doesn't say a word. He turns and walks out.

Jamie sits on the bed under the light and thinks about all the things that might happen in a situation like this, all the stories in the newspapers about things that happened to other people and were never supposed to happen to her.

Then Jamie's mother walks into the room. With her mother is a different man, a man with a gun.

'Jamie,' says her mother, 'these men are now in our house. Just co-operate with them. Give them everything they want. Don't fight.'

Her mother's voice is tinged with panic, but controlled.

'Okay,' says Jamie.

The man asks for Jamie's cellphone – he wants to check, he says, who she has called. She hands him the phone. The man scrolls through the numbers.

'Who's this Mrs Hoberg?'

'She's my flute teacher.'

'Why are you calling her at three o'clock in the morning?'

Jamie doesn't correct the man. She doesn't explain that the phone's clock is wrong.

'Come!' says the man.

Jamie gets out of her bunk. She steps down the ladder. She sees that the man is staring at her.

'Can I put on my dressing gown?'

'No,' says the man. 'Take your duvet if you're cold.'

She reaches up and pulls the duvet off her bed. She thinks about her cat. Where has it gone? She thinks that it must have jumped out the window. She wraps herself in the duvet.

When Jamie walks from the bedroom she sees a third man. This man has his hands on her nine-year-old brother's shoulders. He is steering Angus down the passage.

Her brother, Jamie sees, is sleepy and confused. She reaches out and takes him from the man. She holds her brother in front of her body and wraps the duvet around him.

She says to the man, who looks older than the man she saw in her room, 'Please don't hurt us.'

The man nods.

Jamie walks with her brother into the living room and sees that her father is on the floor. He is lying on his stomach with his hands tied behind his back. He has not been harmed but Jamie wants to throw up.

A man says, 'Go down!'

Jamie and her brother lie down. She puts her arm around her brother. A man pulls the duvet over their heads.

They are going to shoot us now, Jamie thinks. Execution-style to the back of the head. She wonders whether they will shoot a nine-year-old boy. She tries to imagine what it will feel like to be shot, if it will be painful. If she will be made to watch as her family is killed.

Events now become unclear for Jamie. She knows they have taken her mother away but she doesn't know where. She remembers a story about a man who was the father of two small children: the story was in the newspapers a few days (or was it a few weeks?) before. The man's throat was slit, and his children ran to their mother and said, 'Mommy, daddy's dead.'

Are they going to kill my father in front of me?

Jamie can feel Angus shaking beside her. She regains control of her senses. She squeezes her brother. She realises that she's uncomfortable, that her knees hurt. It's an absent thought: *God, I'm uncomfortable.*

A man asks her father about the BMW. 'Does your car have an immobiliser?'

The man's accent is heavy and her father doesn't understand the question. The man kicks her father.

'Hey, motherfucker, does the car have an immobiliser?'

'I know,' says Jamie. She stretches her arm out from under the duvet, to show the man which button to press. The man smacks her hand. She pulls the hand back and remains silent with her thoughts.

God, they're going to rape me. Please God, let this be over.

The men are coming in and out of the living room now. A man comes in with a box of bullets. 'Hey, you, where's the gun for these bullets?'

'I sold it,' says Jamie's father.

The men kick her father again. They hit him on the back of the head.

'You are going to die now!'

Angus hasn't cried yet, but now he gives a dry, choking sob.

Jamie says: 'Please, listen to me. Please listen. He sold it. He caught me playing with it when I was little, and he gave it away.'

The man slaps her.

'You lie, you shit! Where's the gun?'

He slaps her again.

The men begin to fiddle with the television. They unplug the cables and lift the box and pass it back and forth from one to the other. They pass the television over Jamie's father. From her position under the duvet, she sees boots and jeans and hanging cables. Then something heavy falls on her back and rolls off. She thinks that maybe the men have dropped the television on her back. But when she looks out from under the duvet she sees that the men have dragged her mother into the room and thrown her onto the floor. Her mother is now lying on the living room floor next to her father.

A man returns to the subject of the gun.

'We are going to kill your wife. Stop lying to us.'

The man pulls Jamie's mother up again.

Jamie's hair is loose; it is still slightly wet from the shower and it falls over her face and eyes. She brushes the strands aside and focuses on the place on the carpet where her mother was lying. She sees a pool of blood next to where her mother's head was. She whispers to Angus, 'Don't look.'

'Why?' her brother asks, and looks.

———

I ask Jamie to stop. It is now past 2pm and I need something to eat. And while it seems that she could go on without a break to the end, I need most of all to clear my head.

I lean back and breathe in and look around. A young mother with an infant in a pram is sitting at the table behind us. At the table next to us a couple talk in whispers. It is a warm winter's day and the sky is a far-away blue.

I order a sandwich and another soft drink. I talk to Jamie about school and about her hopes of a place at Cambridge. She tells me she's been thinking about becoming a lawyer one day.

I tell her that I think she'll make a great lawyer; that if this story is any indication, she has a good mind for detail and a remarkable ability to detach.

My sandwich arrives. I eat it slowly.

'Are you sure you're not hungry?' I ask.

She's sure, Jamie says.

Eventually I can stall no longer.

––––––

There is a moment of calm in the living room. The other men have taken Jamie's mother away and one man remains behind to watch over Jamie and her brother and father. The man is silent for a while and then he speaks.

'You know, you guys, I love you. I don't want to hurt you. God loves everyone. I'm like God, I love everyone. But my friends, they will kill you. You must give them everything you have.'

Jamie seizes the opportunity to talk to the man. 'I know you guys have a shit life,' she says. 'I know it's hard for you.'

'It's money,' says the man. 'It's the money. Money fucks everything up.'

Angus speaks now too. 'Ja, I know you guys need money. But you mustn't hurt us.'

Jamie starts to think of all the things she owns that are worth money. 'Fetch my blazer,' she says, 'it's in my room, hanging on a hook. There's a badge there. It's worth money. It's pure copper.'

The man goes to her bedroom and brings back the blazer. Because Jamie is one of the top students at her school, her blazer is full of badges. The man pushes the blazer under her eyes. 'Which one of these?' he demands. 'Which one?'

Jamie points to the badge.

'What about the others?'

'No, they're not worth anything. They're worth maybe twenty rand.'

Jamie remembers her flute; she tells the man about it. 'It's solid silver.'

'Yes, you must show me. You must show me.'

'It's in my room,' she says, 'you can take it.'

She also tells the man to take the statue on the cabinet, an African figurine carved by a Knysna artist.

'No,' says the man. 'We can leave you with some memories.'

'Thank you. You see, you're a nice guy.' Then: 'What if the security company comes? Will you kill us?'

'We will kill *them*,' says the man. 'We don't care about them. We'll kill them. This is the way we live. If the police come we will kill them too. Or they will kill us. We don't care.'

The other men return now to the living room, again they ask about the bullets. Then Jamie feels a hand grab her arm. A man is pulling her up. Her first instinct is to recoil from the clammy hand. But she doesn't. She doesn't want to provoke the man. She stands up, her hair covering her face. She squeezes her brother once and goes with the man. She knows where she's going and what's about to happen. She doesn't want to leave her brother.

Jamie is led down the passage. Her mother is lying on the floor of the passage, next to the cupboard with the household valuables. The men have stripped her mother down to her pyjama pants and spaghetti top. She is barely recognisable to Jamie. She is covered in blood, her hair wet with it, saturated. It looks to Jamie as if her mother has lost an eye. She is surrounded on the floor by birthday cards – she is a collector of birthday cards – which are all smeared in blood.

The man leads Jamie past her mother and into her bedroom. Jamie sees her flute on the dressing table. 'Here, you guys can take this,' she says.

'We can take what we want,' says the man.

He picks up the flute and looks at it. 'This is useless to us. What will we do with it? We want gold. We want money and guns.'

'I know,' she says. 'We'll give you everything we have.'

The man stares at her for a long time. When he talks again it is with a grimace. 'I'm HIV positive, you know. My life is over. But you, you are young. Your life isn't over. So give me what I want.'

The man locks the door. The other men try to come in. 'No,' says the man to his colleagues. 'Fuck off, fuck off.'

It sounds to Jamie as if the men outside are using her mother as a battering ram. The door stays shut.

Jamie hands the man all the costume jewellery she has on her table. She reaches into her bag. In her wallet there is only twenty rand. She hands him the note.

Then the man hits her, not hard, on the top of the head – an openhanded slap. 'No, this isn't everything. Where's the gun?'

Jamie goes to her cupboard and finds more jewellery in her jewellery box. The man says again, 'I'm HIV positive.' He takes her hand and places it on his crotch. 'You see how much I want to fuck you?'

The man talks once more about the gun. She offers him her watch. 'I have a watch,' she says, 'it's in the bathroom.'

The man listens through the door to make sure his colleagues aren't outside and then he turns the key and leads her to the bathroom. He quickly locks the bathroom door. The watch is not there. 'Oh,' says Jamie, 'they must have taken it already.'

The man is looking at her. 'I don't want to give you HIV. Do you have a condom?'

'No, I think my father has some.'

Jamie wants to escape, to get away. The man ignores her reply. He pushes her into the shower. 'Take your pants off,' he says.

———

Once more I ask Jamie to stop.

'I'm in uncharted territory here,' I say to her. 'I need you to be very sure about what you want to tell me.'

She says that she has given this a lot of thought; that she sees no point in glossing over the details. She refuses to live as a victim, she says.

'It happened,' she says again. 'And I'm not going to pretend it didn't.'

I nod.

In the same detached and mature tone she has employed all afternoon, she takes me through those twenty minutes in the bathroom. She speaks slowly, waiting for me to transcribe one sentence before moving on to the next. I don't look up until the scene is complete. When we are done, Jamie answers a question I have not asked.

'And yes. I was a virgin.'

———

The man wipes himself on Jamie's sleeping shirt and throws her pants into the shower with her. He shuts the shower door. He urinates into the toilet bowl and washes his hands.

Jamie sits for a long time in the shower. The noises outside continue. When she gathers the courage to slide open the door, the man has gone.

She waits in the bathroom. After a while she hears from the passage the broken voice of her mother. 'Jamie, let us in.'

'I can't,' Jamie says. 'He locked the door and took the key.'

The man, Jamie thinks to herself when she says this, has prevented the other men from raping her.

One of the men bangs on the door. 'What did he do to you?'

She doesn't respond.

The man asks again, more aggressively.

'He raped me!' she shouts.

Jamie's thoughts are in conflict: *I don't want to be the only one left alive*, and, *This happened to me, I survived.* She sits in the bathroom and listens to the men as they run up and down the passage; takkies squeaking, sliding, through the blood on the floor.

Then she hears her father's voice outside the window. She hears the BMW start and the gate open.

Her father, shouting: 'Jamie, Jamie, are you okay?'

'I'm fine! Where's mom? Where's Angus? Are they okay?'

'They're fine! We're all okay!'

'I can't get out,' screams Jamie, 'he locked me in! Can you kick the door down?'

It now feels to her as if she is in a cage. She has to get out of the bathroom. She opens the window and sees her father running past with a carving knife. 'Dad!' she shouts. 'Where the fuck are you?' She thinks to herself that this is the first time she has sworn in front of her father.

She hears the voice of her brother: 'Jamie, where are you?'

'I'm in the bathroom. Are you okay?'

'I'm okay,' says Angus. 'I've got to go to the loo.'

Jamie decides to climb out the window. Halfway through she sees Zodwa, the domestic. 'Don't!' Zodwa says. 'You are going to hurt yourself.'

Jamie hears herself laugh.

She comes back into the house through the front door and finds that her mother is in shock. 'Jamie,' says her mother, 'they hit me on the head. They stabbed me in the neck. I'm going to die.'

Jamie shakes her mother and looks into her wounded eye. She comforts her mother. Then she starts to shiver. She leaves her mother and runs into her bedroom and puts on her dressing gown and slippers.

Zodwa is kneeling beside her mother when Jamie returns. It is apparent to Jamie that Zodwa doesn't know what to say or do.

'Mom, they raped me,' Jamie reminds her mother. Her intention is to shock her mother out of thinking she is going to die.

Jamie's father is on the phone now, calling the police. For some reason the police demand the Paterson's home phone number. For some reason, when her father repeats the number, they can't get it right. Eventually her father swears and hangs up.

Jamie stands beside her father as he lifts up her mother and carries her out to the second car. Jamie follows, and gets into the front passenger seat. Reneke, Zodwa's boyfriend, takes the wheel. Angus sits on Jamie's lap and Zodwa sits in the back, holding Pippin. Jamie's father is also in the back, talking softly to her mother.

The house is left unlocked.

As they drive out the gate they see the neighbour, a police reservist. He is wearing his bulletproof vest. He heard noises, says the neighbour, and he has come to investigate. 'What happened?' he asks.

Jamie tells Reneke to just continue driving. She gives him directions to the Morningside Clinic.

Upon arrival at the clinic Jamie's mother is wheeled straight away into the emergency ward. Jamie sits with her father and brother, Reneke and Zodwa, in the waiting area. They wait in silence, five of them, with the dog. Then her father starts pacing. And Jamie decides to call her music teacher; she needs to speak to a human voice that's not involved.

Jamie's father also makes a call, to his friend Richard Davies. When he hangs up, he says, 'I'm so sorry, Jamie. I'm so sorry.'

Jamie says to her father that it's not his fault.

She looks for the face of her brother, and sees that he has moved onto Zodwa's lap. 'You can cry, you know,' she says to him. She goes to him and hugs him. Which is when Angus starts to cry.

At the insistence of her father, Jamie now enquires about the procedure for herself. She identifies herself as a victim of rape, and is told she needs to take antiretrovirals and antibiotics for STDs. She must also take the morning-after pill. Further, so that the police will have sufficient evidence, she is told that she must undergo a forensic exam.

The staff at Morningside suggest that she be taken to Sunninghill, where they are better equipped to handle such cases. She doesn't want to leave her mother, but she knows she has no choice. She says she'd like to say goodbye to her mother before she goes.

From the door of the theatre Jamie sees her mother and the next moment looks away. A surgeon is working in deep concentration over her mother, stapling a large flap of skin back down to her scalp.

Jamie returns to the waiting area to find that Richard Davies and his wife Peta have arrived. Jamie asks Peta to look after her mother when she wakes up. With her father and brother, she walks out to Richard's car. Richard drives them to the Sunninghill Clinic.

Jamie is led into a special room in the clinic's rape unit. A doctor and a nurse enter the room. There is also a man named Ernie in the room, a representative of the family's medical-aid scheme.

Jamie protests and Ernie leaves. She is then submitted to a barrage of questions. When she has answered their questions, the doctor and the nurse, a pair of dour and perfunctory women, bring out the sexual assault box. They remove a comb and gather evidence from Jamie's hair. They scrape her fingernails. They start to perform a pelvic exam, but she stops them when it becomes too painful. They draw blood from her arm for testing.

The doctor and the nurse now leave the room together. Jamie sits on the tall narrow bed, swinging her legs like a child. The doctor returns and says she wants to keep Jamie's pyjama pants as evidence; she asks Jamie if she has a change of clothes. Jamie says she doesn't, so she is given a hospital gown and a white cotton blanket.

The nurse returns to the room with a handful of pills. She explains to Jamie their purpose. Jamie, having read about this before, asks about the side-effects of the antiretrovirals. The nurse lists the side-effects as if she is reciting a list of grocery items. Then she hands Jamie a glass of water. 'Take them as fast as you can,' she says. Jamie does as she is told and instantly vomits. The nurse opens a box of anti-nausea pills and fetches an IV bag.

'Don't,' says Jamie, 'I think I may be allergic.'

'No, no,' says the nurse, 'you can't be allergic.'

The drip is hooked up to a vein in Jamie's arm. Within seconds she begins to swell and to itch. She begins to have trouble breathing. The nurse gives her an antihistamine. The drug courses through her body until she feels it in her fingertips.

Later, two overweight police officers enter the room. They have come to take Jamie's statement, they say, but somehow they seem uninterested. Then Richard barges into the room. 'She's not giving a statement now,' he says 'Leave her alone.'

Jamie is overcome at this point by profound exhaustion. She is desperate for sleep. She wraps herself in the hospital blanket and goes out to Richard's car and is driven to Richard's house. She is led to a bedroom and she passes out.

She wakes at 8am. She says she wants to go to school. She doesn't realise how ridiculous this sounds. She has a shower and borrows an item of Peta's old clothing – a shapeless one-piece denim suit, which she wears all day.

It is a few minutes before 4pm at the coffee shop in Norwood. I have finished my packet of cigarettes. I ask the waiter for change and go inside to buy another box. I am jittery, unsure of what my obligations are with a story like this, uncertain now about whether I even have a right to tell it.

I open the new box of cigarettes and discuss my reservations with Jamie.

In the same dispassionate tone, she tells me more about the journalists she has spoken to – about the difference, in her mind, between a story that responsibly exposes a real and horrifying facet of South African life and a story that simply exploits for shock value. She tells me about an experience she had recently of the latter: a local magazine, she says, which was shameless.

'Which do you think mine will be?' I ask, not altogether joking.

She smiles anyway.

I tell Jamie I'd like to speak to her again in a few months, after I get back from a trip to the States. I say it would be helpful if she could expand on her motives, maybe even write them down.

She says she'd be happy to do both.

Before I drop her at home, we talk briefly about a young man she has been seeing. He is in his final year of school, she tells me, and so far things are going well.

I ask: 'Do you think a guy that age can deal with what you've been through?'

'I don't know,' she says, 'I hope so.'

———

In early June 2008 Laurie and I embark on a month-long trip, a sort of delayed honeymoon, to North America. Our first stop is New York, which is in the throes of a heat wave, and after four days of sweating in the crowds downtown we decide to take a boat-ride out to the Statue of Liberty and Ellis Island.

In the foyer of the Ellis Island Museum, on a display surrounded by stacks of turn-of-the-century suitcases, I read the following: 'Since 1600, over sixty million people from throughout the world have immigrated to the United States, creating a multi-ethnic nation unparalleled in history.'

The display goes on to tell me that twelve million immigrants landed

on Ellis Island between 1892 and 1924, and that the building I am standing in now was once the nation's chief gateway. 'Today,' says the display,
'over one hundred million Americans can trace their ancestors back to
that twelve million.'

The display, I'm surprised to note, does not leave me indifferent. Taken
with the Statue of Liberty in the bay outside, the words carry an unexpected resonance.

Would I want to be part of the current batch of immigrants?

Later, Laurie and I go into the museum theatre, to watch old footage
of Russians and Armenians and Slovaks and Jews who felt blessed to arrive here; a man in the film who says, 'If they send me back, I jump in the
water.'

Then after the film, during question time, an American in the audience
who asks something as significant as it is laughable.

'What is immigration?'

And the answer from the employee of the US National Parks Service,
a young woman fresh out of college, who says, 'Any time someone goes
from one country to another country, that's immigration.'

Say what you want about the myopia of some Americans, I'm thinking,
they live in a place they never have to consider leaving.

The boat takes us back to Manhattan, and Laurie and I lean against the
railing on the lower deck and try to locate the spot in the skyline where
the Twin Towers once stood. My thoughts are pulled predictably in the
opposite direction: nowhere is safety a guarantee, nowhere is a long un-
troubled life assured.

That same night, we go to dinner with friends at a place in the East
Village, a restaurant on the corner of Second Avenue and Fourth Street
with outdoor tables and a view of the passing foot traffic. Young people
walking by in their tens and hundreds and thousands, and on the faces of
these young people and in the way they walk, a dominant expression – the
look, the strut, that says, 'I am here, and there is nowhere else in the world
I would rather be.'

I'm veering, wholly capricious, convinced now that somehow I need to
make myself one of them.

At the table with us is a twenty-six-year-old American journalist, a smart and driven man who is beginning to get regular bylines in the *New York Times*. He has just returned from a two-month assignment in China, and he tells me about it, and at the end of his story he says, 'Still, it's great to be back in the free world.'

I nod, and admit to him that a big part of me is envious, but when the conversation turns to South Africa I veer sharply back again. He was in South Africa last December, he says, a few days in Johannesburg but mostly in Cape Town. 'How can anyone still live there?' he wants to know.

How can anyone still live there? Were his eyes open? Did he see anything? Forget the mountains and the bush and the ocean and the sky, did he go into a bar and talk to people? Did he see that despite their horror stories there was something about them that was vital and alive? Did he sense the wisdom in their attitudes, notice that maybe they were heirs to an ancient dictum: it could all go for shit in the morning so I may as well live now? Forget the smell of Johannesburg after a thunderstorm, forget the fathomless silences of the Karoo or the shade of an umbrella thorn on a Zululand ridge, did he get any of *that*?

And if not, then what the hell did he see?

———

July 25th 2008 is Professor Alan Paterson's last Friday in the office. I find him at his desk in the medical faculty building, a sunless space down a flight of stairs and through a maze of corridors and security gates. The professor, when I walk in, is leaning back in his chair with his hands behind his head, staring at the ceiling. It is a pose of severe introspection, perhaps dejection.

Files lie strewn on the carpet, waiting to be packed in boxes. Solemn classical music plays softly on the stereo.

Alan invites me to sit at his visitors' table and he takes the seat opposite, indicating that he is ready for me to begin.

As I have already felt with his daughter Jamie, I feel somehow that I am being granted access here to an intensely private moment. Partly to offset my discomfort, I say to Alan that this must all be very difficult for him.

He nods. 'I think half of me just wants to go already. But there's a lot of unfinished business. All the research, you know.' He expands, saying that there's a huge amount of follow-up to be done on liver biopsies, especially as they relate to HIV. 'Which I don't think anybody will do now.'

There's a short silence. Alan notices that I am taking in his office – the shelves of books and papers that line the walls, the microscope in the corner, the framed photographs of graduation ceremonies.

'It's amazing how much stuff one accumulates,' he says. 'There's ten years' worth of stuff in here.'

From next Thursday, he says, the plan is to clear debris from the home. 'That's twenty years' worth,' he adds.

Alan starts at the University of Newcastle on October 1st, he says. He is going alone to reconnoitre, to see how far the British pound stretches. His objective is to be set up and ready when the family arrives – Jamie and Angus will be at school in South Africa until late November, and Bronwyn will first go to Hong Kong, in December, to re-establish her ties with the ballet world, then she will bring the children over.

'We're playing it by ear. I know Britain fairly well, but not from the point of view of working there.'

There is reason to be optimistic, though, says Alan. He recently had a conversation with a colleague, who told him that his salary puts him in an elite category – up amongst the top one per cent of earners in the north of England.

'I don't quite know what that means, but it was said positively. Which is what our problem is here, we don't value our professionals.'

I register the import of Alan's last observation, and choose to let it slide – it's no secret that health minister Manto Tshabalala-Msimang undervalues the contributions of white doctors, and it's a matter that we've discussed off the record at some length. To venture back there now would be to divert from my purpose this afternoon: to try and glean something of the outlook of a man who is in the process of leaving a country he has lived in for fifty-seven years.

So I focus instead on the first part of his response. 'Overall, then, you're hopeful about the move?'

'I'm apprehensive, but yes, I'm hopeful that we'll get to the other side and get through the weather and the rain and live a decent life. And that I can do a forty-hour week, and have time for my family, like a sane person.'

In an effort to probe further, I paraphrase for Alan a statement that JM Coetzee made on Australian television shortly after he emigrated to Adelaide.

'Coetzee said a while ago that leaving a country is like the break-up of a marriage. Would you agree with that? Does this feel like a divorce?'

Alan gives this thought for a moment and nods his head. 'We received a liver from a donor at 5am this morning. I was thinking it was going to be my last in the country. I had a feeling of deep regret.'

He shares with me more of his apprehensions.

'I have big concerns about going to the north of England. I understand the concerns of my family, I really do. I just hope I can find a standard of living that is better, despite the rain and the cold.'

He says that his wife feels the cold intensely, and that she is likely to feel the loneliness of starting again in a new place, and I get an image in my mind of the small and slender woman who was so gracious and welcoming when I sat in her living room in May.

'We looked at perhaps living in Durham,' Alan says. 'Bronwyn at the time was not unhappy with it. But she's unhappy now because you watch Sky weather and Newcastle is always five degrees colder than London.'

He tells me about a man he knows who owns a cabin in the Lake District. 'I'm hoping there are advantages,' he says.

Then: 'The work will be much the same, but more programmed than the general chaos we are living with in South Africa.'

I suspect what the answer might be, but I decide here to risk a diversion. 'Has government made any sort of gesture?' I ask. 'Any attempt to persuade you, the last liver pathologist left, to stay?'

Alan shakes his head. 'No, I don't think they even know, quite frankly.'

He recalls for me what happened when the Department of Health decided a few years ago to transform the old, apartheid-stained South African Institute of Medical Research into the National Health Laboratory Service, at which he himself is chief pathologist until next Thursday.

'The guy who drove it was, to put it bluntly, full of crap. He made

statements like, "Pathologists are not really that necessary." He was a political animal. We lost more than fifty pathologists in a short space of
time. We approached the head of the NHLS with the list of names, and
they promised they would take action, but five, six, seven years later no
action has been taken.'

Alan, I know, could go on – which is why I need to bring the conversation back to my brief. 'Have you sold the house yet,' I ask.

'I'm not going to sell,' he says. 'I'll wait it out; the market is not that
great.'

But for Alan the house – despite what has happened in it – seems also
to be the site of his strongest attachment.

'If we sold, we would cut all our ties. That would be too final.'

After a pause, he adds, 'If we find that Newcastle is an idyllic place, we
would sell up. But even then I think we would be coming back. Because
the one thing that doesn't change in this country is the sheer beauty of
it.'

Why always this word? I'm wondering. Why do so many emigrants, in
the months before they leave, keep referring to *this* aspect of the country?
One answer – the best answer I can come up with when I think about it
later – may be that beauty implies an uncontaminated connection. You
can talk wistfully about the landscape of your birth precisely because of
its immutability: it isn't man-made, it's pure and inanimate, it's the element in your identity that was there before you and the element that will
remain when you're gone.

But Alan, as if having to remind himself consciously of his reasons for
turning his back on them, moves on quickly from the subject of South
Africa's graces.

'If the country sinks beneath the waves,' he says, 'we're outside of it.
Then again, I have a lot of colleagues and friends who can't get up and
go. So I don't think I'll be the vilifying ex-pat who takes joy in watching
the slide.'

It's a statement that's easy to accept; Alan, as far as I'm concerned, is
not the sort of person to indulge in *schadenfreude*. 'Still,' I say, 'there is
a sense that white South Africans wind each other up, a sense that we
cultivate each other's fears, to quote from an article I read a few months

back. Aren't you worried that your decision to publicise your story – and sitting here with my notebook, I'm of course heavily implicated in this – but aren't you worried that you may be fuelling the pessimism?'

Alan at first is philosophical. 'Obviously a lot of people were shaken when they read about what happened to us. And a percentage *will* re-evaluate their futures. It doesn't make me feel good, but it doesn't make me feel bad either. You know, it happened to us.'

I'm hearing the echo here of Jamie's words, and I'm thinking that the fact of certain events is sometimes the most one can say about them, when Alan raises his voice in growing frustration at the question. He points his finger towards the door and lists the stories he knows from just this part of the building, the stories that come to mind when he walks down the corridors.

In the next office, a pathologist who was held up by gun-wielding thugs; five corridors down, a man whose wife and son were hijacked; further away, the ghost of someone who was first on the scene when his neighbours were burnt by boiling water for their valuables; the next office again, a man who left for London after he was held up in his driveway with his child in the car.

'It just goes on and on. All on the third floor here. It just goes on and on.'

He exhales, lowers his voice again.

'I was listening to this show on Classic FM about crime and perception,' he says. 'Somebody on the show had done a survey, and he made the obvious point that South African blacks are as traumatised by the violence as whites. In terms of negative perceptions this is not a white thing. So to say our reaction is fuelled by sentiment? I don't think that's correct. I think the opposite. This sense that it's all a myth, that we should not speak, is a little Pollyanna-ish.'

He stands up and searches in his drawers and folders. 'I want to show you something,' he says. He finds what he's looking for, and as he hands it to me he says it's the only official acknowledgement he got after the attack – a letter from the office of the minister of safety and security.

I read it, and to be fair it seems like quite an acknowledgement. But then I get to the last line. The letter is addressed to Professor A *Peter*son.

I hand the letter back to Alan and look around the office some more. Tacked to the whiteboard I see a picture of Kermit the Frog beside the line: 'Time's fun when you're having flies.'

Alan smiles at me smiling, and he relaxes in his chair.

'You've got to take care of yourself and your future,' he says. 'Which I've never done, which is why I'm not rich.'

I ask, 'Was it for ideological reasons that you never went into private practice?'

'Ja, I wanted to teach. I wanted to research. I like teaching.'

In Newcastle, he says, he will be making more money than he's ever made in his life. The job is a research position, something that British universities place a big premium on, and he will be given emeritus status.

Alan says he doesn't yet have a place to stay when he lands; he's searching for one now on the Internet, preferably a short-lease two-bedroom flat. Before the family arrives, he says, he wants to find a house outside Newcastle.

'I'm thinking of a more rural, village-type life. Which is possible in the north.'

He has a clear picture in his mind, he says. He wants to listen to Elgar and Vaughan Williams, to smoke a pipe. 'Land of hope and glory, that sort of thing.'

'That's the image you have?' I ask. 'That would be a good thing?'

'My grandmother had an infatuation with England,' says Alan. 'I grew up looking at postcards of York and Durham and Edinburgh. When I was a kid I always wanted to go there. The ordered bales of hay, the fields and streams.'

———

Not to put too fine a point on it, or to question in any way the authenticity of feeling and experience of the many South Africans who live elsewhere (whether they have emigrated; whether they are here physically and only in their minds have left), but in the last few years the Radium Beer Hall in Orange Grove might have become my own land of hope and glory.

Touted as one of Johannesburg's oldest pubs, the Radium's pressed-steel ceilings, parquet floors and wrought-iron railings speak to you when you enter of raucous nights stretching back decades into the past of this (once and always) mining town. The west window looks out onto Louis Botha Avenue, a street that seethes with traffic and commerce and life, a scene that reminds you, viscerally and unflinchingly, that you are in Africa. Turn to your left, and you'll see that the bar at which you stand is a many-times-varnished two-tier slab of fine teak, affixed to which are elaborate taps that dispense a range of gold and dark and amber drafts. Behind the bar, on the wall above the shelves holding the hard liquor, hangs a pair of signs that reflect the forthright persona of Manny Cabaleira, proprietor for the last twenty-three years: 'Do not embarrass yourself and management by asking for credit,' and, 'Credit will only be given if you are ninety-five years old and accompanied by your parents.'

And while this is comfortably adequate, in a city where the most popular drinking venues are antiseptic suburban franchises and hazardous township shebeens, to recommend the Radium as a pub of atypical distinction, it is in Manny's collection of framed newspaper posters – a collection that adorns the Radium's north and east walls – that the singularity of the place is truly located.

Posters like 'After mass action satisfaction' and 'Braai the beloved country', which play, in turn, on a cigarette advert and Alan Paton's classic novel to expunge from the country some of the tension that threatened, during the transition, to tear it apart. A poster like 'Berg hikers stoned', which takes a story about an alleged assault in the Drakensberg and suggests that perhaps the victims (as so many of us have done in those mountains) had been sampling the local weed. A poster like 'Your bra can kill you', which transforms a peculiar consumer alert into a regrettable national truism – in this land your friend (your *bra*) may be less than he seems.

But there is a deeper level to Manny's collection. Given his careful placement of the posters in ordered and descending rows, the eye reads the items left to right, top to bottom, as if reading a page in a book. So it inevitably happens that after a few pints a narrative emerges, and although the narrative may change from one night to the next, it is always uniquely and wholly and uncannily South African. It is always a narrative that points to the things that divide us, and beneath that, always, to the intractable irony that this is where we unite.

Like 'Tokolosh took my virginity', a poster from the country's most widely read daily, a poster that divides and unites precisely because the *tokolosh*, a mischievous and jealous demon, is accepted as fact across large parts of southern Africa – although not, as a rule, by whites. Yet there it hangs, next to posters about legendary rugby tests and shamed cricket stars.

Or 'Lesbians lose appeal', which refers to a lost case in a protracted legal battle over the constitutionality of same-sex marriages, a poster that divides and unites in the irreverent fun it pokes at its subject and the tacit acknowledgement that non-exclusion is what our new constitution is about.

Read with 'Strange days indeed', a reference to the other-worldliness of the negotiations and clashes and renegotiations that culminated in Nelson Mandela's inauguration as president in 1994, the posters – if you look at them long enough – flow into one another in an endless interplay of meanings.

Blood, sex, music, disease, miracles, murder, poverty, race, profit, beauty. These are the narratives of post-apartheid South Africa that hang on Manny's walls. They are bewildering and illogical, impossible and bizarre, and still they cohere – because whatever the country is, it is not London or Durham or the East Village on a humid evening in June.

Here's the thing. Where better than home for a person to confront the enigma of identity? Are there bars in Australia where the 'I' and the 'other' are packed in together so tight? Would a pub in Newcastle or New York offer an opportunity to perceive so clearly the markers and symbols that make up a South African self?

For, land of hope and glory though it may be, the Radium is not an integrated bar. Each night the black patrons occupy their stools near the door and the street, and the white patrons congregate further in, and it's a ritual that doesn't much change. But each night there is a meeting in the middle, where a veteran of the apartheid armed forces might have an honest conversation with an ANC stalwart, or a white man might buy drinks for a black woman, or vice versa, and for a couple of minutes the heaviness of three-and-a-half centuries of history lifts and the visions of Mandela and Tutu seem not so far-fetched.

And the next morning you wake up and ask again the question: What are the rules of engagement when the truths about our individual selves are so fluid and yet written so indelibly on our skins?

———

On a Monday in August 2008, with this question – or some version of it – in mind, I get into my Golf and drive to Glenhazel to visit Dana Druion, my wife's first cousin. Dana, I have heard, has recently taken into her home two foreign African families, one Zimbabwean and one from the DRC, and what I urgently want to know is: *Why?*

Why has Dana, a member of a tight-knit religious community that could best be described as insular, involved herself so completely in the problems of the secular world?

My notebook is already out as I park in the driveway. Dana's house is on Northfield Avenue, the main thoroughfare that bisects the orthodox Jewish suburb. Like the majority of houses on this street its exterior wall displays the blue-and-yellow colours of a security company that, since my investigations last year, has become ubiquitous.

'GAP,' proclaims the sign. 'Glenhazel Active Patrol … Crime can be beaten: it's your call …'

I lock the car. It's a warm late winter's morning and Dana leads me through her house and onto the back patio. There's a large pool in the centre of a neat lawn; bed linen drying in the sun on garden chairs; high-tensile burglar-proofing throwing symmetrical shadows over the wide panes of sliding doors.

Dana brings a tray laden with bran muffins and orange juice and asks me to unfurl the umbrella. The dog, a grey Doberman crossbreed, settles itself at her feet.

In an affectionate and sincere voice, she gives me her answer.

'My response to the xenophobia was dictated by the fact that I'm a Jew,' she says. 'This resonates very powerfully for me with the Holocaust. A short time ago, Jews were in the same position. Nobody wanted them.

They couldn't go anywhere. That's the first thing.'

I look up from my notebook. 'And the second thing?'

'The second thing is that I missed apartheid. In the 1976 riots I was fourteen. I remember being vaguely aware that there was injustice and trauma, but I was never fully aware.'

Dana tells me that she didn't go straight to university after school. She says she went instead to Israel, to a seminary for religious Jewish women. Soon after she returned to South Africa she got married, and in 1982 she enrolled at Wits University. As a student, while in training to become a social worker, she gave birth in the custom of her faith to a succession of children – her first responsibility was to her family, she says, and so she never became politically active.

'I think it's always concerned me that I never played my role,' she says.

A statement that is also a fullstop.

I take a bite of muffin and a sip of juice. I ask Dana to talk me through the events that led her to this point.

A week after the xenophobic violence broke out, she says, she got a phone call. 'It was from a social worker, a woman who refers all her trauma counselling to me. At that stage, like a lot of us, I was feeling quite disturbed by the images on TV and the broadcasts on 702. And so when she asked me if I would volunteer at the Cleveland Police Station, I agreed right away.'

Every day for almost two weeks, says Dana, she arrived at the police station, and together with another nine volunteers she helped distribute food, clothing and blankets to over a thousand displaced refugees.

The refugees were all staying in tents, she says, except for Patrick and Lydia Nhopi, whose only child had died, and Tony and Claudia Muderhwa, who had with them a hydrocephalic son. These families stayed inside the police station, in the storeroom, where the supplies and donations were kept.

Dana was in and out of the storeroom many times each day, she explains, and so she befriended the two couples. Then, on the Friday morning of the first week, while she was away at a decor exhibition – she had been searching for a light-fitting for her chandelier – her cellphone rang. It was Patrick, who wanted to tell her that he had just buried his daughter.

Dana was overcome that the man would choose to share with her such devastating information. Her close identification with the fate of Europe's Jews, she says, her knowledge that during the final years of apartheid she had sat idle, had by then occupied a prominent place in her consciousness.

She heard herself ask Patrick, 'Would it help you and your wife to come and stay at my house?'

'Yes,' said Patrick. 'Yes. Thank you.'

'And you can mention it to Tony and Claudia too,' Dana said – because how could she ask one family and not the other?

That Friday night, says Dana – although she didn't watch because it was *shabbos* – Tony appeared on the evening news. He had seen policemen stealing supplies from the storeroom, and he'd decided to go public. The policemen later threatened to pay him back for this, and early on Saturday he had to leave the station and go into hiding. And then some time on Sunday she got a call from Tony, saying he was okay and asking if she would come and fetch him.

'By Monday they were all here,' she says. 'I was anxious …'

'You thought someone might come looking for Tony?' I interrupt.

'No. I was anxious because I didn't know if I was doing them a service or a disservice. By removing them from the community of refugees, I thought I might be depriving them of government help.'

'That was almost three months ago,' I say. 'What do you think in hindsight?'

'I think there was nothing for them. There was nothing provided in the camps.'

She takes me now to find Tony. I follow her down the steps and into the garden. She opens a door to a room underneath the main house, a room filled with PC towers and monitors and electrical appliances. There are two mattresses on the floor between folded piles of clothing. A child with a large misshapen head is strapped into a walker, and when he sees us he smiles.

———

Five hours later I am back in the Golf, heading up Northfield Avenue. My throat is parched and my shirt is damp with sweat. I have just heard a story that could have been taken from the Book of Job, and my mind roils with thoughts (vividly biblical) of absolution and culpability and judgement.

I had sat mute as, near the end of his account, Tony excused himself, stopped talking, and cried. And then I had lifted my pen when his desperation became something else.

'Being a foreigner is not a sin,' Tony had said. 'But for them, they take it like it is being an animal. You can't even speak. Even if they spit on you, you must keep quiet.'

So the question I had arrived with, the question formulated over many nights of staring at the walls in the Radium, sprouts a whole new branch.

Who are these people who will not allow Tony to speak? What are *their* stories? How many times have *they* been stopped from speaking? Is voicelessness an endemic national condition?

And another: At what historical juncture is blame assigned? Are whites doing something meaningful when they take into their homes people whose presence is unwanted by so many? How do such actions compensate for past deafness?

And another: What does an ethnic affiliation with genocide mean? Why, so few years after the Holocaust, did the vast majority of South African Jews remain silent about apartheid? Is it acceptable, ever, to do nothing?

Which becomes: If I was only sixteen when Mandela was released, is it acceptable that *I* did nothing? But then why was I so ready to do nothing when I thought that the man in the queue at Bishop Verryn's church had asked *me* for shelter?

As I leave Glenhazel, I remember that Antjie Krog wrote a passage in *Country of My Skull* – a book ultimately about the failure of the Truth and Reconciliation Commission to achieve the bulk of its mission – that dealt with Jews and Germans and the issue of reparation.

I get home and lie down with the book on the big upholstered couch; on page 130 I find it.

Yes, Krog is writing about FW de Klerk's refusal to explain the past, about the last white president's more pressing need to stop the TRC from destroying his wounded National Party, when she takes a Jewish colleague aside and asks, 'What kind of reparation was done by the Germans?'

The man provides Krog with a lengthy list: pensions, free transport, German leaders kneeling at Jewish memorials, enough money to play a decisive role in the full industrialisation of Israel.

A list that Krog can't help comparing to the unimaginative document on reparation workshopped by the TRC. 'They could come up with nothing more inspired than a lump sum of money,' she writes.

A few lines later, Krog tells the reader that she knows better than to ask the Jewish man whether any Germans were forgiven on the basis of reparation. 'Is contrition in the form of reparation then just as futile as denial?' she wonders.

Then the remarkable paragraph from which the book takes its name begins:

'And suddenly it is as if an undertow is taking me out … out … and out. And behind me sinks the country of my skull like a sheet in the dark – and I hear a thin song, hooves, hedges of venom, fever and destruction fermenting and hissing underwater. I shrink and prickle. Against. Against my blood and the heritage thereof. Will I for ever be them – recognizing them as I do daily in my nostrils? Yes. And what we have done will never be undone. It doesn't matter what we do. What De Klerk does. Until the third and fourth generation.'

——

And now it seems certain that the second generation will have Jacob G Zuma as its president.

It is September 12th 2008. This happens to be the anniversary of the death in detention of Steve Biko, an event that notoriously left justice minister Jimmy Kruger cold. I am in the Golf on the way to St John's, to pick up Jamie Paterson for the next in our series of interviews, and on 702 is a live broadcast out of the Pietermaritzburg High Court – Judge Chris Nicholson is about to derail the state's long-drawn-out attempt to prove Zuma guilty of corruption.

'The court has gained the impression that all the machinations to which

I have alluded form part of some great political contest or game,' says Nicholson, nearing the end of his 115-page judgment. 'There is a ring of the works of Kafka about this.'

I turn right onto Carse O'Gowrie, past the square grey monolith of Johannesburg General Hospital. I'm rapt, immersed in the implications of what I'm hearing. Nicholson's findings, it is blindingly obvious, are damning in the extreme of President Thabo Mbeki; following on from the judge's premise of ulterior motives, his finger is pointed squarely at the head-of-state.

I drive through the gates of St John's and down the tree-lined entrance and into the parking lot. While waiting for Jamie to finish her lesson, I call Phillip.

'What do you think?'

'Crisis averted,' he says. 'This is the best possible outcome.'

'You reckon? But JZ got off on a technicality. What the court still hasn't dealt with was whether he took the bribes.'

'Ja, but …'

After a short debate, I end the call in hesitant agreement with Phillip. There have been minor outbreaks of violence in the days leading up to the judgment, and given the major violence that would surely have erupted had the decision gone the other way, I accept that Nicholson, in his (wholly plausible) assertions of top-level interference, has arrived at an effective compromise.

And so the next line in my notebook is inevitable: Is compromise the most our legal system should strive for?

Jamie emerges from her classroom and gets into the car, and I tell her what's just happened.

She's surprised, she says. 'But to be honest I really don't follow politics that closely.'

In ten minutes we are at the coffee shop in Norwood, seated under the same tree at the same outdoor table as last time. We order drinks; I ask Jamie my first question.

It has to do with a cartoon that's appeared recently in the *Sunday Times*, an illustration by the country's foremost satirist – Jonathan Shapiro; pen name 'Zapiro' – that depicts Zuma, belt unbuckled, about to rape a blindfolded Lady Justice, who is being held to the floor by top officials in the ANC-led alliance.

The cartoon has caused a national outcry, has ruptured an artery at the raw heart of South African race relations, and for the past week Zapiro's defence of himself has been as frantic as it's been consistent: justice is always depicted as a woman, he's said, and in this country her violation has been patently imminent.

Notwithstanding the explanations, however, the core of the matter – as far as I'm concerned – lies in the backlash.

Why is the image so explosive? How does it qualify as taboo? What do we *see* when we look at an illustration like this?

And most immediate: What did Jamie see?

Says Jamie: 'It was actually lying in my bathroom, the bathroom where I was raped, when I saw it. But I had heard about it first. I was prepared.'

'And?' I ask. 'How did you react?'

'I chuckled.'

'*Really*? Why?'

'I don't know, I suppose it was the dark humour.'

She pauses and sips her drink.

'I haven't thought about it much,' she continues, 'but maybe in a way it is an accurate portrayal of what's happening in this country. Because there is no justice.'

I'm compelled to push further. 'Talk to me about the image itself. If we leave aside the politics, what Zapiro shows us is rape. Actually, he shows us gang-rape. He shows us five men and a woman.'

She is composed, reflective. 'I mean, that's the ultimate way to get a reaction, isn't it? There are other ways he could have got a reaction, but that is the ultimate. And obviously, you know, it happens all the time. It happens to people like me, and it happens to poor black women in KwaZulu-Natal, Limpopo, everywhere.'

I follow the question through. 'Yes, it does. Although here, race is the burning issue. Zapiro drew five *black* men, and even if Lady Justice was black too, the fact of the matter is that *he* is white. From that perspective then, why are people so shocked by this cartoon? Why are people so shocked by *your* story?'

Jamie shrugs, as if the answer is self-evident. 'Well, if you're white, it's your deepest fear, isn't it? That black South Africans will rise up and take revenge for the injustices they had to suffer. You know, I remember in grade three a girl in my class coming up to me and saying, "Jamie, when Mandela dies, the black people are going to come and kill us." And that was before I really knew anything about apartheid and what had happened.'

I'm silent. There it is, the answer of the second generation. Then: 'The only way a girl in grade three could say that is if she heard it from her parents, right?'

Jamie nods. She proceeds to tell me about a trip that the family took to Mpumalanga recently; they stayed near Komatipoort, she says, on the Mozambican border. 'I saw a lot of Mozambicans there. They were so friendly. They had no bitterness. But over here you go into a shop and it's almost as if you're resented. Just for being white. And I sort of understand it. Maybe I'd feel the same. It's like, your parents and grandparents suffered while white people stood around and watched.'

I ask, 'Are you looking forward to living in a place where this isn't a concern?'

'I'm looking forward to feeling safe. I'll come back for holidays, but of course my memories of South Africa will always be tainted by that one night.'

To ask Jamie to connect that one night with what she's just said about injustice and revenge is a step too far, I realise, a step that ventures into forgiveness for the unforgivable.

I light another cigarette and change tack.

'So, how are you preparing to leave? Where's your head at?'

'It's a bit confused at the moment,' she says. 'The family is going through a really tough time. My mom had a minor breakdown in the middle of the Department of Home Affairs. We got to the front of the line and we had the wrong forms. She burst into tears. You know, the stress of what we're doing, my dad off already in two weeks. Anyway, it was ironic. They're so inefficient there but they were so nice to her. They took her into the office and they gave her a box of tissues. They gave her a big hug.'

I smile. *This crazy country.*

Out of a sentiment I can't quite grasp, I say, 'Tell me, maybe it's a stupid question, but why do you want to start your university career at Cambridge? Why not do an undergrad at Wits or Cape Town, and then go overseas later.'

She doesn't answer the last part. 'Cambridge is the best law school in England,' she says. 'Possibly even the best in the world, behind Harvard. Still, if I don't get in it's not going to be a tragedy. There's probably a lot of pressure there.'

Jamie has been advised not to include her story in the application documents, she informs me. She was considering attaching copies of the newspaper articles, and while she doesn't exactly know the reason behind the advice, she knows why she wanted to divulge the rape in the first place. 'Because I got through it, I want to use the experience to my advantage.'

Her return to this theme prompts me, 'Why don't you dwell on the trauma of rape?'

'It's not my personality. I try not to be a person that dwells too much. The worst thing that could happen to me is that people treat me differently. Aspects of me have changed, but I'm not a different person.'

'Your response is far from the norm. You know that, of course.'

'Absolutely. People have asked me in interviews whether I would advise other women to speak out. There's no way I would offer any advice on that sort of level. People's minds and their emotions and the way that they deal with things are so completely unique, I wouldn't be arrogant enough to impose my own … I don't know, my own approach.'

Jamie has five copies of a book called *I Have Life: Alison's Journey*, she tells me, a bestseller about another South African rape survivor. 'People arrived on our doorstep with lasagne and that book,' she says, laughing at the memory. But sarcasm, however light, is not her *métier*. 'I used to be very secure in my view of the world,' she goes on. 'Somehow, I'm more confused now. I don't know what to expect. Which is not worded very well, I know.'

'No, I think that's worded just about right.'

I can't help recalling my own worldview at eighteen. What did I know? Everything. The country was burning: hostel dwellers and township residents and apartheid police were engaged in a last-gasp battle for its soul – and from my home in the suburbs I knew … everything.

'Seems to me your eyes are wide open,' I say. 'You understand that something out there isn't joking. Not many white suburban South Africans get that at eighteen. I certainly didn't.'

She sits back and considers this. 'Possibly,' she admits. 'But a big part of me feels I should be doing more. It comes back to why I spoke out. And that's sort of in conflict with the selfish side, the side that wants to run away and be without any responsibility other than to myself. You know what I'm trying to say?'

'Totally.'

'When I talk to people, I'm suddenly filled with this desire to do, to fight. And then I go home and get involved in all kinds of stupid teenage things, like the dance that's in a week's time. You live in this bubble. Still, it's also different for me. Nobody else I know is in my position. I can say something and someone else will listen.'

I'm reminded that it was Jamie who got St John's to put together a charity drive for the xenophobia victims. 'Whatever happened with that?' I ask.

'I didn't do much. I'm getting more credit than I deserve. I just stood in the school office and said, "Why isn't anybody doing anything?" Then I set out some details. And then a couple of weeks later I got a call, saying we need to go and collect the boxes. I went down to the junior school, and there was an office full of blankets and food and old clothes. My friend has a Land Rover. We did three trips taking the stuff back up to the high school. St John's then organised for the Red Cross to come and collect everything.'

I look at my watch. It's time to go. On the fifteen-minute journey back to the Paterson home in Sandhurst Extension, not a word is said.

Alan is in the front yard when we arrive. He's wearing shorts and sandals and an open-necked shirt. He is in good spirits, and invites me inside for a beer.

Seated opposite each other on the couches in his living room, Alan and I talk about the weather. Nowhere in the world do you get spring afternoons quite like this, we agree. Then he tells me how ready he is to start his new life in England.

Regicide.

For six days in late September a political drama unfolds the likes of which has not been seen in the country since the public stabbing of prime minister Hendrik Verwoerd in 1966.

Regarding that historic event, Christopher Hope once observed: 'The assassination is one of the very rare instances when South African politics approaches the status of classic tragedy. More usually it resembles a violent, tear-stained farce.'

There is nothing farcical about President Mbeki's removal from office by senior members of his own party, a decision made during an all-night vigil of the national executive committee to which he was not invited. This episode too seems worthy of Shakespeare.

What began at Polokwane has come to fruition in the aftermath of the Nicholson judgment; what last week seemed an effective compromise has turned out to be its opposite.

Why, the country collectively wonders, could the Zuma faction not hold off for six short months? Why not wait for Mbeki to finish his term?

To members of the empowered classes, the answer, when it emerges, is especially chilling. Simply put, the hardline elements in the Zuma camp have smelt blood. Zuma himself has reportedly said, with reference to the findings of Nicholson, 'There is no point in beating a dead snake.' But Julius Malema, the newly elected leader of the ANC Youth League – a man more provocative even than his predecessor Fikile Mbalula – has taken the statement a step further: 'Fine, we are leaving this dead snake, but we must bury it.'

And 'bury it' they do.

On the afternoon of Saturday September 20th, ANC secretary-general Gwede Mantashe, flanked by national chair Baleka Mbete, confirms to the world in a press conference that Mbeki has indeed been recalled.

The next night, Mbeki addresses the nation.

He reminds us that South Africa is a land where grim poverty exists side by side with extraordinary opulence, that the dignity of all must be respected; he speaks of the continent in terms that echo Fanon, declaring that 'Africa and Africans must not be *the wretched of the earth* in perpetuity'; he appeals, after announcing his resignation, for courage and resilience in the months ahead – 'gloom and despondency have never defeated adversity'.

He shows us, one last time, what he might have been.

———

For the following four days the empowered classes veer wildly between hope and despair as fact and rumour encircle one another in a maelstrom of uncertainty.

Zuma can't yet be instated as acting president – he is not a member of parliament – and so at first the choice looks likely to be Mbete. Far from ideal. But might not the interim leader be Kgalema Motlanthe, as the press suggests on Monday? If so, fantastic. And who will Motlanthe select to his cabinet? Most will hardly be missed, but finance minister Trevor Manuel must surely remain – only *he* can reassure the nervous markets. And yet unbelievably, on Tuesday morning, Manuel resigns. Couldn't be worse. The currency plummets, the All-Share Index takes a creaming. But has Manuel really resigned? Seems he was only following protocol, acknowledging a debt to Mbeki – he is available, he says, to serve under a new president. If asked.

On Thursday evening, as Johannesburg's weary intelligentsia gather after the workday at Wits University to digest all that has occurred, the needle is holding steadily to 'positive'.

Motlanthe is in, Manuel is in, Manto Tshabalala-Msimang is out. The belligerent health minister who alienated scores of highly skilled specialists, the Mbeki loyalist who considered beetroot a more effective HIV treatment than antiretrovirals, has been replaced; the appointment in her stead of Barbara Hogan is cause for real celebration.

In the university's Great Hall, smiles all around. Once again, South Africa has stared into the abyss and prevailed.

Not a tragedy but a romance. Not *Macbeth* or *Coriolanus* but *Henry VIII*.

'Ladies and gentlemen!' The thousand or so members of the audience quieten down; our attention turns to the stage.

There are five men up there, and three of them – the three South Africans – reflect in their speeches the dominant mood. With minor deviations on the theme, their consensus is that it could have been infinitely worse, that our relief is not misplaced. Adam Habib, the vice-chancellor of the University of Johannesburg, even goes as far as to say, 'I believe this is a fundamental affirmation of the strength of our democracy.'

But the other two men demur. They are Tawana Kupe, dean of the Wits faculty of humanities, who is Zimbabwean, and Achille Mbembe, professor at the Wits Institute of Social and Economic Research, a Cameroonian.

They suggest, through their demeanour and their words, that we South Africans are closer to atavism, closer to the malaise that affects some of our compatriots to the north, than we think.

Kupe, the debate's moderator, adopts the understated approach; Mbembe, however, is as animated and direct as he was when I last heard him speak at the xenophobia colloquium in May.

Says the man from central Africa: 'The way Mbeki has been forcibly removed ... without him ever being called upon to defend himself, with very few of his comrades and beneficiaries of his largesse courageous enough to testify on his behalf ... is not simply reminiscent of the Stalinist culture the ANC brought back from exile, it also has the hallmarks of the sorcerers' feasts of yesteryear – a cynical, blind sacrificial ritual, of the kind we find in so many primitive religions all over the world.'

In his trademark emphatic style, Mbembe has the audience instantly in his thrall.

'By ousting Mbeki, the ANC hopes to protect itself from its own violence – that which comes from within the party itself, from brothers who turned enemies once the racist state that underwrote white minority rule in South Africa had been dismantled.'

It's not what we want to hear, but it sounds inescapably like truth. Why have we been so quick to forget the act of vengeance that brought this about?

'A fundamental phenomenon of primitive religion is to bring mass hysteria to a high pitch and to hurl the spirit of the mob onto one totemic individual, who is then turned into a surrogate victim. It might well be that the ANC's mode of operation and the culture of its politics have always been akin to those of a primitive religion.'

Today Thabo Mbeki. Tomorrow – who?

'Inflaming passions, sentiments and emotions in the search for scape-goats of all kinds – imperialism, counter-revolutionaries, foreigners, the judges, the media, intellectuals and so on – will not bring about the radical transformation of the basic conditions of existence poor South Africans aspire to.'

Fine. But what's the solution? Is there one?

'A grand opposition coalition that would constitute a progressive alternative to the ANC is urgently needed. It won't emerge without a radical deracialisation of South African politics, culture and institutions.'

Impossible. The best we can hope for is that Motlanthe somehow retains the presidency after next year's elections; Motlanthe, he's the man to save us.

'A major electoral reform ought to give back to the citizenry the power to directly elect its representatives: the president, members of parliament and municipal authorities.'

Never gonna happen.

'Anything else is but a collective exercise in delusion.'

You Guys Don't Get to Say That

ON THE LAST FRIDAY of September the *shabbos* meal is held at my parents' place in Houghton. It's an informal affair, there are only eight of us at the table: my mother and father, my ninety-year-old grandfather and his companion Zara, my uncle Tony and aunt Sandy, Laurie and me.

We don't talk politics.

Usually, when something as momentous as the events of the last week has occurred, the intra-family debate begins with pre-dinner drinks in the TV room. But tonight, in the dining room, after the *Kiddush* has been recited and the wine passed around and the bread cut, the discussion still hasn't moved beyond its opening theme.

Australia.

Sandy has just returned from another trip, a trip she makes at least once, and often twice, a year – to the eastern suburbs of Sydney, to visit her sons Gary and Derek and her grandsons Josh and Sam.

Gary, we've heard, is doing well in his sales position; Claudia is running the jewellery business from home; the boys are growing so fast you wouldn't believe. 'You should see them, Kev. They're dinkum Aussies.'

I smear the chopped herring over a thick slice of *challah*. 'And Derek?'

'Don't you know?' says my uncle. 'Derek's been in Israel. His company sent him to Tel Aviv to set up a new division. It's a helluva job.'

Still impossible, I find, to think of Derek without thinking of Richard. Naked next to the freeway, shivering, terrified. A settled image after two-and-a-half years, it sits like a dull stone at the base of my skull: an image brought into focus now by Tony's proud update on the surviving twin.

And yet we don't talk emigration either.

While Sandy's application has been approved, while she's ready to leave on the next flight, Tony's going nowhere. What would he do? He's in his mid-sixties, for God's sake, his entire life is in Johannesburg, his friendships, his business networks. In Sydney, what would he do? Spend all day in a cramped flat, watching the cricket, waiting for the grandchildren to walk through the door?

A subject best left alone.

The main course is served. Chicken *à la* king and brisket and basmati rice. We eat and we talk about other things (who got married; who died; no politics) and we refill our glasses. And then Tony reintroduces the evening's theme.

The last time he was in Sydney, he says, in February, he played a round of golf with three South African ex-pats, three guys who left the country in the early nineties. They wouldn't stop, he says; they'd been following events online. 'The "communist" government, the crime, the Eskom blackouts.'

On the tenth tee Tony had had enough. 'Hang on a minute there, fellers,' he said. 'You guys don't get to say that, not in front of me. The country was very good to you all. If you stop and think about it, it put you on this golf course where you're standing now.'

A story uncharacteristic of my uncle.

I lay down my fork. My applause is vigorous, heartfelt.

CHAPTER 8

Strange Ways Indeed

THE INVISIBLE SKYSCRAPER STILL stands, still invisible.

The city, like the country it describes, is still in drag: a cheap dress hangs over the ageing body, not quite hiding the secret beneath.

But a stalemate has been reached in Johannesburg's urban heart – and the poor, for once, are the beneficiaries.

In late October 2008, at a table in the Wits University canteen, Stuart Wilson, the human rights paralegal from Manchester, explains the situation.

'You remember San Jose?' he asks.

The last time we met, Stuart had been laughing madly at the gearbox in my Alfa. Today, the Englishman's manner is brusque. He has a law exam to write in two days: it's clear he wants this interview done with as soon as possible.

I answer his question dutifully. 'You took me there last March, after we visited Saratoga Avenue. The crumbling apartment block in Berea.'

'Yes, well, we went through three courts with that building. An agreement was endorsed by the Constitutional Court about a year ago.'

Stuart has before him a chicken salad, from which he does not raise his eyes as he speaks. He swallows a mouthful. Then: 'The San Jose matter has set something of a precedent regarding evictions of the inner city destitute.'

Bent forward over his lustreless meal, he gives me the history.

In 2006, says Stuart, the High Court effectively decided that the city could not sacrifice its poor in the name of urban renewal. 'What the judge told the city was, if you can't offer alternative accommodation, you can't evict.'

I wait once more as he swallows.

But when the case got to the Appeal Court, he continues, the city was given wide discretion as to where it could place the San Jose residents. 'Meaning, if you want to dump them in an informal settlement twenty kilometres away, go ahead.'

Another mouthful.

Of course the city had first-rate legal representation, says Stuart. Three weeks before the start of the Constitutional Court hearing, on the advice of its counsel, it filed a fresh set of evidence – to the effect that it was re-visiting its renewal plan, implementing policies favourable to the poor.

'The strategy worked,' Stuart avers. 'The Constitutional Court decided that the city's position had changed. It was all smoke-and-mirrors in the end, though. The city had nothing like a policy for the thousands of poor people it wanted to evict. And it still doesn't.'

I'm confused, not sure at all where Stuart's going with this. 'I don't get it,' I say. 'I don't see who wins.'

He sets aside his meal, sits back and folds his arms. I have his full attention now, but his tone remains abrupt. 'The Constitutional Court ordered the parties into settlement negotiations. In the course of those negotiations, our clients in San Jose were offered the occupation of two other buildings, also in the inner city. To start with, we didn't accept the terms. The city didn't specify as such, but it was clear they wanted to extract as much money from us as possible.' Eventually, says Stuart, agreeable terms were hammered out. 'We could occupy the buildings, at rent of no more than twenty-five per cent of the residents' average household income, around six hundred rand per month, until more suitable housing was found.'

A flash of insight; I think I'm beginning to understand. 'So you're still there.'

'Yes, we can more or less stay in those buildings indefinitely. My own view is that we'll stay there forever. The only alternative the city can offer us is public housing at a reduced rate. And at the moment, politically, the city can't go anywhere near a policy that smacks of classic welfarism.'

Now, I sense, we are approaching the nub of the matter. 'Why's that?'

'The million dollar question, isn't it? The way I see it, the city doesn't want any sort of relationship with the poorest and most vulnerable of its citizens. It's as cynical as that. It regards itself as a business. Its product is a self-sustained, commercially oriented, private property urban core. In that situation there is no place for people who can't pay rentals.'

My mind is working overtime. The city would rather become landlord to the very people it wants to evict than give up on its self-image? It would rather fool itself that it's New York than admit to itself that it's São Paulo? It would rather suffer in disguise than live as what it is?

Stuart picks up on my bewilderment; he provides a final piece of background.

'The one thing the Constitutional Court did decide is that people can't be moved from their homes without meaningful engagement. That means going into the buildings, interviewing people, finding out their income, seeing if a solution can be found without an eviction. This is a proposition the city is still completely freaked out by, and since the San Jose judgment there hasn't been a single mass eviction.'

Not one? I ask Stuart about 7 Saratoga Avenue, about Themba Jacky Koketi and the other residents of the carpet factory.

'It's the same story,' he says. 'The owner can't evict until the city provides some kind of answer on what it can offer as an alternative. The city hasn't been specific on what it can offer, so they're still there.'

'Including Themba?'

'Including Themba.'

Stuart's bearing visibly changes; he lightens up, allows some warmth into his voice. 'That's kind of the lesson, isn't it? What would've happened to Themba had he been evicted? Maybe he'd have gotten his honours degrees, maybe not. Maybe he'd have wound up a hobo. But the point of preventing the eviction was to take that worry away from him, to give him some sort of agency. My own view is, had he been evicted, he would have dropped out. I hesitate to say this, because he's such an ingenious guy. Still, preventing that scenario is the direct value I see in the work that I do.'

———

Beyond the gate, in the courtyard of the former carpet factory, a man in brown overalls sits with his back to a wall. He returns my wave but does not get up. Aside from him, the courtyard is empty; I take my phone from my pocket and dial Themba.

'You're here? I'm coming now.'

Themba unchains the gate, ushers me through, chains it shut again. I follow him to his room. On the narrow bed is a tracksuit top, which he puts on and zips to his throat before steering me back outside. 'People are sleeping,' he whispers, 'behind the partitions. We will wake them.'

We climb onto the roof of a disused garage, using as footing an exposed rusted pipe. The day is grey and cold, casting an added pall over the concrete and brick that surrounds us. We sit side by side, our legs dangling off the edge.

And then, as I open my notebook, balancing it on my thigh, four pistol shots reverberate in quick succession off the buildings to the north.

Crack! Crack! Crack! Crack!

Instinctively I jerk around, searching for the source. 'Themba, that's not fireworks, is it?'

He turns around too and looks calmly in the direction of Hillbrow. 'Ya, that is a gun. Maybe rubber bullets.'

The attempt to assuage me – if that's what it is – works well at first. Themba appears unfazed, as if gunfire in these parts is a daily (hourly?) occurrence. So I draw in a deep breath and tell myself that the shots are not as close as they sound.

And I resume as if nothing has happened.

I ask him how things have been at 7 Saratoga Avenue since my last visit.

'In terms of the housing situation,' he says, 'it is the same. Nothing much has changed. Stuart has won the case, so we are no longer going to be evicted. If we must leave this place, we must get alternative accommodation. And also, the police do not harass us any more. We have been staying here in peace.'

Peace, I'm thinking, is a relative notion.

But peace, whatever its properties, is not what I have come to discuss. More immediately, I want to know about Themba's plans. 'I heard you passed your exams,' I say. 'When are you starting work?'

'Ya, I am done with my exams. I start work in January. I will be working for the Department of Social Development, who gave me a bursary for the extra year.'

Themba, I've already learnt, now has two postgraduate degrees. In 2007, he graduated with his honours in psychology; this year he's added to that an honours in social work. Which means that this twenty-eight-year-old from an off-the-map village in rural KwaZulu-Natal, this man who is a product of South Africa's largest and most hindered economic class – insufficiently schooled, impoverished, cut off – is supremely qualified to work in areas that are critical to the country's progress.

'I'm not clear as to what I'll be doing,' he says, 'whether I'll be working as a clinician or as a probation officer. They will place me where there's most need.'

His preference, he says, is to be a probation officer.

'I like to help people who are in conflict with the law, so that they can do something with their lives. I strongly believe that an individual has the capacity to grow if they are given a chance. An individual can change his own life.'

In his account to me of the vision, Themba freely employs the language of his training – words like 'facilitation', a phrase like 'effecting change'.

'People are the experts of their own situation,' he says. 'You can build on their strengths in consultation with them. That is the best way.'

He shares with me more of the details – how, ideally, the community must be co-opted into the programme; how the community 'acts as the front line' – and I then ask him where he places what he envisages within the wider context.

I begin this line of questioning with a vivid memory from the previous visit. 'Is that sheet of paper still on your wall?' I ask. 'The one with the quote from the judge in Zuma's rape trial. How does it go? "If you can control your body and your sexual urges, then you are a man, my son"?'

Themba throws his head back, laughs hard. 'Ya, that's it. It is still there on my wall.'

'Why?'

'Well, I suppose with regard to Zuma and what has been happening around him, for me he hasn't acted in a proper way. You know, for a long time I have doubted his intellectual capacity. Even if there was a conspiracy, how come he fell into it? Maybe they used that woman to trap him, but why did he fall for it? His moral judgement is very questionable when it comes to leadership. And I know that he is the man the ANC has chosen, but it cannot be good for the image of our country. If it can maybe be Motlanthe, it would be better.'

I have a follow-on question for Themba; I'm hoping he can give me some insight into a matter that I haven't properly thought through for myself.

In the weeks since the ousting of Mbeki, the month-and-a-half since the Joburg intelligentsia gathered in the Wits Great Hall to hear Achille Mbembe declare that the country's best hope (given the atavistic nature of its ruling party) was a 'grand opposition coalition', a new party has indeed been formed in South Africa. The party would soon take the name 'Cope' – a clever abbreviation of the official 'Congress of the People' – but for now it goes as 'Shikota express', a reference to former Gauteng premier Mbhazima 'Sam' Shilowa and former ANC national chair Mosiuoa 'Terror' Lekota: two men, robustly jeered by the Zuma faction at Polokwane, who following Mbeki's axeing took the bold step of breaking away from the liberation movement.

What, I am keen to hear, does Themba make of Shikota express?

'No,' he says. 'I don't like it at all. The leadership ...'

Crack! Crack! Crack!

Three more pistol shots from the apartment buildings behind us. Again Themba does not flinch – does not even turn around – but I am now starting to sweat.

'Take Shilowa, for instance,' he says. 'Even as leader of Gauteng province, South Africa's powerhouse, he didn't do much. If he was a real leader, why didn't he sort out those things he is talking about fixing now? These people are after power and their own interests. They manipulate the poor and they are supported by the elite.'

I am aching to flee, my self-interest demands that I scuttle for the car, but somehow I manage to sit tight. Themba has hit his stride now; he has much to say on the efficacy (or otherwise) of ANC economic policy.

'It is another form of the neo-liberalist policies pushed to us by the IMF and the World Bank. It is serving the interests of *those* people. Fine, there has been big growth under Mbeki, but the social inequalities have been building. For me, that has been the issue fuelling the xenophobic attacks. People can deal with poverty, but not with social inequality. The economy of this country is concentrated with the few ... If the ANC can focus on the poor, our country can develop. But if you don't invest in human capital, growth is an illusion.'

To hear such words from a man whose life is lived in the fullest shadow of their implications, from a man who is not in the business of empty slo-ganeering, is to be struck afresh by their force. So, while my sweating can't be helped, I rationalise again the fear that has moved from my intestines to my throat – *ridiculous to think those bullets could be turned on me, a passive observer, a white man with a notebook* – and I focus on a theme.

'Themba, you talk about the xenophobic attacks. Did you witness it? Did you experience any of it first-hand?'

'Ya, some of the people staying here, and some in that church over there' – he points to the church next door – 'they were very scared to go out. Most of the people in these buildings are Zulus. They knew the Zulus were behind the attacks.'

Themba says he saw people beating up Somalians on Saratoga Avenue; he says he saw people looting. 'It was a mixture of criminality as well,' he says.

'And being a Zulu man yourself, how did this affect you?'

Themba nods. 'I'm glad you're asking that,' he says. 'It made me feel terrible. I'm not xenophobic. I strongly believe that as Africans we need to appreciate our diversity. So for me it was a serious concern. You see, this thing of colonialism has been instilled in us. Borders, artificial things, are dividing us. No policy can stop this thing now. It is an ideological matter.'

'But did the attackers not try to recruit you? I mean, knowing that you're Zulu?'

'No. They didn't try. They know I'm educated, that I think differently. They knew I would talk against it.'

I have to ask it: 'Themba, tell me again, because I need to be sure. Can we really identify a dominant ethnic group as the force behind this? Can we really say it was the Zulus?'

He stares out at the city, sighs heavily. 'Ya, I suppose it's true. Remember, I was there. I was also one of the volunteers for the Centre for the Study of Violence and Reconciliation. I visited those refugee camps, to assist and to counsel. We assessed the situation, we knew who was behind it.'

Themba pauses for a long moment.

'I was very traumatised by what happened,' he says. 'I had dreams about it. Some were saying in the camps, "No, it's better to die." And a few of those people, they knew I was a Zulu. I told them. And they accepted it. Not all of us are the same, you know.'

He shakes his head and goes on. 'One afternoon, when I was here at Saratoga Avenue, I went out to look. The streets of Johannesburg were clean. There was nobody outside. The foreigners, you see, they had their information – they knew the Zulus were coming from the Jeppe hostel. When you think about it, there must have been a third force behind this thing. It must have been planned.'

Maybe. Probably. Anyway … enough.

Enough of this fucking subject. Enough.

Themba, whether or not he's auditioned for the role, whether or not he's aware of his place in my psyche, is an archetype of the possible: the outlook less inevitable, the consciousness more imaginative. Dare one use a word like *hope?*

He tells me, when I ask, that he is going to move out of Saratoga Avenue as soon as he banks his first pay-cheque.

'Here there is no water,' he says. 'You become tired of looking for it and fetching it. It's a big problem. It would be difficult for me to develop myself if I stayed. Also, there is still no electricity. This last year I've gone a lot to the computer labs at the university, sometimes I've even slept there. How can a person develop himself like that? Because the next thing I want to study is maybe a few courses in management.'

Crack!

A gunshot, timed to perfection.

Closer. Jesus, it's getting closer.

I can withstand it no longer. I can wait just as long as it takes for

Themba to tell me of his relief – 'I used to live in constant fear … I used to think I couldn't carry on … but now I am done … now I can make my way up … now it will be easier …' – and then I need to secure for myself my own relief.

My apartment in Killarney is less than three kilometres from the former carpet factory in Saratoga Avenue. It is a journey, at this time of the afternoon, of less than five minutes. I drive up the hill and wave at the security guard at the front gate. I park in the garage behind a second gate. I stand on my balcony and smoke a cigarette.

The jacarandas are in full bloom; a blanket of purple shrouds the northern suburbs.

———

Distance (n): the length of the space separating two people, places, or things.

The following days are given over to wrestling with an abstract noun.

Three kilometres: the length of the space separating Kevin from Themba, Killarney from Saratoga Avenue, panic from relief. Three thousand metres; each one a light year.

What, then, is the length of the space that separates black from white?

In early November, in a newspaper column in *The Weekender*, this most banal and yet still most profound of South African questions is posed by Jacob Dlamini, a black journalist furthering his studies abroad.

'It is not often that I think about the fact that there are very few white South Africans I can honestly call friends,' Dlamini muses, from a desk somewhere in North America. 'The thought is just too depressing and a personal mark of our collective failure to forge a united nation.'

The full column, entitled 'White compatriots judge Zuma by his blackness', has been helpfully cut out and kept for me by a colleague (white), and so I take it with me to the office of the man who – now that I am thinking in such terms – may be called my own 'closest black friend': Tawana Kupe, the recently appointed dean of the faculty of humanities at Wits University.

Tawana and I first met in Grahamstown, in early 2000, where he was then assistant professor at the Rhodes University journalism school. I enrolled in his signature class – postgraduate media theory: a comprehensive debunking of the great journalistic myths (reportorial objectivity, editorial independence, etc.) – and two years later, when I commissioned him as a contributor to the media trade journal I edited, our association spontaneously became one of long lunches, shared confidences and spirited debate.

Today, as the first black dean of a pivotal faculty in Johannesburg's largest tertiary institution, my friend presides over a fiefdom that to all intents and purposes is contemporary South Africa in microcosm: a convocation of races, nationalities and ethnic affiliations brought together by circumstance, and divided, in the main, by choice.

The view of the non-integrated cliques, in other words, from the tall windows of his corner office.

'I am going to embarrass you a bit,' Tawana says, after he has read the Dlamini piece and considered its thesis. 'When I came to your thirtieth birthday party five years ago, I was one of two black people there.'

Which is fair enough. As far as I'm concerned, with all that support for the point on the campus grounds outside, further elaboration is unnecessary. But for Tawana, a Norwegian-trained social scientist, data is lifeblood.

He tells me about a recent function held by a white colleague – he was the only black person present; another function held by a black friend – no whites.

'My sons and I often eat at Sofia's in Rosebank,' he says, 'and I seldom see other blacks. Not because they can't afford it, but because the black elite eat elsewhere.'

A handful of similar examples follow. Anxious to move beyond the data, I stop Tawana. I have come here in the hope that my friend will explain some mystery, give me fresh insight, show me how to look at the problem in a new way. So I ask him whether, as an outsider, someone born and schooled in white-ruled Rhodesia, he thinks that certain South Africans may be overly concerned by this unextraordinary state of affairs. 'It's an ancient phenomenon,' I say, 'people tend to stick to their own. Why should we be any different? Is it really so terrible, as Dlamini puts it, that we have failed to forge a united nation?'

But because there is no mystery to explain, Tawana can't tell me what I'm desperate to hear. He can't offer a single viewpoint from which race in South Africa is provisional or secondary.

He can tell me only how it is: how race continues to undermine the legitimacy of South Africa's social institutions; how our education system and corporate sector still bear the hallmarks of white privilege; how the TRC was in effect a symbolic gesture that could never possibly eradicate 350 years of oppression; how the vast majority of whites today – whether they admit it to themselves or not – are living off the fruits of accumulated plunder.

'And unfortunately there isn't much that you as a white person can do about it,' he says. 'I'll give you an extreme example. Let's say you decide, out of your conscience as an enlightened white South African, not to apply for a job – because you know that if you do apply, thanks to your superior education, you're likely to get it. You understand that I'm not talking now about an affirmative action job, I'm talking about a job that goes to the person who is most qualified. So if you decide not to apply, what you're actually doing is committing race suicide. And what about the next white person who comes along and chooses not to commit race suicide?'

What about him? Would he be the typical white South African, the guy who refuses to acknowledge the past? Or would he be the typical human being, the guy who acts according to the dictates of self-interest?

Would he be me?

And what about Stuart Wilson? There's a guy who's *done something*, even if he isn't really a South African. Or is that not what Tawana's suggesting? Is my friend suggesting rather that the idea of *collective* white sacrifice is absurd?

These are my thoughts as I leave Tawana's office. The rest of the discussion had focused on Barack Obama and the post-racial ideal – 'What do they mean by *post*? Is this thing over?' – but my heart hadn't been in it. I had been mired in a paradox, and the talk of Obama seemed far away.

I close the heavy wooden door of the dean's office behind me. I walk out onto the east campus concourse, sit on the steps of the Great Hall. I watch the non-integrated cliques walk by, the white and Asiatic and black students in their small exclusive groups. And suddenly I remember that there is at least one sense in which the distance from white to black is not so unassailably far.

We do have something in common, I'm thinking.

In the years since the destruction of apartheid, in this new time where crime has no colour – where the police force does not have as its sole objective the protection of a privileged race, where all are equal before lawlessness and disarray – our fears have begun to coalesce.

Are we not now uniformly afraid, for the first time with uniformly good reason, that our blood-bespattered history will overtake us and swallow us all whole?

The place where I sit, I realise, is about halfway between my apartment in Killarney and Themba's room in Saratoga Avenue. Is the distance from one to the other really no distance at all?

———

December 16th, a national holiday in South Africa.

On December 16th 1838, four hundred and seventy Afrikaners killed three thousand Zulu *impis* at the Battle of Blood River. The Afrikaners may have had the advantage of gunpowder, but the day was nevertheless commemorated as a great victory, a sign of God's grace. It came to be known as *Dingane's Day*, for the defeated Zulu king.

In 1952, to further politicise that long-ago battle and to consecrate the Afrikaner's relationship with God, the National Party renamed the holiday the *Day of the Covenant*.

On December 16th 1961, the ANC abandoned its philosophy of nonviolent resistance. The movement's newly formed armed wing, Umkhonto we Sizwe, bombed government buildings in Johannesburg, Port Elizabeth and Durban.

In 1995, Nelson Mandela, the country's first black president, renamed the holiday the *Day of Reconciliation*.

On December 16th 2007, delegates at the Polokwane conference, arguably the most conflict-ridden event in the ANC's ninety-five-year history, demonstrated their overwhelming support for Jacob Gedleyihlekisa Zuma.

And now on December 16th 2008, the losers at the Polokwane conference, led by former Mbeki loyalists Mosiuoa Lekota and Mbhazima Shilowa, officially launch the breakaway party Congress of the People, thereby presuming to offer an alternative to de facto one-party rule.

Like many families in Johannesburg today, my wife's family takes advantage of the holiday and the flawless Highveld sky to gather for lunch in the garden – to sit outside and to laugh at each other's jokes and to redeem the complimentary pleasures of summer in Africa. We are not unaware of the history of this day, but it isn't something we talk about. We are just here, content, living our lives.

Then, the next day, I receive from a friend a copy of an article published in *Harper's*. Written by expatriate South African poet Breyten Breytenbach, the piece takes the form of a letter addressed to Nelson Mandela. After describing in tragic detail the implosion of his forsaken homeland – the homeland for which he languished seven years in an apartheid prison – Breytenbach writes the following:

'I must tell you this terrible thing, my old and revered leader: if a young South African were to ask me whether he or she should stay or leave, my bitter advice would be to go. For the foreseeable future now, if you want to live your life to the full and with some satisfaction and usefulness, and if you can stand the loss, if you can amputate yourself – then go …'

It takes me a long time to discover what I think of these words. They sit with me, nag at me, on a road-trip through the Karoo. They are there with me in the boundless nights of the vast interior, they echo across the silent desert floor, they lose their bite and become hollow as, in Cape Town now, I watch the sun melt once more into the sea.

The new year ushers in all the hopes and expectations that every new year brings. And back in Johannesburg, when I look again at the words, it's with the new year's eyes. Their meaning is no longer to be found in what *I* think of them, but in how I understand them through the lens of the lives I have witnessed.

Might not Themba Jacky Koketi achieve in South Africa the 'usefulness' of which Breytenbach speaks? Might not Stuart Wilson? Are they both not engaged in the task of imagining some kinder future, of making that future manifest in the physical world? Is this not perhaps 'satisfying' for them? Or should Stuart return to Manchester and Themba to … where?

Should Rob Caskie seek a place where he's guaranteed not to meet the same fate as David Rattray? Would that be his most prudent course? Or should he remain where he is, in full voice beneath the umbrella thorns, paying homage to his murdered friend by transcending the lessons of history?

The Solomon family whose little boy was shot … would Breytenbach think they were living life 'to the full' if they were back in Israel, or Wisconsin? Yes, the Solomons pay the price of surveillance cameras, electrified fencing, armed guards in double-cab four-by-fours. But then they say that behind all those walls is the most caring community in the world.

And how about Timothy Maurice Webster, or Carol Dyantyi? Would the Aids orphans in Soweto prefer it if *they* weren't around? Would these children prefer not to have guidance? Would that allow them more time to train-surf, to play *spara-para*?

Are any of these questions worth asking?

There are, though, the other lives – for whom Breytenbach's words present some trouble, for whom the phrase 'amputate yourself' might hold some resonance. What would count as amputation, for instance, to Tony and Claudia Muderhwa? What 'loss' would be too great for them to bear? To go back to Bukavu, to the easternmost province of the DRC, where as Breytenbach himself laments in the selfsame piece – 'the mass raping of women' continues unabated? Or to stay in South Africa, where to be a dark-skinned foreigner is a sin?

It is better here, they think. It is much better here.

Maybe one day the Patersons will agree.

Maybe one day Breytenbach's 'foreseeable future' will be over, and Jamie Paterson will ride into town with a Cambridge law degree, and Derek Bloom will sit again at our *shabbos* table. Maybe then we will have new means of embracing the world, new limbs in place of the figurative ones we have lost – just from being here, just because these are our ways of staying.

References and Further Reading

The following material is either quoted directly in the text, or served as narrative and thematic inspiration during the composition of *Ways of Staying*.

Biss, Eula. February 2008. 'No-Man's-Land: Fear, Racism, and the Historically Troubling Attitude of American Pioneers'. *The Believer*. See www.believermag.com/issues/200802/?read=article_biss (accessed 13 March 2009).

Blair, Jon (producer/director/writer). September 2007. *Murder Most Foul*. Documentary screened on special programme of *Carte Blanche*, M-Net.

Breytenbach, Breyten. December 2008. 'Mandela's Smile: Notes on South Africa's Failed Revolution'. *Harper's*.

Capote, Truman. 2007. *In Cold Blood*. London: Penguin.

Coetzee, JM. 2002. *Stranger Shores: Literary Essays*. London: Vintage.

Coetzee, JM. 2007. *White Writing: On the Culture of Letters in South Africa*. Johannesburg: Pentz Publishers.

Dlamini, Jacob. November 2008. 'White Compatriots Judge Zuma by his Blackness'. *The Weekender*.

Fanon, Frantz. 2001. *The Wretched of the Earth*. London: Penguin.

Frost, Robert and Robert Faggen (ed.). 2007. *The Notebooks of Robert Frost*. Cambridge, MA: Harvard University Press.

Fuller, Alexandra. 2003. *Don't Let's Go to the Dogs Tonight*. New York: Random House.

Godwin, Peter. 1996. *Mukiwa: A White Boy in Africa*. London: Picador.

Godwin, Peter. 2006. *When a Crocodile Eats the Sun*. Johannesburg: Picador Africa.

Hope, Christopher. 2004. *White Boy Running*. London: Picador.

Johnson, Shaun. 1994. *Strange Days Indeed*. London: Bantam Books.

Krog, Antjie. 2002. *Country of My Skull*. Johannesburg: Random House.

Krog, Antjie. 2003. *A Change of Tongue*. Johannesburg: Random House.

Malan, Rian. 1991. *My Traitor's Heart*. London: Vintage.

Marinovich, Greg and Joao Silva. 2000. *The Bang-Bang Club: Snapshots from a Hidden War*. London: Basic Books.

Mbembe, Achille. 2001. *On the Postcolony*. Berkeley, CA: University of California Press.

Mda, Zakes. 2007. *Ways of Dying*. Cape Town: Oxford University Press.

Mphahlele, Es'kia. 2004. *Down Second Avenue*. Johannesburg: Picador Africa.

Ndebele, Njabulo. 2007. *Fine Lines from the Box: Further Thoughts about Our Country*. Johannesburg: Umuzi.

Paton, Alan. 2003. *Cry, the Beloved Country*. New York: Scribner.

Poplak, Richard. 2007. *Ja, No, Man: Growing Up White in Apartheid South Africa*. Toronto: Penguin.

Steinberg, Jonny. 2005. *The Number*. Cape Town: Jonathan Ball.

Thamm, Marianne. 2002. *I Have Life: Alison's Journey*. Johannesburg: Penguin.

Vladislavić, Ivan. 2004. *The Exploded View*. Johannesburg: Random House.

Vladislavić, Ivan. 2006. *Portrait with Keys*. Johannesburg: Umuzi.

Acknowledgements

I am indebted above all to the remarkable people whose stories appear in these pages. I hope the final product justifies their trust.

Ways of Staying would not have been possible without the intervention and encouragement of two individuals: novelist Jo-Anne Richards, whose intuitive grasp of the writer's psyche saw me safely through more than one crisis of confidence, and non-fiction author Richard Poplak, who – aside from awakening me to the finer subtleties of the craft – convinced me that it was *this* book I needed to write and not some other. I am fortunate to know them both.

The Wits Institute of Social and Economic Research (WISER) provided a quiet haven and supportive environment in which to complete the final chapters. It has been a privilege to call myself a Writing Fellow at the institute, and I wish to acknowledge a debt of gratitude to the entire staff.

To Branko Brkić, Phillip de Wet and Tanya Pampalone, my friends and former colleagues at *Maverick* and *Empire*, I am grateful for each minute of caffeine-infused debate on the internal mechanics of good narrative journalism. I am especially grateful, however, that for over two years Branko sent me out on assignment with instructions to put the theory into practice. The magazines closed too soon, but I am confident this won't be the last book to revisit the valuable material they generated.

The contribution of *Ways of Staying*'s editors, Ivan Vladislavić and Andrea Nattrass, has been immeasurable – were it not for Ivan's mastery of structure and Andrea's belief in the primacy of detail, it would have been a much diminished work. That said, where mistakes appear, they are mine alone.

Terry Morris, managing director at Picador Africa, has been a committed advocate of the book since first she saw two-and-a-half chapters in rough draft in May 2008. I am deeply appreciative of the professional and enthusiastic manner in which she and her team have shepherded *Ways of Staying* through to publication.

For their close and perspicacious readings of early drafts of the text, I am thankful to Annari van der Merwe and Laurence Hamburger. Michael Titlestad likewise gave generously of his time and expertise – his insights helped shape the work more than he perhaps realises.

Importantly, I would like to thank my uncle Tony, aunt Sandy and cousin Derek for their warm and helpful attitude to this project – they have been consistently tolerant, despite the pain my requests and questions may sometimes have caused. I am lucky, too, to have such caring and devoted parents, Michael and Valerie, whose support (as always) has been unconditional.

Finally, I owe an incalculable debt to my wife, Laurie, whose artist's empathy and saint-like patience has sustained and inspired me throughout.